GETTING THE CHURCH ON TARGET

GETTING THE CHURCH ON TARGET

by
Lloyd Perry

MOODY PRESS
CHICAGO

THE MOODY BIBLE INSTITUTE
OF CHICAGO

ISBN: 0-8024-2922-X

Moody Paperback Edition, 1981

Third Printing, 1981

Printed in the United States of America

Contents

Introduction

These are dangerous days for the organized church. If it continues just to try to preserve society rather than to redeem it, to give its blessing to questionable enterprises, to substitute fellowship for service, and to prize man's opinion more than God's revealed truth, then it should give heed to the parable of the unfortunate frog.

The unfortunate frog is a cold-blooded animal. Its temperature fluctuates with the temperature of its immediate surroundings. One particular frog was placed in a kettle of water which was on top of a stove. The water was gradually heated. Since the frog was cold-blooded, it had no mechanism to detect temperature changes. Gradually the frog's body temperature increased with that of the water. While this heating process was going on, the frog was free at any time to jump to safety. But since he was oblivious to the change taking place, he saw no reason for such drastic action. Eventually the unfortunate frog was boiled to death, totally unaware of the dramatic though gradual changes taking place in and around him. This could be a very meaningful parable for today's church. It is time to be alert to what is taking place and to make some changes.

Reform involves the improvement or amendment of what is wrong. Revival pertains to the restoration of life and strength. Renewal seeks to bring back to an original condition of freshness. Revitalization looks ahead rather than backward. It envisions a goal-directed church organization that correlates our profession and our practice. The church needs revitalization.

The concern of this book is church revitalization. The process of revitalization has four steps: diagnosis of the church situation, organization, implementation, and assessment. In this process there is a need for explicit rather than implicit goals. The motivation for individuals becoming involved in church activities should be intrinsic rather than extrinsic; it should arise from theological commitments, interests, and concerns rather than power, status, and prestige. Provision should be made for all segments of the constituency to have a voice in the plans and procedures. Processes should be developed to take advantage of energy and resources.

Both the clergy and laity have been collecting slivers under their fingernails as they have scraped the bottom of the barrel for new ideas for renewing the church. Some are beginning to realize that lasting, healthy changes do not come by employing fascinating fads, tailor-made plans, or high-pressure procedures but by clarifying.

In the search for new ideas for church revitalization, there has developed a new interest in church management. Laymen have been disturbed as they have entered the organized church for service and have discovered the deficiency in management understanding and procedures. Pastors have realized that much of their time in the pastorate is spent in administrative activity. They sense the general inadequacy of their seminary training to equip them to meet the challenges of this area of work.

This book is designed to provide an introductory survey of the broad area of church management, or administration. A recent sabbatical year of study under such men as Robert Worley of McCormick Seminary and Alvin Lindgren of Garrett Seminary stimulated my research in an extensive bibliography. At that time I collected a file of materials and quotations dealing with numerous subjects from differing theological perspectives. Both clergy and laity will find a wealth of ideas from many sources. These sources have been identified whenever possible. Any missing identifications have been by oversight, not by intent.

Church management should be preventive as well as therapeutic. This book should serve as a thought-provoking, practical administrative guide for pastors and laymen. It is intended to be a sourcebook of ideas, a stimulator of discussion, and a survey text for classes in church administration.

We are reminded that no rearrangement of bad eggs is going to make a good omelet. It is not the external circumstances but the heart of man that really counts. In all these things, seek God's will—not that you may look at it but that you may do it.

CHAPTER 1

Having God's Man in God's Place for Ministry

For the first time in American church history, the major church groups have stopped growing and have started to shrink. In 1967, the ten major denominations started their downward trek, and they have kept going since that time. Between three and four thousand parishes dissolve or merge every year. The "signs of death" as cited by Lyle Schaller in his book, *The Local Church Looks to the Future*, are making an appearance. The churches are concentrating their resources on member-related activities. An excessive amount of time is spent in holding anniversaries in order to recall the good old days. The church has lost touch with the community in which it is located. City churches are longing for the suburbs in hopes that a change of scenery will restore life.

The church is one of the last organizations to ask for help when it is in trouble. There are cover-ups which can be employed to delay the time of real decision. As long as we can show that one person was added to the rolls in the year, we can argue that the thousands of dollars were well spent, since the value of one soul cannot be counted in dollars and cents. This type of reasoning does not always make sense when that individual was merely transferred from another church roll to ours.

There are those who confuse the invisible Church with the visible church and keep whistling in the dark as they rely upon the fact that the Church belongs to Christ, and He has promised that it will never perish. In reality, the local, visible churches are perishing. Some attempt to cover their true spiritual depravity by building a new building. There is the hope that the large monument on the corner will offset the fact that the sense of mission has faded. The church business can be carried on by an elite minority, thus making it practically impossible for the true conditions to become known. Few seek help until they realize that it is really needed.

If a problem in the local church should be discovered, then there is a supposed cure which has been applied in many situations through the years: blame the condition upon the minister and get rid of him. Some do this in a kind way and some use "the axe." The scapegoat is isolated and sent to die in the desert. There are times when the minister is responsible for the problems. It should be remembered, however, that when you have a losing team, it does not always become a winning team by firing the manager. If the pastor is God's man in God's place for ministry, the church should be careful about dealing with God's annointed. We are not just playing games where we can change personnel by whim. We are dealing with God's work, where we should be involved in change of personnel only within the scope of His will.

An effective pastor is a very important factor in getting a church on target. He should be God's man in God's place in God's time. There is a unique place for him to fill. Three analogies give insight into his responsibilities. He is a bond servant carrying out the commands of his master. As a shepherd, he provides food, protects from foes, and makes preparation for the future. He serves as a steward managing the affairs until his Master returns. He rejoices in the privilege of being a co-laborer with Jesus Christ.

Changing times have brought many changes in the life and labors of the pastor. In days past, he maintained a unique position in the community because of his professional standing and education. This has changed. He can no longer expect that position and authority will come to him automatically because of age, profession, education, or culture. Many in the community will have an advantage in one or more of these areas. His authority must now, maybe more than ever before, be centered in his position as a spokesman for God. His authority must be based upon "thus saith the Lord."

The pastor is expected to be a preacher, counselor, teacher, administrator, theologian, public relations expert, fund raiser, and churchman. The multiplicity of tasks confronting him causes the pastor to have real questions regarding his role. Many pastors have considered their most pressing personal question to be the matter of the purpose and ministry of the church. The bells are still ringing. The rheostats are taking the lights up and down. The doors are still opening and closing. But the machinery has caused the real mission to become clouded and sometimes even lost.

This age of revolutionary change and tension is making unprecedented demands upon the time and resources of the pastor. It is imperative that he make a careful analysis of his motivation for entering the ministry and also of his concept of the church. He needs to have a realistic view of the pastoral office. A good analysis prior to becoming involved may help to lessen the confusion later. The pastor not only needs to know God's job description for his task, but he should try to make certain that this job description is understood by the local church.

The Pastor

An evangelical pastor is expected to be an informed man, thoughtful, apt in independent investigation, and well oriented in respect to all truth. He is to be a man of integrity, truthful, honest, self-controlled, and morally pure. He is to be a man who is emotionally mature. He should be gracious, cheerful, positive, and cultured.

As a Christian, he should be committed to Christ, sensitive to the Spirit of God, and faithful in using the means of grace. He must be rooted in biblical truth, conscious of his position within historical Christianity, aware of his responsibility to the whole Christian community, and constant in his witnessing for Jesus Christ.

As a servant of Christ in the church, he ought to be oriented sympathetically toward the problems of his contemporaries and be alert to ways in which God's Word may be applied in specific concrete situations. He must be able to communicate the Gospel effectively. He should be able to provide challenging leadership. There should be a positive relationship maintained with the denomination in which he labors, and he should be appreciative of the traditions and contributions of other denominations.

As a member of society, he should be alert to the world in which he lives. This should result in his opposing the evil and promoting the good. He should be ready to assume his responsibility to the community in which he resides.

James D. Glasse, in his book *Putting It Together in the Parish,* has a section dealing with competence in the ministry. He emphasizes the operational understanding of the ministry. The first of the five competencies discussed is that of relating effectively to congregations in their particular social, economic, political, and cultural context. The second competence is that required in the management of the organization. This includes such matters as goal setting and the development of leadership. The pastor must be able to help individuals mature through teaching, counseling, and helping them in spiritual living. The fourth competence involves the development of the pastor's own personal and professional resources. The final competence is in the matter of leading people in worship.[1]

It is important for the pastor to recognize and develop the spiritual gift or gifts given to him by the Holy Spirit. Several of these gifts have special relevance to the pastor and his ministry.

The gift of *teaching* is mentioned in Romans 12:7, 1 Corinthians 12:28, and Ephesians 4:11. It is the divine enablement whereby a believer is able to communicate the Word of God by explaining and applying the truth of the Scriptures.

The gift of *pastor-teacher* is mentioned only in Ephesians 4:11. This carries with it the idea of feeding, protecting, and expressing concern. This gift carries in its meaning the thought of giving special attention and self-sacrifice to those under his shepherding care.

The gift of *evangelism* is mentioned in Ephesians 4:11 and pertains to the divine enablement of the believer to proclaim the Gospel and witness the result of men being born into the family of God. The gift is the same in mass evangelism and in personal evangelism.

The gift of *exhortation* is accompanied by the divine enablement whereby people respond practically to the sharing of the Word. It is the gift which provides the ability for a man to disciple another in the things of the Lord. It is the ability to stimulate faith in others.

The gift of *administration* involves the ability to rule within the body of Christ. In 1 Corinthians 12:28, the gift is designated "to govern," meaning to guide. In Romans 12:8 the word means "to preside, rule, or govern."

The gift of *helps*, in Romans 12:7, refers to service, or ministry. In 1 Corinthians 12:28 it is a word meaning "to lay hold of" or "exchange." In both cases, it carries the meaning of one helping to carry the burden of another. God gives some believers a special sensitivity to the needs of others and the ability to do something about these needs.

The Pastoral Office

The offices of bishop and elder are the same (Titus 1:5,7), and the pastoral office (Eph 4:11) belongs to the bishop-elder category. There are two classes of elders: the teaching elders, who also rule, and elders who rule but who ordinarily do not teach. The pastor must truly be a gift of God to the church (Eph 4:11). His personal, moral, and spiritual qualifications must be recognized by the church (Ac 20:17-35; 1 Co 12:1-11; 1 Ti 3:1-7; 4:13-16; 2 Ti 1:6; 2:2; Titus 1:5-9).

It is the duty of the teaching elder to declare his understanding of the Word of God concerning the great issues of our day. It is his duty to teach the stand of the wider church, denominational and national, on these issues. It is also his responsibility to raise all the important moral problems he feels to be inherent in these positions. The congregation, with the leadership of the pastor and in relation to Scripture, will seek to find the will of God through His Word.

It is the minister's task to bring the judgment of God as well as the comforts of His grace upon the congregation and its life. It is his task to make the glory, judgment, and love of God real in the midst of the community of men. He must bring to bear on the concrete issues of life the reality of God's presence through His Word of judgment and promise. The pastor is a witness to the Lordship of Jesus Christ.

The minister must learn to share leadership and responsibility. It is his task to equip the laity for its mission. The minister must develop the skill of making conflict creative and rewarding enough so that it will not be resisted as being evil. He must develop the skill of encouraging trust and honesty. He must be able to facilitate communication and promote dialogue. The development of these skills is discussed at length in separate chapters in this book.

The pastor must provide the congregation with preaching and worship, teaching, pastoral care, and administration. The Bible divides the tasks of the minister into two classifications. He is to feed the flock of God and take oversight thereof (1 Pe 5:2). As the overseer, or bishop, his first duty is to rule (Ro 12:8; 1 Th 5:12; 1 Ti 5:17). This means that he is to superintend or preside over the congregation. As the teacher, his duties are largely educational. Their exercise should produce a well-informed, spiritually wise congregation. He should give attention in this educational ministry to reading, teaching, and preaching (1 Ti 4:11,13; 2 Ti 4:1-2). The ministry of shepherding and teaching should be carried out without desiring personal glory.

The Pulpit Committee

The process of finding God's man for God's place in God's time will vary, basically because of differing denominational practices. Where no denomination is involved, the local church has greater freedom but also faces greater problems.

The most critical experience of the pastor's adjustment in his vocation comes when he faces his first church. That first church can either make him or break him, humanly speaking. He may be tempted to throw his weight around before he has any.

If the church which is seeking a pastor is a "good" church, there will be an abundance of interested aspirants. If the church is a star of lesser magnitude, there may still be a number who in desperation will seek to fasten their wagon to even this small star. Pulpit committees normally prefer to seek the man rather than having the man seek them. The problem on both sides, however, is what is God's will in this whole matter.

Three suggestions may prove helpful in discovering God's will. We can discover His will in His Word. His will never contradicts His Word. His will can be discovered through the works of providence. God is in charge and can and does make "all things work together for good to them that love God, to them who are the called according to his purpose" (Ro 8:28). His will can be discovered through the witness of the Spirit. He gives that feeling of either confirmation or dissatisfaction within the soul whereby the child of God has an inner assurance that something is or is not His will.

The pulpit committee may be elected by the congregation or designated by an official board of the church, or the official board itself may serve as a pulpit committee. In a church where the center of power rests in the congregation, it is recommended that the congregation elect the pulpit committee.

The committee should be small in number and representative in membership. A pulpit committee of five regular members and two alternates should be adequate for a medium-sized church. The two alternates should attend all meetings and should vote only when one of the regular members is absent. Some steps should be taken to make sure that the membership of the committee is representative. The five members may consist of two from the ruling board of the church, one from nonoffice-holding membership of the church, one representing the interests and concerns of the youth, and one member at large. It is wise to have both men and women on the pulpit committee.

The written ballot can be divided into sections, with several nominations for each committee post. The nominations may be made by the nominating committee of the church or by the official church board if no nominating committee is provided in the church constitution. Before a name is included on the ballot, the individual should be contacted to make certain that he will serve if elected. Additional nominations can be made from the floor.

Once the committee has been elected, its first task is to elect a chairman and a secretary. It is normally wise to have one of the two members from the ruling board of the church serve as chairman. He will be the one to make the reports of progress to the church. The secretary of the committee will be responsible for correspondence with all the prospective candidates, the mailing and receipt of questionnaires, and the keeping of the minutes for the committee. Reports will also have to be prepared for the church.

The committee should begin its work by studying the biblical purposes of a church. This will lay the foundation for establishing a job description for a new pastor.

The purpose of the church should be noted in the church constitution. If they are not, then the pulpit committee should ask the church to clarify in writing what the puposes of the church are, since they will expect the pastor to guide them in the fulfillment of these purposes.

The pulpit committee will want to make a careful analysis of the Scriptures to determine the spiritual gifts desirable in a potential candidate. Some pulpit committees have had a tendency to establish human boundaries such as age or marital status. When this is done, potential candidates are often automatically eliminated from consideration because of personal biases rather than scriptural grounds.

When a church needs names for consideration, the denominational office or officials can often supply a list of names of men who might consider a change. This is one of the blessings gleaned from being part of a denomination.

The committee may turn for help to Christian colleges, Bible schools, and seminaries which have placement departments. It is their responsibility to work with churches and ministers seeking God's man for God's place.

The members of the congregation may be invited to submit names of possible candidates to the committee. It should be made clear that these names will be given careful and prayerful consideration, but all may not be contacted, for any number of reasons.

There may be pastors who can supply names of men who might consider a change of pastorate. In some cases, the pastor giving the name may not want his name made public.

The pulpit committee may, at this point, have several names before it for consideration. Some on the committee may know some of these men already, and they can share some information. The committee should at least know where the men are presently serving. If they are in a denominational church, the committee can check the yearbook and discover the size of the present church, salary, and several other meaningful bits of information.

The names can then be sorted into groups. The most likely prospects are placed in group one. This group will contain the names of those who on the surface seem to have the best potential for service in this type of church. The leading of the Holy Spirit will be an important consideration at each decision point.

A preliminary questionnaire will be formulated and sent to this first group. The questionnaire should be simple and easy to complete. The committee will want to know whether the potential candidate would under any circumstances feel that he could consider a call at this time. If there is a possibility, then he should describe his general spiritual history, educational background, and church experience. When the committee receives this preliminary questionnaire, some of the names will be automatically excluded from further consideration. Dependent upon the response from the first group, the committee may want to select a second group of names and send the preliminary questionnaire to those men also.

When, after prayer and study, three or four names surface as strong possibilities, the next step should be taken. This involves the formulation and sending of a more extensive and exacting questionnaire. This will request more specific information regarding personal spiritual background, academic preparation, professional experience, pastoral record, denominational connections and cooperation, and three or four names of individuals who would be able to provide further insight regarding the potential candidate. The committee should also request a short statement of faith and list a few specific items to be considered. This not only will assure the committee of getting the specific information they desire but will also give the possible candidate some hint as to the type of church that is considering him and the matters which they consider of special importance.

When an individual has taken time to complete such a questionnaire, the committee should make certain that appreciation is expressed for his work and that he is notified regarding the general progress they are making as they search for God's man for that church. This questionnaire should put God's spotlight upon one or two individuals who seem to be special possibilities.

The next step in investigation is visiting the church where the possible candidate is now serving. The committee should go unannounced and try to be rather inconspicuous in the congregation. After the morning and/or evening services, the committee may want to caucus and decide whether they would like to meet personally with the potential candidate to get to know him a bit better.

If they decide they would like to have further contact with him, they can arrange such a meeting. After finding out whether he is still open to a change of pastorates, they can give him a copy of their church constitution, a statement of faith, a description of the purposes of the church, a job description, and other information which they feel would be helpful. The potential candidate should be given time to consider this material and to seek God's leading and enlightenment.

After some days have passed, the pulpit committee should contact the individual. If he is interested in pursuing the matter further, a meeting can be arranged where he can discuss matters with the pulpit committee. The pulpit committee should be prepared to lead in this discussion. A good way to begin is to ask the guest for his testimony regarding his commitment to Jesus Christ. After the committee has asked questions and provided information, the potential candidate may then be given the opportunity to ask questions that he may have. At this point, both the pulpit committee and the potential candidate will have gained much information. The committee must now decide whether they want to invite him to candidate at the church. If it is mutually agreed that this shall take place, then some careful planning should be done.

The pulpit committee and the church should remember that the candidate is not to be judged just on the basis of one or two sermons preached within the church but rather on the basis of the thorough examination and recommendation of the pulpit committee. He is also to be evaluated on the basis of his general rapport with the people.

The ideal length of time for a candidating experience is two consecutive Sundays and the week in between. This gives the candidate an opportunity to preach at least four times and conduct a midweek service. It also provides time for a church fellowship time. The candidate will also have an opportunity to visit some of the homes and become acquainted with the church and neighborhood. The pulpit committee should take advantage of every opportunity to give the church people a chance to meet and converse with him.

The church is responsible for caring for all of the expenses incurred by the candidate during this visit, together with a stipend to provide for the pulpit supply in his home church. This money should also cover the visit of his wife and even his family, if possible.

The Pastoral Candidate

There are several items which the pastoral candidate will try to clarify through quiet observation.

1. Do the people carry their Bibles to church? Do they use them during the Scripture reading and sermon?
2. Is there a genuine sense of freedom while preaching in the church?
3. Are there people of all ages and sexes in the congregation?
4. Is the church favorably located with regard to the shopping district and housing developments?
5. Is the congregation lower class, middle class, or upper class?
6. Is there potential for growth and room for expansion?
7. What is the number and nature of services scheduled for the coming week and month? Check the bulletin, church literature, and tract rack.
8. Is there any evidence of the church's impact upon the community?
9. Who appears to be the church boss? Who really runs the church?
10. Does the congregation appear to be of one mind in supporting the denomination? Check the bulletin, mission list, and literature.
11. Was the previous pastor held in high esteem? What might have been his reason for leaving?
12. Do the people appear to be hungry for the Word of God?
13. Is there a church study for the pastor?
14. Is the parsonage suitable for the pastor's family?
15. Does the attendance at prayer meeting give evidence of an interest in spiritual development?
16. What is the general cultural and educational background of the congregation?

17. How is the church equipped with regard to heating, air conditioning, ventilation, and lighting?
18. How is the church equipped with regard to visual aids, cloak rooms, and parish house?
19. Is the church located in a good neighborhood?
20. What appear to be the major hindrances to the success of this church?
21. What is the average attendance at the various services?
22. What is the quality of the work of the church staff?
23. Is an attitude of friendliness evident? Are people greeted upon entrance to the church? Upon leaving it?
24. Does the quality of congregational singing indicate at least moderate musical talent within the church?
25. Is there a spirit of reverence before the service? Or is there talking or restlessness?
26. Do the ushers, choir, and organist appear to have made adequate preparation for the service?
27. Are there a Sunday evening service, Sunday school, youth organization, and other scheduled activities?
28. Are there an adequate music department, qualified organist, choir director, and good hymnal?
29. Do the people seem to enjoy coming to church?

The pastoral candidate should try to learn the answers to the following questions by discussing them with responsible people. He should make it clear that at this point he is only seeking information and not expressing personal desires.

1. What are the statistics on church membership and attendance?
2. Is a parsonage provided for the minister?
3. Are parsonage utilities paid by the church?
4. Does the church make any provision for secretarial help?
5. Does the church make any provision for the pastor's car expense?
6. Does the pastor get an annual vacation? How many Sundays or how many weeks?
7. Does the church have a budget? What items are included in it? Do the members have copies?
8. Is the church interested in missions? How much does it give?

9. What is the financial condition of the church? Is the church in debt?
10. Are there plans for building in the near future?
11. How does the church raise money?
12. Does the church have a constitution? Obtain a copy if it does.
13. Is the church incorporated?
14. How long has the church been without a pastor?
15. Is there a known reason for the previous pastor's leaving? How long was the previous minister there?
16. How well is the Sunday school organized? Has the leadership received training?
17. Does the church own any audiovisual equipment?
18. Is an excessive amount of visitation required of the pastor?
19. Can the pastor rely on deacons for aid in visitation?
20. How many and what meetings will the church expect the pastor to attend?
21. If a call to the church is accepted, would it be for an indefinite period of time? What is the church procedure for severing relationships with its pastor?
22. Are there responsibilities which the church expects to place upon the minister's wife or family?
23. Does the church provide a nursery?
24. How many men have already been considered for this pastorate since the former pastor left? How many men have been offered a call and refused it?
25. Does the church make provision for moving expenses?
26. Is there an assistant to the minister? What are his duties? To whom is he responsible?
27. Is there a deacon available to accompany the minister on emergency night calls?
28. Does the church have a policy regarding open or closed communion?
29. Does the church have policies regarding divorce? Remarriage? Membership? The holding of office?
30. Do all the deacons believe in and practice tithing?
31. Does the church pay the organist, choir director, secretary, assistant pastor, song leader, sexton, and other staff?
32. Has the church ever had a membership visitation program?

33. What day of the week does the church consider the minister's day off?
34. Does the church have a policy regarding the use of the church for weddings and funerals of nonbelievers and nonmembers?
35. Has there been an increase in the church attendance and budget during the past five years?
36. What are the church organizations for youth, young couples, and adults?
37. What is the church's attitude toward lodges, councils of churches, drinking, smoking, dancing, church fairs, bingo, church suppers, and other activities?
38. What type of special evangelistic services does the church expect to promote? How often?
39. To what extent is there cooperation with other local churches?
40. Is there a doctrinal statement and church covenant to which the pastor and people must adhere?
41. What is the church policy regarding offerings being taken by outside speakers? How much does the church pay supply preachers?

The pastoral candidate should provide the pulpit committee with information pertaining to the following:

1. His attitude toward the privacy of his home
2. The hours he expects to spend in study without interruption, except for emergencies
3. The name he prefers ("Pastor Smith," not "Joe" or "Reverend Smith")
4. An understanding that the wife is not the assistant pastor
5. His position on tithing
6. His attitude toward marriage of divorced people, mixed marriages, and marriages of nonbelievers
7. His practice of premarital counseling
8. His attitude toward church finance, suppers, sales, and other fund-raising activities
9. His attitude toward denominational meetings
10. The extent to which he will cooperate with other churches
11. His attitude toward missions and giving to them

12. The procedure he will follow when leaving town for twenty-four hours or more
13. What he believes to be biblical preaching
14. The procedure of obtaining permission from the church board before accepting outside speaking engagements
15. A summary of his doctrinal position
16. His position regarding baptism, Lord's Supper, and dedication of infants
17. His view of the specific responsibilities of deacons
18. The desire for a private telephone line
19. The possibility of his teaching a Sunday School class
20. The desire for his office to be private
21. The desire that no one should speak for him, privately or publicly, unless he specifically asks them to do so

At least a short period of time should elapse between the candidating experience and calling for a vote by the church. This will give time for extended prayer on behalf of both the church and the candidate.

The vote for the calling of a pastor should always be by secret ballot. The number of votes necessary for extending a call is normally set by the church constitution. Absentee or proxy votes are not normally accepted. The votes should be counted and the results made public at the meeting. Note that we have been dealing with only one candidate; therefore there is no competitive voting. When the voting is complete and the findings have been declared, the church should move to notify the candidate at once.

If the vote is favorable, the candidate should be given the count which was taken on the first ballot, and he should be assured that a letter giving the specifics of the call will be in the mail in a few days.

The formal letter of call should include information on such matters as housing or housing allowance, salary, length of vacation, car allowance, moving expenses, utilities covered, insurance, and other matters discussed and agreed upon by the then potential candidate and the committee. This letter of specifics is important and should be formulated with care. If the pulpit committee has any questions about specific items within the letter, they should go back to the church for clarification.

The candidate will normally need from one to two weeks to come to a settled conviction regarding the Lord's will in connection with the call. If more time is needed, he can ask for an extension.

If the candidate feels led to accept the call, his present church should be notified on or before the date of the reading of the acceptance letter in the new church. The letter of acceptance should be gracious and general, with the exception of noting the time when he plans to arrive on the new field. The letter of acceptance will indicate that a letter of specifics will follow, which will be shared with the church at a later time. This letter will include the matters mutually agreed upon by the candidate and the committee. It is important that the entire church family know of the agreements which have been made with the new pastor.

As soon as the new pastor has accepted the call, the pulpit committee should send notices to all potential candidates who were kind enough to complete questionnaires, advising them that a pastor has been called.

The church should call its new pastor for an indefinite period of time. A yearly vote takes away a sense of security on the part of the pastor and his family. It also tends to add a note of instability to the work of the church. It will take a new pastor at least three years to get to know a small church and at least five years to get to know a larger church. The church family should plan to be tolerant and give the pastor time to survey the situation as well as time to build.

The Pastor and a Call to a New Parish

As for the pastor who has accepted the call, his church constitution will normally note the amount of time required between the giving of a resignation and the actual consummation of his ministry there. Some denominations advise as much as three months. Several feel that this is too long a period and that thirty days is a more reasonable length of time.

This interim period will be a very busy time for the pastor. All of the people who have been planning to have him and his family over will now realize that this must be done immediately. He may find that his family will be entertained for one or two meals each day. He must also proceed to pack his books and belongings. If his new charge is many miles away, he will have to decide whether to sell some of his present furniture and buy new at his new location or pay for the moving of his present furniture.

After he has read his resignation, he is a "lame duck" pastor. Everyone realizes that he is merely filling the gap until the next permanent pastor can be interviewed and invited. People will be hesitant to join the church during this period, since they have no assurance of the future direction of the pastoral ministry of the church. The church constituency will be hesitant to institute new programs, since these might not fit into the plans of the new pastor. For these and many other reasons, the pastor who has resigned should not remain more than thirty days before moving.

The pastor who has resigned should not participate in the process of seeking his successor, but he should do all he can to help prepare the way for him. The church should be in good condition. A list of members should be available for the new pastor. The new pastor will appreciate little hints that will help him in calling and shopping.

A pastor should let his people know that when he leaves their church, he is really going to leave it. He will want them to show the same support and loyalty to the new pastor as they have shown to himself. He will pray for them, but he should not make regular trips back nor in any way take part in solving future problems that may arise. Correspondence with the members of one's former church should be held to a minimum. If there is correspondence, no references should be made to church problems and future possibilities in the church just left. When a pastor leaves a church, he should leave it alone and not dabble in its life and activities. He should help former parishioners forget him so that they can more effectively center their attention on the work of the Lord through their new pastor.

The Pastor and His New Parish

As the new pastor heads toward his new field of service for Christ, there are several matters which he hopes his new parishioners will keep in mind. It would be presumptuous for him to give such a list to the church, but if someone else made this list available for the new church to take care of, it would be a great relief to the new pastor.

A check must be ready for the movers when the van arrives. Most companies will not unload the furniture until they are paid. They will charge rental until the check is forthcoming. If the pastor is delayed in arriving, the furniture should be unloaded but not unpacked, since the contents of the boxes are personal.

It would be a pleasant surprise for a new pastor to walk into the pantry of his new parsonage and find it stocked with canned goods. Some churches even arrange a schedule for bringing a hot dish to the parsonage door once or twice a day during the first week.

The new pastor will need a complete set of keys to the church, the parsonage, and any other church buildings. He will also appreciate knowing where the keys are kept for the church closets, offices, and vehicles.

He will want a private telephone line. The church may be able to arrange this for him or have someone available to go with him to the telephone office and to help him contact other utility offices in the community.

He will be concerned about any responsibility which he may have for the bulletins for the first Sunday and in the future. It will be helpful if he does not have to worry about the bulletin for the first Sunday.

He probably will not want to be called Reverend but prefer to be referred to as Pastor. It is normal that the pastor not be referred to by his first name nor his wife by hers, except when they are in very small, private groups of adults.

It will be difficult for the new pastor to find his way around the community. Perhaps a deacon could give some help in this matter by providing a map of the community with significant markings locating such buildings as schools, hospitals, shopping areas, and town or city offices. One of the deacons may also be available to go with the pastor on emergency calls at night.

He will appreciate being taken by his parishioners to his first denominational meetings and conferences. They will then be able to introduce him to the group as their new pastor.

Everyone knows that the pastor is relatively ignorant about the church when he arrives. It has been suggested that he seek as much information as possible about the church. Since he is new in the parish, people will not feel he is prying. The pastor's main concern for the first few months is gathering information. There will be many meetings that the new pastor and his wife will be expected to attend, especially during the first few weeks in the new parish. If there are small children, the cost of babysitting can mount up. The church might provide some help at this point, both in personnel and in finances.

As a new pastor, he is desirous of knowing the church "secrets." Many churches have unwritten rules which are actually followed but which the pastor has no way of knowing unless someone tells him. These may include such policies as: no divorced people can hold office in the church; an evangelistic invitation must be given at the close of each service; the morning service must end promptly at noon; no one can serve on a board or committee unless he can be present at all meetings. Any number of other items may be included in this list.

There may also be rather unique services which this church has held for years. It would be helpful for him to know of these well in advance. One church, for instance, cooperated each year in a community service for burning Christmas trees. Another church held an early morning service each Christmas day. Another church always had at least one series of revival meetings each year. Some churches may even have a speaker engaged for special meetings in the future. The new pastor's ability to unearth these secret procedures and customs and his ability to deal with them constructively may have a very positive effect upon his ministry at that church.

Each church has its own identity, its uniqueness arising from various factors. There may be geographical barriers dividing the parish or geographical oddities which will definitely influence the church activity. There are sociological factors, so it is important to know who lives in the community and how long they have been there. The cultural, racial, and ethnic factors will have an influence upon programs which may be started and special features which need to be emphasized, and in some cases will pose problems for the membership committee. There are value systems, traditions, and habits which will exert an influence. The church may hold a certain viewpoint on such issues as smoking, movies, and lodge membership. Every church operates on the basis of its history; the past experiences of the church will have its influence upon present and future activities and plans. The size of the church building and church membership will also be significant; for instance, a large building may demand an undue amount of money from the budget to keep it functioning.

The new pastor will find it helpful to make a list of the community resources available. These may be discovered by checking the telephone directory, or the city register, or contacting the chamber of commerce. He will then want to list beside each the reason for considering that resource important and how he can contact that resource. Once a relationship between church and community is established and developed, it can work both ways. Both the church and the community can profit.

Any increase in attendance during the first year should be evaluated with wisdom. It does not necessarily mean that the work of the new pastor is better than that of his predecessor. The fact that a pastor is new in the community will in itself bring a temporary increase in attendance and enthusiasm. Remember the old adage, "A new broom sweeps clean." Just novelty and curiosity may be the reasons for increased attendance. Pay more attention to an increase in attendance after a year rather than after the first month.

The pastor should make certain that he becomes known as a calling pastor. He will want to call on his entire membership during his first year, if at all possible. That first call is a get-acquainted call and should not be of extended duration except in rural localities. The pastor's wife might want to accompany her husband on this first round of visits. This will strengthen the emphasis on getting acquainted. The pastor will have to cut down on the number of calls after his first contact with the congregation since he cannot keep his feet going constantly through the parish and also have his head back in his study preparing messages from the Word. Both the pastor's feet and his head must share in the ministry.

During the first few months on the field, the pastor and his wife should provide opportunity for the church people to see the interior of the parsonage, perhaps by holding an open house. Most human beings have an inborn curiosity. The new parishioners will be interested in discovering how the new pastor and his wife have decorated the parsonage. Rather than making the parishioners think up excuses for getting inside the parsonage, a new pastor should let them know he is going to invite everyone to come. They will then give him some time to settle, knowing that he has promised to invite them soon. The parishioners will appreciate his willingness to let them see his home since he as pastor will be visiting in their homes.

The pastor should use the first few months to gather information regarding the church's past and present accomplishments and failures. The procedures followed by his predecessor may not at first seem wise to the new pastor. As he discovers the procedures of his predecessor there may be a temptation to dub him an ignoramus. But he should wait a while; the former pastor may have been far wiser than the new one thinks. Time often adds its touch of wisdom. There may be unique features in that particular church which necessitated particular procedures.

A new pastor will have to listen on many occasions to a discussion of that which the predecessor did and did not do. He must listen, but he should say little. Remember that if they talk about the former pastor after he has gone, they will probably talk about the new one when he leaves.

Most churches have a church controller, or "church boss." This individual may not even be in an official position, but he has extensive influence within the church. The pastor should find out who he is and assist him in maturing spiritually. Remember, it may take a long time to discover this leading individual. He or she may stand back in the shadows at the beginning and show his real identity only about the time of the first church business meeting. But if he is growing spiritually, he will support needed programs and will also lead others to support them. When this individual speaks publicly or privately, he will sway the opinions of many of the voting members.

The pastor will want to be cautious in selecting helpers during the first year. First impressions are often misleading. Many who appear to have potential for service do not possess the ability to carry a project through to completion. Many will want to establish close friendships with the pastor and his family during the early months, but only time will indicate where wise friendships can be formed. "Pine log" friendships burn brightly for a time but do not last.

God never makes mistakes, but pastors and pulpit committees are fallible. We would have less cause for concern and fewer problems if we could always be certain that God's man was in God's place for ministry. It is more profitable for a pulpit committee to spend a long time and seek special spiritual guidance in joining the pastor and the church than to have to go through the agonies of being forced to sever the relationship later. A pastor should be selected with prayer and care. The pastor and the church must both be on target.

Additional Reading

Gillaspie, Gerald W. *The Restless Pastor*. Chicago: Moody, 1974.
———. *The Empty Pulpit*. Chicago: Moody, 1975
Reinboth, Oscar H. *Calls and Vacancies*. Saint Louis: Concordia, 1967.
Turnbull, Ralph G. *A Minister's Obstacles*. Westwood, N.J.: Revell, 1946.

CHAPTER 2

Clarifying Purposes, Goals, and Objectives

Growing churches have clear-cut purposes, goals, and objectives. They are not content to have motion without meaning. It is a maxim of educational philosophy that philosophy governs materials and methods. In church work we should not begin by formulating a plan or establishing a program but by determining the purposes. If we aim at nothing, then that is what we will hit.

Dean Kelly, in his book *Why Conservative Churches Are Growing,* states that one reason for the growth of conservative churches is that they are willing to put more time and effort into their cause. Another reason for their growth is their willingness to subordinate their personal desires and ambitions to the shared goals of the group.[1] For full effectiveness, all of the work of the church must be integrated into a unified program with meaningful purposes at its core. The achievement of God's purposes, not mere activism, should be the concern of the church. Some churches seem to struggle merely to survive rather than to achieve a purpose.

Clarifying purposes and establishing goals are lost arts in churches, homes, and individual lives. Our purposes and goals, conscious or unconscious, largely determine what direction our lives take and whether or not we find freedom and fulfillment as individuals and members of the human family. Clear purposes and goals force people to become specific in their thinking.

Purposes and goals are the key variables in revitalizing a church. When we are dealing with these, we are dealing with power. You do not find meaning in a purposeless organization. Purposes and goals provide insights into an organization's character and thus to its behavior. The definition of purpose should influence the actions and attitudes of every person in the congregation. Establish the purposes first, and then proceed to program and performance.

The purposes of a church are often listed near the beginning of the church constitution. Constitutions do not provide thrilling reading material for members of a church, and therefore the purposes are not reviewed very often. They were formulated in the past by those no longer present. The present constituency may have disregarded these purposes almost completely and proceeded to follow unofficially a new set of purposes. These purposes are often merely assumed and do not appear in written form. This may result in many sets of purposes being operative within a single church.

In order to discover how knowledgeable the church people are of their real purposes, one could distribute the form entitled "*Questionnaire on Congregational Purposes*," which is included in the appendix. Church members need to be challenged to think through the reason for their existence and church activity.

Clarifying General Purposes

In establishing purposes, the church has a distinct advantage over many organizations. It has the Bible as a foundation for faith and practice. God has made clear the purposes for His Church. The first divine purpose is service. The Church is the paramount instrument through which Christ accomplishes His will in the present age (Jn 15:16; 1 Co 12:27-30; Eph 1:22-23; 3:10*b*). The second purpose is to exalt the moral glory of Christ, who became visible to men when He became incarnate (Jn 1:1,14). The Church is the body through which He is now manifested, as His physical body was when He walked among men (Jn 17:10, 22-23). The third divine purpose is to exhibit to the entire world the wisdom and grace of God, showing what God can do for sinners (Eph 2:6-7; 3:8-11). The fourth divine purpose is fellowship; the Church was created for fellowship with Christ her Lord in the present and in eternity future (Mt 28:20; Jn 17:24).

Alvin Lindgren, of Garrett Seminary, sets forth the purposes of a church in terms of functions. The first is *koinonia,* which includes shepherding, counseling, fellowship, healing, and ministering. Another function is worship. This includes proclaiming the truth, dramatizing beliefs, and ceremonial remembering. The third function is promoting a missionary spirit. This includes outreach, witnessing in the world, and the transformation of oppression systems. The fourth function is fostering growth. This includes personal spiritual development, learning, and interpreting the Christian faith. It also involves finding new methods of expressing the Christian faith.[2]

A pastor taking a course at a seminary in the Midwest was asked to write what he considered to be the five purposes of a Christian church. His list included the following five with their corresponding Scriptures.

1. To worship God (Eph 1:3-14; 1 Pe 2:5-10)
2. To sustain and upbuild the faith of the members (1 Co 12:23-25; Eph 2:22; Titus 2:14)
3. To engage in mutual service (Eph 4:11-15)
4. To win others to Christ (Mt 2:8, 19-20; Ac 1:8)
5. To interpret today's happenings in the light of God's revelation (Ro 15:4; Eph 3:8-11)

One seminary asked thirty-eight of its graduating seniors to list what they considered to be the outstanding purposes of a church. Their first fifteen purposes were in this order:

1. Evangelism
2. Worship
3. Preaching the Word
4. Training members to live by the Word
5. Instructing the members in the Christian truth
6. Administering the ordinances
7. Fellowship
8. Teaching Bible doctrine
9. Bringing glory to God
10. Missions
11. Guiding Christians toward spiritual maturity
12. Prayer

13. Perfecting the saints
14. Training leaders
15. Providing opportunity for service

Fred Dickason, in his class lectures at Moody Bible Institute, has suggested that the church has three purposes: to express the glory of God, to evangelize the world, and to edify the saints.

A church constitution will normally list three or more general purposes for the church. These are often forgotten when the members of the church plan their programs and activities. These purposes are so broad that it becomes difficult to demonstrate the relationship between each segment of the church and one or more of these general purposes.

We suggest that the church begin with these general purposes but not stop there. It is our aim to become more specific and active. The second step is to proceed from general purposes to specific areas of concern. The third step is to formulate goals for each of these areas. The fourth step is to establish objectives which, when completed, will fulfill the goal. We might illustrate the four steps by the following diagram:

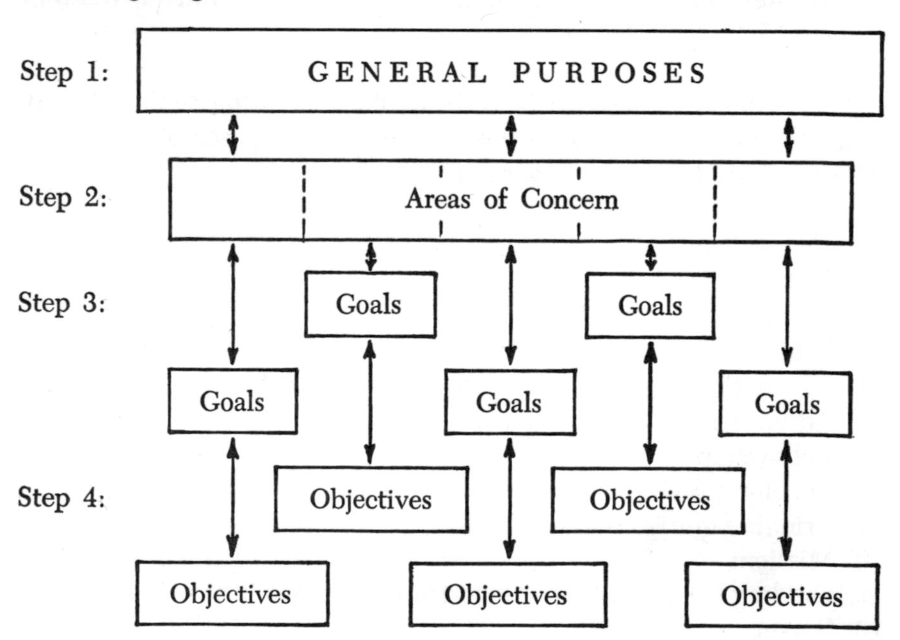

The church can use this diagram as a guide for the formulation of goals and objectives. List the general purposes of the church, such as winning the unsaved, edifying believers, godly worship, meeting the spiritual and educational needs of the youth, and any others. Then list the areas of concern within the church life. These areas of concern might include property, transportation, finance, education, hospitality, administration, outreach, spiritual life, and worship. Before proceeding, we must clarify the nature of goals and objectives.

Definition of Goals and Objectives

A goal is a state of being toward which one is heading; it is qualitative in nature. The formulation of a set of goals must be followed by the formulation of a set of objectives. Objectives are steps taken to achieve a goal. They are quantitative in nature, and their effectiveness can be measured. One can determine whether or not an objective has been accomplished.

Now that we have distinguished between goals and objectives, we can illustrate the four-step process set forth in the diagram as follows:

Step 1. Select one of the general purposes: *winning the unsaved*

Step 2. Select an area of concern: *youth activities*

Step 3. Select a future state toward which you are heading: *young people who know how to lead an individual to a saving knowledge of Jesus Christ*

Step 4. Determine a step which can be taken so that the goal noted in Step 3 can become a reality: *provide someone able to train youth for evangelistic work to lead four of their meetings and instruct in soul winning.*

We can now reread this diagram and see what has been done. By providing someone able to train youth for evangelistic work to take four of the youth meetings for instructional purposes, we will be taking a step toward our goal of having a group of young people in the church who will know how to lead an individual to a saving knowledge of Jesus Christ. This objective and goal will involve several areas of concern: youth activity, education, outreach, and spiritual life. We now have a specific objective and goal involving various areas of concern which will help us fulfill one of the general purposes noted in Step 1, winning the unsaved.

Classification of Goals

Amitai Etzioni, in the book *A Comparative Analysis of Complex Organizations*, suggests that there are several classifications for goals. The first of these is *organizational* goals. These represent the state of affairs which the organization is attempting to realize. They can be determined by an examination of specific aspects of the organizational process, such as the budget. Examining the budget will highlight the priorities in the allocation of means. In a church, it will give a fairly good indication of the goals and purposes of that church.

The *stated* goals can serve as a clue to the actual goals. The stated goals are the ones spelled out for promotional purposes. A church will sometimes publish in its literature certain statements and slogans to attract others to the church. Those who come sometimes discover that these indicators of purpose and goals do not really reflect what the church is doing.

The *order* goals are associated with discipline in church work. The order, or discipline, goals attempt to control participants by segregating them from society and by blocking them from further deviant activities. Some merely segregate deviants; others segregate and punish; and still others eliminate deviants altogether. The order goals in a church are sometimes unpublished. They are, however, just as real and binding. These order goals may include practices which the members should follow, or they may list practices from which the members should abstain. There may be an attempt to produce a church of positive Christians or a group of separatists who will be bound together by that which they do not do.

The economic goals usually concern producing commodities and services supplied to outsiders. These are prominent goals in most churches; however, there appears to be more emphasis on establishing economic goals which will provide for the membership rather than for outsiders, although one might consider missionary financial goals as supplying services to outsiders.

Organizations have *cultural* goals which may be evidenced in the attempts to preserve cultural heritage and transfer it from generation to generation. These goals have been evidenced in bilingual churches where many older congregations have continued to maintain worship services in their mother language in order to keep the cultural image.

Social goals are served by organizations that satisfy the gregarious needs of their members.[3] Many churches put a very high priority on these goals.

Etzioni's classification pertains to secular organizations more directly than to church organizations; there are many similarities, however, between them.

Establishing Goals

When a church is healthy, its purposes and goals are explicit and can be examined by all the members. The goals should be acknowledged by as many as possible within the church. By this we mean that they should be determined by as many as possible rather than being determined by just a few and passed to the others. Goals for a group are more likely to be achieved when the whole group is involved in setting them. Personal involvement is important.

The first step in establishing goals is to clarify the task itself. Your task is to have as many people as possible establish goals for all areas of the church life: property, transportation, finance, education, hospitality, administration, communication, outreach, spiritual life, and worship. Then all activity will be aimed at making the goals a reality. It is important not only that the task be clarified for the committee but that the church family be made cognizant of the importance and extent of the task.

The second step is to gather from the church family information as to their hopes and concerns for each of the areas listed. There should also be a consideration of resources, traditions, limitations, needs, and scriptural guidelines. One method of gaining some of this information is to have brainstorming sessions in which people are invited to share ideas without comment or evaluation. After the session, a committee can organize and evaluate the material collected. The accumulated material should be shared with the church family at a later time. Be sure that this whole process is not dominated by the committee; it is for the entire church family.

The third step is combining the collected information according to each particular area to which it pertains. The areas serve as classification headings for the hopes, concerns, resources, traditions, limitations, needs, and scriptural guidelines.

The fourth step is the formulation of one or more goals for each area. These goals should accord with Scripture as well as reflect the concerns of the constituency. These area goals must be viewed in respect to the overall purposes of the church. As these area goals are established, there must be a concern for the individual, a concern for the fellowship, and a concern for the work of the Kingdom. As several goals may be formulated in each area, the process of determining priorities must take place in order that first things may be accomplished first.

There are several basic types of organizational orientation. The first might be called *task* orientation. This is concerned primarily with the performance and activity of the moment. *Control* orientation, on the other hand, is related to government, authority, and decisions. The primary concern is not to accomplish something but to do whatever you do in the correct way. We advocate a third type, *goal* orientation. This means that everything done must contribute to the stated goal. Unfortunately, churches often start out with goal orientation but end up perpetuating an organization rather than pursuing a purpose or goal. The ideal is to have a goal-directed, achievement-oriented church organization that embodies our theological commitments and serves our moral intentions.

Establishing Objectives

Objectives must be compatible with the general purposes of the organization. They should be dynamic, promoting action. What actions, when carried out, will make each area goal a reality? It is important to consider the maturity and capabilities of the members of the group. It is not practical to establish objectives which are out of reach of the group. The objectives should be varied enough to meet the needs of individuals within the organization but not so numerous that they diffuse the effort to a level of ineffectiveness.

These objectives should be cooperatively determined. There is no one pattern for accomplishing this which can fit every situation. Good administrative leadership is needed at this point to bring about an expression of the creative, cooperative, and self-generating zeal of all the members.

The Importance of Purposes

There is a close correlation between the fulfilling of purposes and good administration. Good administration demands that the administrator share with the group its understanding of its purposes. In church administration, the pastor must know what the purposes are, and the congregation must be kept aware of them. The administrator must coordinate and initiate activities and experiences which will carry out these purposes. He must help the people use all of the resources at their disposal in fulfilling the purposes. It is important to keep in mind that the best methods of church management are those which accomplish the purposes of the church.

Organizations have boundary lines which tend to give it identity. These boundaries are directly related to the purposes of the group. The purposes of a group are often so precisely and narrowly delineated that they automatically exclude a certain segment of people. In some groups the boundaries are nearly closed, whereas in other groups there is a large degree of permeability. Boundaries force groups to discriminate as far as new members are concerned; some prospective members are weeded out because they will not help attain the purposes of the group.

The style of the church building should bear a direct relationship to the purposes of a church. The church building is a tool of mission. In considering a building program, begin with the purposes you hope to accomplish in the building. Then consider the program you want to develop to bring the purpose to pass. You should then consider the resources which are available.

A budget is a statement of purpose and a diagram of expectations. The purposes of a church can be seen in its budget. Unfortunately, some churches have overlooked their purposes when formulating the budget. The goals some churches have for budget formulation are keeping the budget as low as possible, securing enough pledged contributions to equal the proposed expenditures, and keeping the actual expenditures within the limits of the anticipated receipts. A level of giving should be developed which is related to the potential of the congregation rather than merely to the covering of the budget. The budget should be a floor rather than a ceiling. There should be freedom for the organization to reach forward to achieve its expanding purposes.

Each group within a church must evaluate its goals in terms of the general purposes of the entire church. The church is a sum of its parts. Each part should reflect the purposes of the whole. Cooperative effort can be short-circuited and productivity curtailed when the goals of organizations within the church conflict with the general purposes of the larger organization. One indication that a group has the capacity to grow is in its ability to divide into parts while maintaining collective unity around prevailing purposes.

The most important thing about a road is where it leads. The direction of a church must be determined and made clear to the constituency. The most important questions to ask about a church are not, What buildings does it have? Who attends? When was it founded? or Where is it located? The most important question is, Why is it there?

Additional Reading

Etzioni, Amitai. *A Comparative Analysis of Complex Organizations*. New York: Free Press, 1961.

Getz, Gene A. *Sharpening the Focus of the Church*. Chicago: Moody, 1974.

Kelley, Dean M. *Why Conservative Churches Are Growing*. New York: Harper & Row, 1962.

Lindgren, Alvin J. *Foundations for Purposeful Church Administration*. Nashville: Abingdon, 1965.

Richards, Lawrence O. *A New Face for the Church*. Grand Rapids: Zondervan, 1970.

Schaller, Lyle E. *Parish Planning*. Nashville: Abingdon, 1971.

Worley, Robert C. *Change in the Church: A Source of Hope*. Philadelphia: Westminster, 1971.

CHAPTER 3

Systematizing Church Management

Students would find it profitable in their preparation for the ministry to spend a year working in some business organization where they could view firsthand the skills of administration as performed by trained professionals. Such an experience would give them an appreciation for good management.

Many activities appear easy until one tries them. Water skiing, for instance, does not look difficult as you watch from the shoreline or read about it in books. But when you actually try it, then you become aware of its difficulty. Management is somewhat similar. You can read about it, but you will never appreciate its complexity until you actually become involved in it.

The pastoral office encompasses at least four activities: personal relationships and ministries; preaching and the conduct of worship; teaching; and administration. In the work of administration, the pastor needs to make things happen. His job is both to facilitate and to initiate activity.

Pastors have various attitudes toward administration. Some rebel, thinking of it in terms of busywork and priding themselves on the lack of organization within the parish. To others, it is a menial chore; it is all right for laymen, but the pastor feels he is above such matters. Still other pastors major in carrying out organizational details and in publicizing the church and themselves. All three of these attitudes toward administration need to be corrected.

Part of the pastor's attempt to avoid involvement in management stems from the fact that few seminaries offer much help in this area.

The pastor feels inadequate and therefore ignores or runs away from his administrative responsibilities.

During World War I, pilots did not have the many flight instruments they have today. When they were in the midst of clouds and haze, they would determine whether or not they were right side up or upside down by the pressure exerted on either their seat belt or the seat of their pants. If the pressure was on their seat belt, they were upside down. Unfortunately, in church work too many approach management from the standpoint of merely checking the place of pressure. And in some cases, an individual may be numb or naive and not feel any pressure at all. It is not wise to put your mind in neutral and merely go where you are pushed.

Many seminaries have neglected the study of management because Christians have been conditioned to accept the natural-leader concept. The "natural" leader generally starts his own organization. Biographies are written about him. Young men are told to emulate him. He does unique things and gets away with them because he is the boss. He is very successful, but usually over a rather short period of time.

Management is a skill, but it is also a tool for the spiritual man. The spiritual man can take this tool and use it for the glory of God. The real issue is whether or not the individual is a spiritual individual. God will bless some things as supplements which He will not bless as substitutes. Management can never be regarded as a substitute for spirituality.

One of the simplest definitions of administration is the one given by Arthur Adams in *Pastoral Administration*: "Administration is working with and through people to get things done."[1] Dr. Lindgren says that purposeful church administration involves the church in the discovery of her nature and mission and in moving in a coherent and comprehensive manner toward providing such experiences as will enable the church to utilize all her resources and personnel in the fulfillment of her mission of making known God's love for men.[2]

The word *administer* comes from the Latin *administrare,* meaning "to serve." This serving function involves discovering and clarifying goals and purposes and in guiding movement toward their realization. It provides the means through which a group can fulfill its purpose. One must know where he is going and why before he can decide how to get there. Administration consists of facilitating the recognition of the purpose of the church, stimulating and coordinating experiences and activities, and discovering and utilizing personnel and resources.

Administration was the term which was used until just a few years ago. The schools which were then schools of administration are now schools of management. In Christian circles, administration, or management, is the stewardship of the talents of the men entrusted to our care.

Qualifications of an Administrator

The first and most basic concern of the church administrator is to have a clear understanding of the nature of the church. Beyond this basic concern, the administrator must have a comprehensive understanding of the field in which he is working so that he can determine what means will contribute to the achievement of the purposes of the group. He also must be able to work well with other persons whose contributions are as important and essential as his own. The administrator must like people and be able to put them to work at a task they consider worthwhile. He must develop the ability to deal with insignificant matters quickly but at the same time not to treat details casually. A capable administrator is known by the percentage of right decisions he makes and his ability to select the right followers. Whatever he does must be done in love. He must recognize the uniqueness of every situation and work with a flexible set of principles, but always keep the goals in mind.

A pastor functioning as an administrator will help carry out the programs and plans of his congregation. He will lead the church in building and property improvement and management. It is part of his task to run an efficient office. He will encourage activities in the many groups organized within the congregation. One of his important functions will be to secure the right leadership to develop the entire church program. The resolution and creative use of conflict also is important. The pastor should not take charge of administration matters as a dictator but as a guide. He should serve as a resource person, necessitating his acquaintance with helpful bibliography and resource people. He should desire to learn from others involved in the same type of activity.

The essence of leadership is mobilizing people on behalf of a particular aim because they desire its realization and want to join in bringing it to pass. Our churches need pastor-administrators who can effectively order, forward, and facilitate the associated efforts of a congregation to realize some defined purposes.

It is evident that many temptations come to the administrator. There is first of all the temptation to be more interesed in programs than in people. He is sometimes tempted to confuse institutional goals with divine purposes. There is the temptation to manipulate rather than to lead. It is difficult for him to forget that he is not a ruler but a servant and steward of the Lord. Another temptation is to substitute busywork for spiritual activities. Someone has suggested that St. Vitus is America's favorite saint. We tend to be hyperactive; we must always be in motion. We seem to feel there are only two types of people—the quick and the dead. But great decisions are not made in busy streets. It is imperative that the administrator slow down and separate mere work from spiritually profitable activity.

Many of the qualities which mark a business executive as worthy of promotion are also profitable for the productive church worker. Some of these qualities are the capacity for hard work, the ability to get things done through people, a neat appearance, self-confidence, an ability to make sound decisions, ambition, and the ability to communicate.

The Administrative Process

There are five basic steps in the administrative process as applied to church administration. The first is the *recognition of needs.* The basic needs must be clearly understood before we can attempt to fill them. Sometimes the administrator sees a need so clearly himself that he proceeds with a plan to meet it and then tries to sell the board on the program before they actually realize the problem. The experience of Nehemiah, as recorded in the second chapter of the Bible book bearing his name, illustrates the wisdom of surveying the situation and recognizing the extent of need before beginning to build.

The second step in the administrative process is *planning*. Planning is thinking, coordinating, analyzing, communicating, and interacting. Planning also involves revising, appraising, and criticizing the proposed plans and suggestions. As many people as possible should be given the opportunity to make suggestions. A clear statement of the problem should be given wide publicity. There is often the danger of being diverted from recognizing the true problem and focusing only on the effects of the problem.

The administrator would find it profitable to study the problem-solving techniques which have formed the basis of the modern discussion method in the book by McBurney and Hance, *Discussion in Human Affairs*. The discussion method has been developed for directing thought in the discussion of a problem. It involves an adaptation of Dewey's analysis included in his process of reflective thinking. The five steps in the discussion method are:

1. The definition and delineation of the problem
2. The analyzing of the problem
3. The suggestions of hypotheses or solutions
4. The reasoned development of the hypotheses or solutions in the preceeding step
5. Further verification[3]

There should be an exploration of many possible solutions and an attempt to arrive at a consensus as to the best one.

It is imperative in planning that we involve people in the decision-making process if we want them to cooperate in carrying out the decision. We must give them the facts and be willing to let them know what we know about the situation. It has been found that if you as a leader tell the people all you can, they will seldom ask that you tell them what you should not tell them.

In planning our concern must not be what we did in the past but where we are at this moment and, with this information, how we should plan for tomorrow. Present choices limit future actions; decisions made now will control the actions of tomorrow. Just as big doors swing on small hinges, decisions which appear small in size may be great in influence.

Lorne Sanny was the successor to Dawson Trotman of the Navigators. In preparation for that position, he read, among many other things, a little booklet entitled *Management*, written by the president of the National Bank of Detroit. This little booklet started him on a trail of discovery of helpful guidelines in management. As a result, Sanny developed four questions related to objectives. He poses these questions to those who serve in the organization with him. The first is, What are your objectives? The second is, What are your opportunities? The third question is, What are your resources? The final question is, What is your strategy for applying your resources to your opportunities to obtain your objectives?[4]

There are five rules for establishing obejctives: (1) consider past performance, (2) set realistic levels, (3) state goals in measurable terms, (4) build an improvement factor into the objectives, and (5) formulate objectives in conjunction with those who are to carry them out.

The third step in the administrative process is *organizing*. This involves the what, when, who, and follow through. We must establish an organizational structure which will help us achieve our objectives. Management organizing is the grouping, arranging, and relating of the work to be performed.

The fourth step in the administrative process is *stimulation and implementation* of action. All workers should be secured early, and adequate provisions should be made for their training. Some so emphasize the results of the program that they ignore or minimize the concern for the growth of persons. One aspect of stimulating action is keeping to a time schedule unless significant circumstances make a change desirable. Keeping the congregation well informed is always a stimulant to action.

If we are in places of leadership, we must make decisions. Hesitancy to do this will breed demoralization and frustration in our ranks. To make decisions involves risk. A logical decision can be made only after the problem is defined. A decision must be valid in terms of the evidence upon which it is based. Decisions we make are valid or invalid depending upon how and when we look at them. Four questions should be asked in connection with decision making:

1. Do we really understand the problem?
2. What are we trying to get done?
3. Is this the way to do it?
4. What may go wrong if we put this decision into action?

In a recent book entitled *Decision . . . Ouch!*, William Krutza suggests that in making decisions we should analyze our feelings, get the facts, consider others, understand ourselves, evaluate our interests, and discover God's will.

The fifth step in the administrative process is *evaluation.* This is a continuing process taking place simultaneously with each preceeding step of the administrative process. Continual evaluation involves controlling the work we engage in, checking the work in progress, and completing it. Once the goal has been identified, the relationships determined, the work assigned, and the decision-making power defined, controlling ensures that we are all going in one direction.

Ordway Tead, in *The Art of Administration,* states that there are several elements which together make up the responsibilities of administration as a total process:

1. To define and set forth the purposes, aims, objectives or ends of the organization
2. To lay down the broad plan for the structuring of the organization
3. To recruit and organize the executive staff as defined in the plan
4. To provide a clear delegation and allocation of authority and responsibility
5. To direct and oversee the general carrying forward of the activities delegated
6. To assure that a sufficient definition and standardization of all positions have taken place so that quantity and quality of performance are specifically established and are assuredly being maintained
7. To make provisions for the necessary ccmmittees and confer-

ences and for their conduct in order to achieve good coordination among major and lesser functional workers

8. To assure stimulation and the necessary energizing of the entire personnel
9. To provide an accurate evaluation of the total income in relation to established purposes
10. To look ahead and forecast as to the organization's aims as well as the ways and means toward realizing them, in order to keep both ends and means adjusted to all kinds of inside and outside influences and requirements[5]

Administrative Efficiency Principles

Herbert Simon, in *Administrative Behavior,* states that the following are some of the commonly accepted administrative principles.

1. Administrative efficiency is increased by a specialization of the task among the group. Administrative efficiency is increased by grouping the work, for purposes of control, according to a purpose, process, clientele or place.
2. Administrative efficiency is increased by arranging the members of the group in a determinate hierarchy of authority.
3. Administrative efficiency is increased by limiting the span of control at any point in the hierarchy to a small number.[6]

Certainly one of the basic principles to keep in mind is that the best methods of local church organization are those which best accomplish the purpose of the church. Good church management recognizes that there is no one pattern which can fit every situation. Good administrative leadership is continuously moving in a world of strategy deeply concerned to assure the "consent of the governed." The aims of the organization are shared in the making. The working policies and methods are agreed to by those involved. All feel free and eager to contribute their best creative effort.

Here are ten suggestions for good management as suggested by the American Management Association. Some changes have been made in the wording, but the basic thought has been maintained.

1. Definite and clear-cut responsibilities should be assigned to each person or position.

2. Responsibility should always be coupled with corresponding authority.
3. No changes should be made in scope or responsibilities of a position without a definite understanding to that effect on the part of all persons concerned.
4. No employee should be subject to definite orders from more than one source.
5. Orders should never be given to subordinates over the head of a responsible executive.
6. Criticisms of subordinates should be made privately and never in front of other employees.
7. No dispute or difference between executive or employee as to authority or responsibility should be considered too trivial for prompt attention.
8. Promotions, wage changes, and disciplinary action should always be approved by the executive immediately superior to the one directly responsible.
9. No executive or employee should ever be required or expected to be at the same time an assistant to, and a critic of another.
10. Means should be provided for individuals to check on their own work. They have a right to know how well they are doing.

Communication in Church Administration

Communication is any process whereby decisions are transmitted from one member of an organization to another. Organizational communication is a two-way process involving facts, advice, and information being transmitted to the decision maker, who in turn transmits his decisions to other parts of the organization. A two-way process of communication must be maintained, however, since the pastor must keep informed of how his people are thinking and feeling. The people must be constantly informed of pastoral changes in policies and procedures which affect their work.

To communicate is to make contact, to inspire, and to receive response. Communication between people involves relationship and information. In general, communication can be said to be a process by which senders and receivers of messages interact in given social contexts. The word *communication* comes from the Latin *commu-*

nis, meaning "common." When we communicate, we are trying to establish commonness with someone. Speech is a unique process of symbolic communication that involves interaction between persons. Christian communication is a distinctive process. It includes both human and divine elements. It is a difficult activity, since it involves all kinds of classes of people and includes a ministry to groups as well as to individuals. Because it is complicated, it takes additional work and sacrifice.[7]

An organization is a systematically organic whole, arranged in interdependent parts. Each part has a special function or relation to the whole. It is through the process of communication that organizations achieve the goal or end which was formerly unavailable to the individual.

Communication within an organization is important. It is a very vital tool of good management. The workers must feel that they are informed concerning the mutual interests in the success of the organization. Leaders should allot time each week to become acquainted with problems within the organization, and a portion of time for discussing these problems should be given in the staff meetings.

Effective communication demands that problems be discussed as they arise. Such discussions should be open and frank, fair and equitable. Staff meetings need to be held not only at a proper time but also in a proper place. An emphasis should be placed upon creating and maintaining good attitudes throughout the discussion. The maintenance of good human relations is an everyday process. There are two essential elements in a good communication climate. The first is an attitude that is people-centered rather than production-centered. The second is an open-door policy in fact as well as in word.

The leaders must recognize their responsibility to listen as well as to speak. The desire to listen to another person exerts a powerful control over our listening behavior. What one expects to hear may affect what he actually hears.

Face-to-face communication is the most effective. There are times, however, when such verbal communication should be followed by writing. The wise administrator delivers instructions and descriptions of responsibility in writing. As administrator, he will also require that reports, evaluations, and recommendations come to him in writing from his co-laborers.

It is comparatively easy for a pastor to allow communication barriers to come between him and his people. Some of these barriers come because of the emphasis upon the dichotomy between clergy and laity. The clergy often is unable to speak the language of the laity.

It has been suggested that there are three major barriers to communication: individual differences, an atmosphere of unfriendliness, and a lack of proper channels. An attitude of infallibility will also discourage and short-circuit communication. The person who has this dogmatic attitude often appears to be more interested in triumph than in truth.

The communicator who is coldly objective or who refuses to disclose his own feelings is likely to be viewed with suspicion. His purpose in communication may be judged manipulative by the receiver. When this happens, communication is subverted.

Ambiguity of authority interferes with communication. The people must know where the lines of authority are drawn. They have a right to a clear and definite job description.

If we are to improve the quality of communication, we must be alert to the situation at hand. We must think through our approach and try to project ourselves into the other person's point of view. We must approach the intended receiver of the message in a friendly, natural manner.

Communication Flow in Administration

The flow of communication must be directed. Whenever possible it should move upward, step by step, through an organization. It should not be necessary for the bottom level of workers to communicate directly with those who are several steps higher in the organization, although this does not mean they should be denied the opportunity if need arises. Communication should move upward in an organization until it reaches one who can care for the matter. If that one can handle the problem effectively, then it does not have to go higher.

One should be a sensitive listener, realizing that not everyone will appreciate the same facts in the same way. A complaint or criticism will not always reveal the true cause for the criticism. The leader must realize that often his workers tell him only what they know he wants to hear.

The flow of communication within an organization will be better laterally, among the workers of the same status, than it will be either upward or downward in the levels of management. More messages will be sent downward than upward. Persons who are low on the authority ladder will be cautious about the messages they send upward. Persons of high status often think that they are being heard more accurately than facts sustain, because persons lower on the ladder often distort messages they receive from above in such a way as to fit their purposes.

Patterns of Communication in Administration

The following diagrams indicate the types of communication patterns most often found in organizations. If one wanted to test the comparative effectiveness of these patterns, he could select different groups to use the different patterns and see which group was most successful in having a message communicated from point (A) to the other members of the group.

Pattern 1 is known as "Custer's cluster" and is the pattern of communication most commonly used in organizations. Pattern 2 involves more time on the part of the participants but conveys the information in a more reliable manner. Pattern 3 is the communication pattern found in an organization which is run by a dictator.

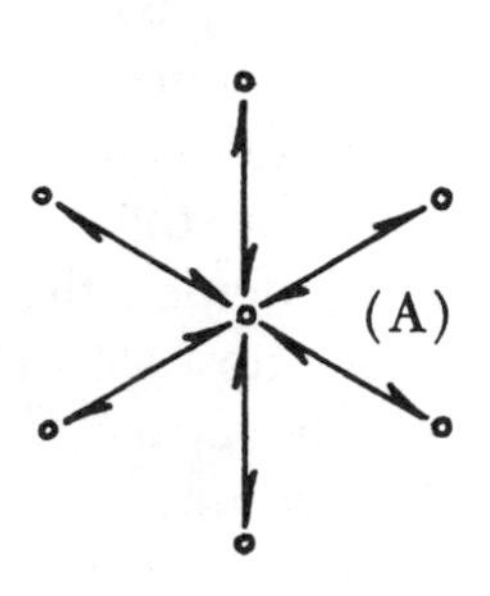

Pattern 1

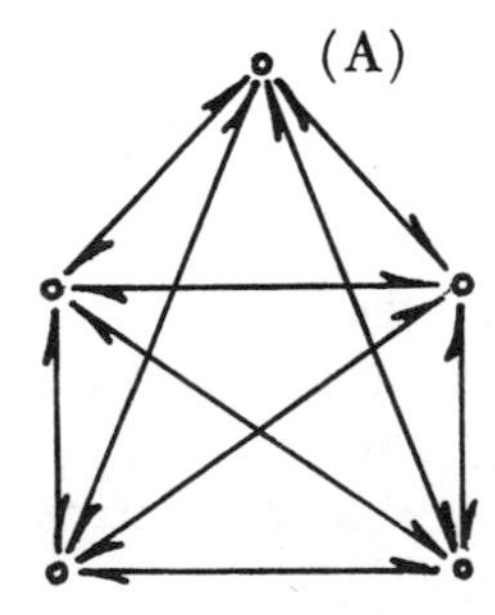

Pattern 2

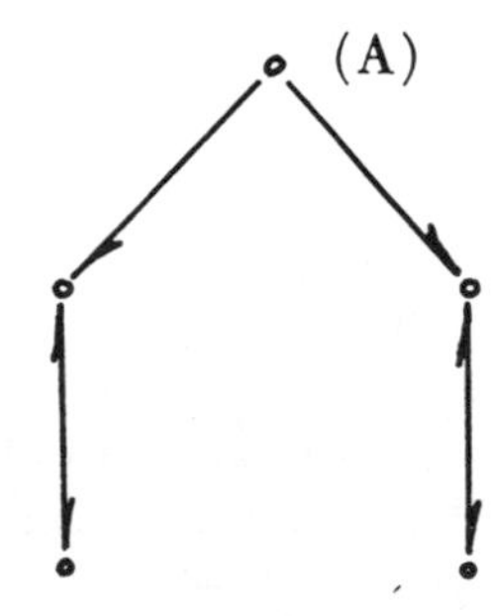

Pattern 3

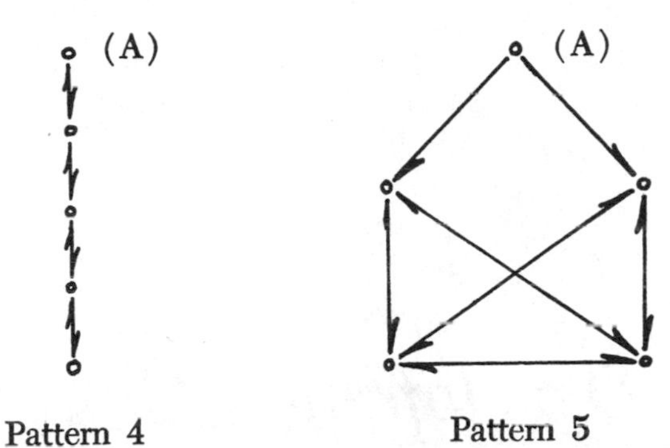

Pattern 4 Pattern 5

Patterns 4 and 5 are least trustworthy, since the message which is originally given at point (A) will probably be distorted before it arrives at its desired destination. The desire in all five patterns is to transmit the message from point (A) to all of the participants. Each time a message goes through a second party to a third party, the risk of distortion is increased.

Shared objectives and shared knowledge are essential to teamwork. The success of an organization is dependent at least in part upon the quality of its communication. Communication is the key to coordination. There must be organized channels for communication, or individualism will replace teamwork and rumors will replace facts. Poor communication is involved in most management problems.

Additional Reading

Drucker, Peter F. *The Effective Executive.* New York: Harper & Row, 1967.

———. *Managing for Results.* New York: Harper & Row, 1964.

Getz, Gene A. *Sharpening the Focus of the Church.* Chicago: Moody, 1974.

Hendrix, Olan. *Management and the Christian Worker.* Manila: Living Books For All, 1972.

Leach, William H. *Handbook of Church Management.* Englewood Cliffs, N.J.: Prentice-Hall, 1958.

Schaller, Lyle E. *Parish Planning.* New York: Abingdon, 1971.

CHAPTER 4

Developing a Church Organizational Structure

To some, the very word *organization* is anathema. They feel that any attempt at organization tends to short-circuit the ministry of the Holy Spirit. It would almost seem that they believe confusion is the mark of the presence and ministry of the Holy Spirit. We do well to remember that in the beginning, God brought order out of chaos. The excesses to which so many have gone in the past in this matter of organization should not deter us from making use of its constructive helps.

When we discuss organizational development, we are attempting to find ways to change the organization from its present state to a better developed state. Organizational development is the strengthening of those human processes or organizations which improve the functioning of the organization so that it can achieve its objectives.

The goal of organizational development is that the organization gain insight into its own processes, develop its own diagnostic and coping resources, and improve its own internal relationships, with the help of an outside and/or inside consultant who functions as a catalyst. An outsider cannot solve an organization's problems, but frequently he can help increase the organization's capability to solve its own problems. This type of help puts the focus on organizational, group, and interpersonal processes and hence has been labeled "process consultation."

The church has been one of the last organizations to be willing to refer problems to a consultant. Business organizations have been doing this for years, but churches have felt it a sign of weakness to seek outside help. Churches have often failed to pay attention to organizational facts. In some cases, they have not evaluated their organization or its progress, and in other cases they have merely ignored the warning signs of danger.

Organizational development is a deliberate effort to improve effectiveness of an organization by planned intervention in the behavior patterns of the total system or organization. It is an attempt to help the organization develop its capacity for self-renewal. Such a process will normally take from two to five years.

High priority is given to team building; an organization is seen as functioning through teams or groups rather than through individuals. A strong emphasis is placed upon goal setting, intergroup relations, and conflict. The communication within an organization is a matter of major concern.

Several factors take on special significance in organizational change. Clear plans for expediting changes are important. These can be made more clearly through organizational charts and comprehensive job descriptions. The process of mapping the church organization will lead to an understanding of relationships and responsibilities. Mapping consists of drawing a diagram (often referred to as a wire diagram) which will, by connecting or nonconnecting lines, indicate the relationship of each group within the church to the others. It will also demonstrate the lines of communication and responsibility between church officers. Each member within the organizational framework will be able to see himself in terms of the total structure. Some groups within the church will have formal connections with other groups, whereas some relationships may be informal. By using different colors it is possible to indicate which groups are most affected by history and tradition and which by the immediate environment. Another color can indicate the decision-making centers.

As the organization is mapped, sources of conflict and dysfunction will also appear, and the chart will clarify where changes can be made.

Once the mapping process has been completed, the lines and colors will provide a meaningful portrait of the organizational framework.

It must be recognized that a leader can work effectively with only a limited number of persons. Authority and responsibility must be clearly understood. The ideal size of an organization must be determined in terms of its purposes and resources.

An effective church organization should promote communication, encourage maximum participation, facilitate feedback, and encourage innovation.

Organizing is the process of defining and grouping the activities of an enterprise, and establishing the responsibilities and relationships of the persons involved, in order to accomplish the ends of the group. This process should be noted for order, efficiency, participation, and provision for unexpected occurences.

The church is a volunteer organization. People may feel free to sit down and do nothing or merely to walk out. Sometimes there are physical, social, or financial factors which force them to participate. But if the motivational power of the Holy Spirit is inoperative in their lives, then the hope of continued productive activity through thick and thin is greatly diminished.

The church is composed of human beings not necessarily tailor-made for specific responsibilites. Patience and tolerance on the part of all concerned is imperative.

Defining the Church

The word *ekklesia* means "assembly," or "congregation," and is translated "church." In the Bible it never has the sense of building or edifice, but very early it came to be used to denote buildings for worship.

The word *ekklesia* is derived from *ek*, "out of," and *kaleo*, "to call." The basic meaning is therefore "called out." The first-century preachers and missionaries referred to a body of Christian believers as an *ekklesia*. The word appears 115 times in the New Testament. After the gospels, which do not use the word except for two occurrences in Matthew (16:18 and 18:17), the word appears in all books except 2 Timothy, Titus, 1 and 2 Peter, 1 and 2 John, and Jude. Though the word is missing in these books, the concept is present.

Two usages of the word are not significant for our study. The word is used in one passage to indicate the assembly of the citizens of a Greek city (Ac 17:32, 29, 41) and is used twice for the meetings of the Israelites in Old Testament times (Hebrews 2:12, where Psalm 22:22 is quoted, and Acts 7:38, where Stephen refers to assembled Israelites as "the *ekklesia* in the wilderness.")

The third use refers to a group of believers in Christ who form a unit of permanent fellowship in a given locality. There are approximately ninety instances of this use in the New Testament. It is often plural, as in Romans 16:16, where reference is made to "churches of Christ" and in 1 Thessalonians 2:14, "churches of God which are in Judea in Christ Jesus." More frequently the single "house church" of the apostolic epoch is so designated (Ro 16:5, 23; 1 Co 16:19).

The final use of the word *ekklesia* is to designate what theologians have called the "Church universal." There are about twenty-five references containing this usage. It appears that the word *ekklesia* denotes primarily the local assembly and that its use was extended to the universal Church. Adloph Deisman, in *Light from the Ancient East*, says:

> The first scattered congregations of Greek-speaking Christians up and down the Roman Empire spoke of themselves as a "(convened) assembly"; at first each . . . congregation was so called, and afterwards the whole body of Christians everywhere was spoken of collectively as "the (convened) assembly." That is the most literal translation of the Greek word [*ekklesia*] This self-bestowed name rested on the certain conviction that God had separated from the world His "saints" in Christ, and had "called" or "convened" them to an assembly, which was "God's assembly," "God's muster," because God was the convener.[1]

The local church has some recognizable attributes and properties. These characteristics are not formally listed in the Bible, but they are demonstrated. For a brief period, the Church universal and local were approximately one, in one place, Jerusalem.

The last seven verses of the second chapter of the book of Acts give us a picture of a vital local church. Spiritual life was the primary and comprehensive mark of this local church. The church gave attention to the apostles' doctrine and was noted for its fellowship, *koinonia*. This loving fellowship had an immediate practical outlet in the apostolic community (Ac 2:44-45). This church combined the intellectual aspect (doctrine) of the church's life and the social (koinonia) with an activity, the observance of the Lord's Supper. Other characteristics were prayer and Christian testimony (Ac 2:46-47).

The church against which the gates of hell cannot prevail (Mt 16:18) is the holy universal Church, the total number of God's elect of this age in heaven and on earth. The teaching of the New Testament regarding the nature of the universal Church may be summarized in two propositions:

1. The Church is a body of believers. It is created by the Holy Spirit, who imparts His own eternal life to each believer-member and who is Himself in a distinct and special way the bond of vital unity between the members themselves and of all with Christ. This proposition is set forth in 1 Corinthians 12.
2. The formation of the Church by the special work of the Holy Spirit was the culmination of a process of revelation and history, all of which lies in the record of the New Testament. This revelation and this history relate to the coming and work of the Holy Spirit.

In the present age, the Church is being formed gradually and silently as God gathers His people out of all the nations. The completion of this Church is fixed at the second coming of Christ, as stated not only by general doctrinal and scriptural considerations but by at least one specific text, Acts 15:15-16. When the Church is complete, Christ will come to remove her by resurrection and translation. This is taught in 1 Thessalonians 4:15-17 and related texts. The Church will come to a blessed consummation when at the "marriage" and "supper" of the Lamb she will be united with her visible Head forever (Eph 5:25-27; Rev 19:6-9; 22:1ff).

The final paragraph of Matthew includes the commission of the Church, which begins at verse 16 and goes through verse 20. The historical setting of the commission is given in verses 16 through 18, and the actual elements of the commission in verses 19 and 20. There is only one basic command in the commission, namely, to make disciples of all nations. Having gone or as you go, two activities will be involved: baptizing and teaching. The commission is to make disciples of men of all the nations.

The Nature of the Church

God's first concern is not what the church does but what the church is. Being always precedes doing. What we do will depend upon what we are.

The church is primarily and fundamentally a body designed to express through each individual member the life of an indwelling Lord and is equipped by the Holy Spirit with gifts designed to express that life. Therefore a congregation, in that it is an organism and not an organization, has a uniqueness and a personality all its own. The purpose and functions of the local church cannot be separated from the definition of its nature.

A. H. Strong, in *Systematic Theology*, has the following definition of the local church.

> The individual [local] church may be defined as that smaller [than the universal church] company of regenerate persons, who, in any given community, unite themselves voluntarily together, in accordance with Christ's laws, for the purpose of securing the complete establishment of his kingdom in themselves and in the world.[2]

The church is a group of people concerned about the quality and characteristics of its life. Some of the areas of concern are: worship; learning about Christian faith; leadership in the congregation; relationships between parts of the church; decision making; communication; the nature and direction of goals; plans for achieving the goals; the church's relationship to the community; and the climate, character, and internal relationships of the congregation.

The church is a constantly changing body and needs continual sources of information about the character and quality of its life. The pastor may sometimes have this information but keep it to himself. When there is no information, there is no way for the congregation to discover the truth about itself as a corporate body. The information needs to be made accessible to the congregation so they can critically evaluate their life.

This evaluation, or assessment, is a public process of relaying pertinent information and acting upon that information. There are two types of assessment. The first is *descriptive* assessment, a "snap-shot" of the congregation or portion of the congregation showing the way in which they are presently expressing their faith. Then there is an *evaluative* assessment, in which some ideal of a congregation living faithfully and obediently is assumed, against which the congregation or aspects of the congregation's life are evaluated.

An assessment of organizational processes is necessary so that corrections and adjustments can be made. (See the assessment tool in the appendix, "How Do I Feel About Our Worship Service?") This assessment of processes will also involve checking decision making, communication, social climate, leadership, systems relations, and structure. The end product must also be assessed. This will involve evaluating goals and objectives, organizational conditions, and feelings about the achievement. True assessment should lead to active dealing with the truth the people find about themselves.

Faithfulness to God depends upon truthfulness in dealing with God, fellow church members, and the world in which the church is placed. Faithfulness to God is manifested when the people are truthful about the character and quality of their own lives. Truthfulness is an indispensable ingredient in the prescription for church revitalization.

Types of Church Organizational Structure

There are three basic types of church organizational structure. The first is the *mechanistic structure.* This has centralization of power, control, and specialization. The rules are passed down from the top, and there is no question where the authority rests. Charles Perrow, in *Organizational Analysis: A Sociological View*, calls this a bureaucratic model. Only the individual at the top of the organization needs to know the goals and purposes. The general workers merely do what they are told and never inquire into the organizational goals. It is recognized that in this type of structure there is some advantage in the area of efficiency. It should be remembered, however, that the bigger and more centralized the organization, the bigger and more pervasive will be the effects of its faults and mistakes.

This type of organization is used in several large, independent churches of our day. The pastor is in complete control. The members and officers do not need to know why, they need only to do. The pastor holds sway as though he will be on the throne forever. Other pastors often say, "I pity the one who has to assume his position when God calls him home. All is well today because the king still lives."

In the *human-relations structure,* the emphasis is upon groups and togetherness rather than individuals. There is a recognized interlocking between the groups. Emphasis is placed upon the need to belong and for everyone to be friendly. The leader does not merely create work but rather becomes a supporter. He pays attention to the needs of the workers. Leadership is a personal ministry. This structure has a tendency to become ingrown. It sees only its members and loses sight of the needs of world. The pastor looks through a microscope rather than through a telescope. It can become a closed corporation.

The third type of structure is the *organic structure.* In this structure, knowledge is shared throughout the organization rather than being kept at the top. Communication is both vertical and horizontal. Three principles are especially emphasized: individual dignity, creative freedom, and self-development. The leader talks, listens, learns, and stands alongside his people. Involvement with the world is emphasized.

Adams, in his book *Pastoral Administration,* takes another approach to organization, or structure, classification. His first classification is the *central organization.* In this, an official board delegates responsibilities to committees. The centralized structure may be set forth in a chart. Committees or commissions are appointed to cover such matters as worship, membership, evangelism, Christian education, stewardship, and finance. Committees may be organized in terms of activities they are to perform and needs they are to meet. Many church organizational structures have one central board, and each board member is a member of a committee. This means that the board has contact with, and sometimes has control over, all the committees of the church. This can develop into a board dictatorship.

There is the organization which is formed to meet the needs of special social groups. The coffeehouse ministry is one which illustrates this type of organization, since it was designed to meet the needs of a group of young people who were finding difficulty in meeting their social needs within the framework of more traditional social activities. This ministry provides the young people with opportunities for meeting others of their own age. They can have fellowship and extended conversation. As Christian young people circulate within the group, they take advantage of opportunities to challenge the non-Christian young people to yield their lives to Jesus Christ as Saviour and Lord.

There is finally the organization involving a covenanted relationship covering every aspect of life. In this, there is a sharing of income, worship, and other areas of life. Some have felt that communal fellowships may be the new vanguard in the church's mission. There are several motivations which may be spurring this interest in communal living. Some communal situations have sought to forge new forms of worship. Others have been formed to satisfy the need for a time of reflection. Others have come together to give a quiet witness to Christian unity. Recovery of the outcasts, evangelism, and spiritual edification have also been motivations for this type of movement.[3]

Types of Church Polity

By church polity we mean church government. The types of church government go from the extreme of authoritarianism to the other extreme of complete democracy.

The four most common types of church government are the episcopal, connectional, monarchial, and congregational. The *episcopal*, or prelatical, is a tightly knit organization with a bishop ruling. The basis of authority is in the apostolic succession of the bishop. This is the form of government in the Church of England. The *connectional* church government is used in the Methodist, Episcopal, Lutheran, and Presbyterian churches. The local organizations are thought of as bearing a relationship one with another and are interdependent. The third system, the *monarchial* form of church government, is one which is ruled by a single individual; it is dictatorial in nature. This form of church government is seen in the Roman Catholic church. The *congregational* form of church government is democratic and gives voice and vote to the people. This is employed by such groups as the Baptists, Disciples, and Seventh Day Adventists.

Church Organizational Climate

The six dimensions of organizational climate include structure, responsibility, risk, standards, rewards and support, and a friendly team spirit. The organizational structure must be appropriate to the members and to the situation. It should offer equal regard both to the task and to the people who perform it.

Edgar Schein, in *Organizational Psychology,* suggests that there are four criteria of organizational health. The first is *adaptability.* This includes the ability to solve problems and to react with flexibility to changing environmental demands. The second is a *sense of identity;* the members should know the nature of their goals. The third is the *capacity to test reality.* This is the ability to discover and correctly interpret the context of the organization. The fourth is the *integration* of the subparts of the total organization so that the parts are not working at cross purposes.[4]

Many churches have problems at all four of these points. Some have a tendency to resist change. Their favorite slogan seems to be, "Come weal, come woe, our status is quo." In some churches it is even difficult to make slight changes in the order of service. Adaptability is certainly not a glowing characteristic. Churches are often confused about their actual goals. Analyzing to discover the facts of church life is not a strong point. It is difficult not to work at cross-purposes when we are not sure of what the purposes really are.

Kilinski and Wofford quote Rensis Likert's *New Patterns of Management,* pp. 140-61, stating that organizations are ineffective when they tend to have low member-involvement and interest. Other reasons for ineffectiveness are the general meetings that are large and formal; little candid, personal interaction between leaders and membership; and members not personally familiar with each other, which reduce the warmth and openness of the interaction. Sometimes members feel that their leaders have little interest in their ideas. They feel that they as individuals have little influence upon the organization. The leaders are more active than in the more effective organizations; therefore, the members have less to do.[5]

There is a tendency to assume that people attending the same church for a number of years know each other. The facts just do not bear this out. A person can be lost in a church for years. We salve our consciences by saying that we recognize faces, but actually we have not cared enough to learn names. Individuals are important. We should take time to recognize them and find out what they think. Good church structures should promote communication and encourage maximum participation. They should facilitate feedback and encourage innovation. Organizations that are effective have high member-involvement. The members feel that they have more influence. Open and effective communication is established and maintained between all staff, boards, and committees. There is a feeling of openness and trust so that individuals feel free to express their opinions. They feel that their opinions are being heard. Maximum involvement is encouraged in decision making. Conflict is dealt with openly; differences are not ignored or buried. We need to put the stethescope to the heart of the church and check its health in terms of these criteria.

Problems in Church Organizational Structures

A problem-free organization is as much a curiosity as a totally normal personality. There are many problems which can arise within organizational structures. Sometimes there is a waste of manpower and financial resources, or a duplication of effort. Many times problems arise as an organization attempts to cope with its constantly changing environment. Problems often arise within an organization when members do not understand its function and dynamics. And of course, all organizations are made up of individuals, who differ widely in their abilities and are neither perfect nor supermen. They are not machines created by and for the organization; they have their own goals, personalities, and interests outside the organization.

A Systems Approach to Church Organization

To look at the origin of systems and the systems approach, we must go back to the 1920s. The systems approach was conceived of in the biological studies, with much of the original work being done by Ludwig von Bertalanffy. In the early twenties, von Bertalanffy became curious about the obvious lack in the research and theory of biology. He advocated an approach which considers the organism as a whole, or system.

But then a further generalization became apparent. In many phenomena in biology, as well as in the behavioral and social sciences, mathematical expressions and models are applicable. The structural similarity of such models in different fields became apparent.

But von Bertalanffy was before his time. The proposal of systems was received incredulously. For the next twenty to twenty-five years, the systems theory was forced underground. But it did not die there. In 1954, the Society for General Systems Research was formed as an affiliate of the American Association for the Advancement of Science. Its program includes four major functions: (1) to investigate the isomorphy of concepts, laws, and models in various fields, and to help in useful transfers from one field to another; (2) to encourage the development of adequate theoretical models in the fields which lack them; (3) to minimize the duplication of theoretical effort in different fields; (4) to promote the unity of science.

The growth and acceptance of the systems approach since 1954 can be readily ascertained by even the most casual glance through the "Systems" listing in a card catalogue. Invariably one finds a multitude of listings which show the relationship of systems to psychology, sociology, physics, mathematics, biology, and so on. Today, without a doubt, the systems approach has caught on.

A system is a set of parts coordinated to accomplish a set of goals. A systems approach is simply a way of thinking about those total systems and their components. The systems approach is basically concerned with viewing the organization in terms of its environment so that decision making can take place in a logical and coherent fashion and none of the errors of narrow-minded thinking will occur.

There are three basic approaches to a system. First of all, we have the *efficiency* approach. This approach involves identifying the trouble spots within a system, especially waste areas, and removing the inefficiency. A second approach is the *science* approach. The proponents of this approach claim that there is an objective way to look at a system and to build a model that describes how it works. This approach is most frequently used in the mathematic, economic, and behavioral sciences. The *humanistic* approach is the third approach. Systems are people, and the fundamental approach to systems consists of first looking at the human values: freedom, dignity, privacy. Plans grow out of situations rather than being imposed on them.

There are at least five basic considerations which must be kept in mind when thinking about the nature of a system: (1) the total system's objectives; (2) the system's environment; (3) the resources of the system; (4) the components of the system; and (5) the management of the system.

While objectives are the logical place to begin, they are, perhaps, one of the more difficult areas to deal with. It is not easy to determine the real objectives of a system. In order to clarify the matter, we should move from the vague statement of objectives to some precise and specific measures of performance of the overall system. The measure of performance of the system tells us how well the system is doing. In our evaluation of objectives, we must be careful that our stated objectives are our real objectives, the ones toward which we are working.

The environment of a system is what lies outside of the system. Since it lies outside the system, the system can do relatively little about its characteristics or its behavior. Environment, in effect, makes up the things and people that are fixed, or given. The environment is both something that determines, in part, how the system performs, and something outside of the system's control.

The resources of the system are inside. They are the means the system uses to do its job. The resources are normally thought of in terms of money, man-hours, and equipment. Resources, in contrast to the environment, are the things the system can change and use to its own advantage. Resources are the general reservoir out of which the specific actions of the system can be shaped.

These specific actions are performed by the components (also referred to as *parts* or *subsystems*). Each component in the system has missions, jobs, or activities. The real reason for the separation of the system into components is to provide the kind of information needed to tell whether a system is operating properly and what should be done next.

The last aspect of the system we must consider is management. The management of a system deals with the development of the plans for the system including the overall goals, the environment, the resources, and the components. The management sets the component goals, allocates the resources, and controls the system performance. Not only does the management of a system generate the plans of the system, but it must also make sure that the plans are being carried out in accordance with its original ideas. If they are not being carried out, it is management's duty to find out why. Also, one of the critical aspects of the management of systems is the planning for the change in plans. Why? Because no one can be sure of having set down the correct overall objectives or a correct definition of the environment or a fully precise definition of resources or the ultimate definition of the components.

Reference is often made to *open* and *closed* systems, and it will do us well to have a basic understanding of these concepts. *Closed* systems are those which are considered to be isolated from their environment. A closed system is static and always contains the same components. An *open* system is one in which there is exchange with its environment, resulting in import and export and the building-up and breaking-down of its material components. An open system is in a quasi-steady state, maintaining a constant mass relationship with its environment while undergoing a continuous change of component material and energies as material continually enters from and leaves into the outside environment.

A final key to understanding the nature of the systems approach is that the system is always embedded in a larger system. We must always remember that effecting a change in a system or subsystem will likely effect another system, subsystem, or the whole system. For example, a cost-cutting plan in one subsystem could raise the costs in other subsystems and thereby raise the cost to the total system. Systems are mutually dependent, a fact we dare not forget.

The diagram which follows illustrates the effect of a systems approach to church life.

Let us take the example of a professing Christian who has been divorced and who smokes. He is seeking active participation in the life of the church represented by this systems diagram. He begins at the input system point, from which he must pass through a screening filter. This screening filter might be the church board or the pastor. In many churches, membership committees serve as a screening filter. He might not get through the screening filter in a church where he could not become a member until he had been freed of his habit of smoking. In other churches he might have difficulty in getting through the screening filter because he has been divorced. If his skin happens to be other than white, he might have additional trouble getting through the initial filter screen due to community or historical influences on the church.

If he does get by this screening point, there may be certain areas of activity which would be closed to him. In fact, in some churches he would have very little opportunity for service. The church might allow him to contribute financially and attend services, but that might be the limit of his service.

If he does get in and feels constrained of the Lord to go into some type of Christian service outside the church, the filter screen at the output point would then take control. Even if he has been set free from the habit of smoking, he might have difficulty joining some mission boards or other Christian organizations. His divorce and the color of skin might be hindering factors.

We are not attempting at this point to be judgmental but only to see realistically what takes place. Everything that happens within a church affects everything else in the church and may well be influenced by community and historical factors. There are few changes which are minor and few problems which have simple solutions.

A Democratic Church Organization

The Greek word *demos*, "the people," is combined with the word *kratos*, "authority," to imply that all authority stems from the

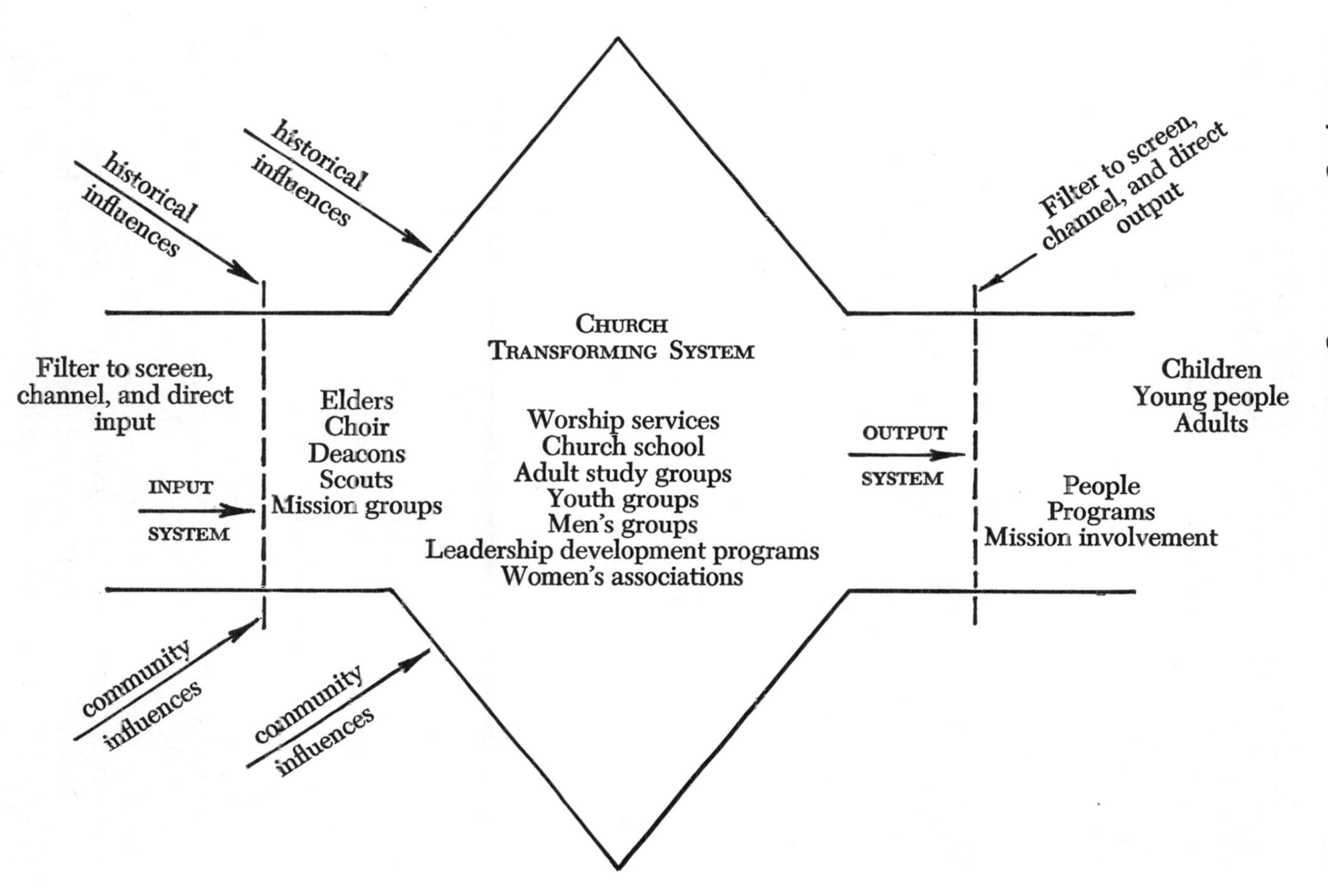
historical influences
historical influences
Filter to screen, channel, and direct input
INPUT
SYSTEM
community influences
community influences
Elders
Choir
Deacons
Scouts
Mission groups
CHURCH
TRANSFORMING SYSTEM
Worship services
Church school
Adult study groups
Youth groups
Men's groups
Leadership development programs
Women's associations
OUTPUT
SYSTEM
Filter to screen, channel, and direct output
Children
Young people
Adults
People
Programs
Mission involvement

people. Democracy is the means by which individuals are able to determine what freedoms they may expect without impinging upon the rights of others.

There is no one body of methods or procedures which is absolutely democratic, but there is clearly a body of ideas which democratic societies have demonstrated to be valid and illuminating.

Ordway Tead gives the following list of identifying marks of a democratic organization:

1. We define, delimit and specify who is to compose the membership or electorate.
2. We identify and specify what internal subgroups seem important to identify as requiring to have their special interests represented and voiced in relation to the affairs of the whole (e.g., the representation of states in Congress).
3. We provide explicitly for the participation of these exigent interests as such in a continuing representative body.
4. We try to assure a leadership for such representative deliberation which drives toward soundly integrative agreements.
5. We seek to provide all representatives with *all* facts relevant to every issue discussed.
6. We strive toward agreements that take account of and incorporate minority opinion just as fully as possible.
7. We try out solutions agreed upon (e.g., new legislation) to see how well they work.
8. From time to time we review the outcomes to see how satisfactory they are (e.g., by constitutional review, by periodic new elections.)
9. We change our adopted practice if experience indicates this to be desirable in the agreed public interest.[6]

There are demands which are placed upon a local congregation if it desires to have an effective democratic church government. A purely democratic church government recognizes that it is the task of the whole church to pursue and preserve unity of action. It is likewise the task of the whole church to preserve pure doctrine, to give the ordinances, to elect officers, and to administer discipline. There must be a respect for individuals, which will demand, among other things, that minorities be protected and that there be freedom of discussion. Decisions must be reached by democratic action. Decisions will often involve a voluntary sacrifice for the common good; personal opinions and desires may have to be put aside for the sake of the group. One of the most important demands will be a devotion to the truth.

A Team-Centered Church Organization

A team-centered organization is one in which the basic unit of communication is the group rather than the individual. There is a great amount of mutual influence among individuals within each group. The group leader is usually warm and accepting of others, and the group members love and accept one another. The group as a whole is responsible for decisions and actions within its particular area. The members participate actively in carrying responsibility. Overlapping memberships assure communication between groups within the organization. When the official board of a church has as its membership the leaders of all major groups, then each group has a communication link to the board.

To build such a team-centered organization within a church, it is first necessary that both the leaders and the general members understand the basic concepts of a team approach and agree that such a team-centered organization would be valuable. There must be a willingness to modify the present procedures of the church which might not fit in with this approach. In some cases the authority to make decisions must be moved from one group to another. The change over to a team approach should be done gradually through a series of meetings.

A Creative Church Organization

Lyle Schaller, in his thought-provoking book *The Change Agent*, gives some characteristics of a creative organization. The primary orientation of such a group is to the contemporary social scene rather than to yesterday or to the mere perpetuation of the organization itself. The primary focus is upon members' needs rather than on products or services. A creative group must be aware that problems do exist. The emphasis is upon problem solving rather than upon institutional maintenance. The people are aware of the importance, relevance, and availability of knowledge from a variety of disciplines that can be utilized by the organization in fulfilling its purpose and achieving its goals. Changes are made in an attempt to gain benefits. One must constantly monitor the pace of change so that the costs involved in bringing about the changes will not outweigh any benefits sought through the change.[7]

In considering organizational development, there has been an emphasis on unity and cohesiveness. This togetherness, which characterizes an effective organization, carries with it the implication that each part of the organization affects every other part. If the church is to get on target, it should move toward that target as an organized unit.

Additional Reading

Burke, W. Warner, and Hornstein, Harvey. A. *The Social Technology of Organization Development*. Fairfax, Va.: NTL Learning Resources, 1972.

Churchman, C. West. *The Systems Approach*. New York: Dell, 1968.

Kilinski, Kenneth K., and Wofford, Jerry C. *Organization and Leadership in the Local Church*. Grand Rapids: Zondervan, 1973.

Schaller, Lyle E. *The Change Agent*. Nashville: Abingdon, 1972.

Schindler-Rainman, Eva, and Lippitt, Ronald. *The Volunteer Community*. Fairfax, Va.: NTL Learning Resources, 1971.

Seiler, John A. *Systems Analysis in Organizational Behavior*. Homewood, Ill.: Irwin, 1967.

Von Bertalanffy, Ludwig. *General System Theory*. New York: Braziller, 1968.

CHAPTER 5

Training for Leadership

There is always a need for good leadership. It is one of the basic requirements for a good program within a church. Harold J. Fickett in his book, *Hope for Your Church* has this interesting statement: "There are three requirements for a good program within the church. The first is leadership, the second is leadership and the third is leadership."[1] A lack of leadership may be part of the reason that in a typical year, an average of at least eight protestant congregations disappear every day as a result of mergers and dissolutions. Churches need more leaders, not more members.

Spiritual leaders are made not by election or appointment but by God. He knows the area of service where He plans to use them and can prepare them accordingly. Effective leadership diagnoses where the greatest readiness and capacity exists to carry out the commitments and priorities of the organization. A good leader utilizes the best-equipped persons to act on those priorities. Organizations which intend to change must develop leaders who can be change agents.

A leader shows the way; he directs the course of another by going before or along with the one he is leading. Once a spiritual leader is sure of the will of God, he will go into immediate action regardless of consequences. The leader knows where he is going and is able to persuade others to go along with him. Leadership is the capacity and will to rally men and women to a common purpose.

True leadership is achieved by giving oneself in selfless service to others. This is never done without paying a price. Count Zinzendorf of the Moravian Brethren was an example of this as he renounced selfish ambition and gave his life to missionary leadership. The summary of his life's philosophy was in his sentence, "I have one passion, it is He, He alone." The Moravian Brethren caught the devotion of Zinzendorf, their human leader. One member out of every ninety-two became a foreign missionary.

The leader will try to make certain that the aims of his organization are such that they can win the loyalty of his group. He will be concerned that all the members of the group are enjoying some of the results and benefits of their work. He will try to make certain that the people have a sense of belonging. Although the people are willing to be led, he will make certain that this willingness is not exploited.

William Carey was unconsciously a diplomat. One of his fellow workers testified of him: "He has attained the happy art of ruling and overruling others without asserting his authority, or others feeling their subjection—and, all is done without the least appearance of design on his part." [2]

The servant-leader demonstrates his commitment to a shared ministry (Lk 22:24-27; Jn 13; Gal 5:13-15; Phil 2:5-11; 1 Pe 2:16; 4:8-11). He gives freely of his resources, encourages evaluation, practices what he preaches, and is honest and trustworthy. The true spiritual leader will never canvass for promotion. The leader is to be like Christ, the servant of all. "Whoever wants to be great among you must be your servant, and whoever wants to hold first positions among you must be everybody's slave" (Mk 10:42-44, Williams)

> The words *disciple* and *discipline* derive from the same root. A leader is a person who has first submitted willingly and learned to obey a discipline imposed from without, but who then imposes on himself a much more rigorous discipline from within. Those who rebel against authority and scorn self-discipline seldom qualify for leadership of a high order. They shirk the rigors and sacrifices it demands and reject the divine disciplines that are involved.[3]

The early disciples coveted a crown of glory but were not ready for a crown of thorns (Mk 10:37). Coronation interested them but not crucifixion. It was necessary for them to change.

Definition of Leadership

The personalized term *leader* and the abstraction *leadership* have been often intermingled without regard to differences. A leader is anyone whose ideas are helping to give direction toward the common goals of the group. The leader is an individual, in any social situation, whose ideas and actions influence the thoughts and behavior of others. Leadership is influence; one man can lead others only to the extent that he can influence them. Leadership is also doing what is necessary for the group's functioning. It will include providing information, clarifying points of view, and summarizing a discussion. Leadership is really a function, not a person.

The distribution of leadership functions in a group occurs in several ways. Usually, in a mature group, members will assume responsibility for group roles necessary for effective functioning. We might list five broad categories of leadership functions: initiating, regulating, informing, supporting, and evaluating. The type of leader who emerges and the type of leading that is employed depends upon the group's purpose.

Qualifications for Leadership

In general, a leader of a democratic group epitomizes the values and norms of his group. The democratic leader is able to perceive the direction in which the group is moving and to move in that direction more rapidly than the group as a whole.

Christian leadership requires a personal commitment to Jesus Christ. One thing precedes great leadership, and that is an unqualified love. There must also be a genuine love for Christ's Church and for people. There must be the ability and desire to grow in the understanding of the Christian faith and in one's relationships with people. The leader must be able to work with others. Christian habits and ideals must be evidenced in his daily life. He must have the courage of his convictions and not be easily discouraged. No pessimist was ever a great leader. There must be talent in line with the proposed task. The leader must be willing to accept and carry responsibility.[4]

Dr. John R. Mott moved in student circles, and his tests for leadership included:

1. Does he do little things well?
2. Has he learned the meaning of priorities?
3. How does he use his leisure?
4. Has he intensity?
5. Has he learned to take advantage of momentum?
6. Has he the power of growth?
7. What is his attitude to discouragements?
8. How does he face impossible situations?
9. What are his weakest points?[5]

A good leader must be aware of the needs which are shared by most of the group members at the beginning of a project or program. Some of these needs are:

1. To know who is who
2. To know where they fit in
3. To know what is expected of them
4. To know what they can expect from their leader
5. To understand the goals and objectives
6. To feel at ease
7. To feel identified with the program
8. To be stimulated mentally

Powhattan James, in his biography of George W. Truett, the great Baptist leader, wrote:

> The Man of God must have *insight to things spiritual.* He must be able to see the mountain filled with the horses and chariots of fire; he must be able to interpret that which is written by the finger of God upon the walls of conscience; he must be able to translate the signs of the times into terms of their spiritual meaning; . . . he must be able to draw aside, now and then, the curtain of things material and let mortals glimpse the spiritual glories which crown the Mercy-seat of God. . . . The man of God must declare the pattern that was given unto him in the Mount; he must utter the vision granted unto him upon the isle of revelation. . . . None of these things can he do without spiritual insight.[6]

A. E. Norrish, a missionary to India, testifies:

I have never met leadership without a sense of humour; this ability to stand outside oneself and one's circumstances, to see things in perspective and laugh. It is a great safety valve! You will never lead others far without the joy of the Lord and its concomitant, a sense of humour.[7]

Types of Leadership

Pure types or styles of leadership seldom exist. Leadership style may be defined in terms of how the leader views his subordinates. A democratic leader may, under other circumstances, become a bureaucratic leader. Various terms have been used to identify leadership styles, and various classifications have been formulated. Some feel that there are basically two styles, the persuasive and reflective. The persuasive leader formulates goals and makes plans and then tries to persuade the group to follow his lead. The reflective leader, on the other hand, seeks to glean from the group the goals which they already hold but may not have put into concrete terms.

Dr. Kenneth Gangel has arranged leadership styles into three categories. The first is the *authoritarian*, which controls all progress to the goal as well as the interrelation of members. The autocratic leader believes he must rule with an iron hand. "He feels that he alone can direct the activities of the group satisfactorily and that because of his greater knowledge or abilities, the task of group membership is to give implicit obedience to his commands."[8] The *democratic* leadership style distributes responsibility rather than concentrating it. When such a leader is absent for a time, the group is still able to continue. Democratic leadership is the closest to the New Testament leadership style. "This is the median approach between the autocratic and free-rein stances. . . . Most of the time he will probably be democratic, but there will be those rare situations in which he should feel the flexibility to slide to the left or to the right, thus adopting temporary postures of free rein or autocratic leadership respectively."[9] The *laissez-faire* leader is really no leader at all. He holds the official leadership position but is actually only a figurehead.

Five leadership-style categories were developed by Dr. Warren Schmidt. The five styles could be arranged on a continuum. At one end of the continuum would be the leader who leads by telling.

The second kind of leader leads by persuasion; he makes decisions on his own and then sells them to the group. The third leadership style is that of consulting; the leader seeks information from an expert before making a decision. The fourth style is the participative; the leader and the group join together in making a decision. This style usually generates more ideas and more enthusiasm, though it can, on occasion, be very time consuming. The fifth style of leader delegates responsibility and decisions to someone else.[10]

As we see these five styles located on a continuum, we note that the greatest amount of authority rests with the leader who tells the group what to do. This authority decreases as we go to the persuading, consulting, joining, and delegating styles. As the authority decreases, the involvement of the members increases. The greatest group participation occurs under the delegating leader, since he removes himself and leaves decisions up to the group.

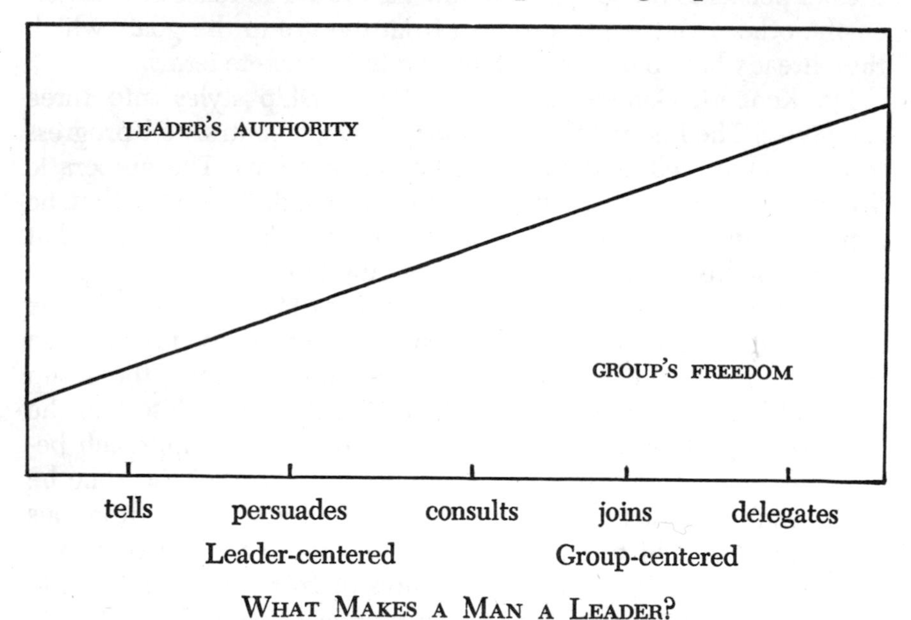

WHAT MAKES A MAN A LEADER?

Gordon Lippitt, in his book *Organizational Renewal*, points out that behavior scientists have come up with several different concepts as they have tried to determine what makes a man a leader. There is first the *great-man theory*. This holds that leaders are born and not made. But this trait approach is quite unsatisfactory, since to this point chromosomes and genes have not been positively related to leadership. The *functions approach* seeks to identify leaders in terms of their functions. These might include decision making, providing information, planning, and providing a symbol for the group. The *situational approach* assumes that there are certain traits and capacities that are crucial for effective leadership in one situation but not in another. There is a need to be flexible in the selection and training of leaders for different situations.[11]

How does one become a leader? In his lectures, Howard Hendricks suggests the following ten ways:

1. He will develop deep personal convictions, not opinions.
2. He will maintain a rigid personal schedule in terms of his objectives.
3. He will subordinate all of his life to his goal.
4. He will be willing to make hard-nosed decisions.
5. He will have a sense of destiny.
6. He will learn to live with tension.
7. He will work more intelligently, not harder.
8. He will become excited about what he is doing and where he is going.
9. He will perceive others by their potential.
10. He will master the art of developing men, not manipulating them.

How can one tell when he has begun to be a leader? Maturity is vitally related to leadership.

A mature person is marked by several characteristics. He has self-discipline and staying power and is able to stand on his own. His life and example are consistent; what he is in public is no different from what he is in private. He is teachable and willing to serve others. He approaches life with a confident, positive attitude. Above all, he has the kind of faith that does not fear to take risks.

William Sangster said, "The church is painfully in need of leaders. I wait to hear a voice and no voice comes. I love the back seat in Synod and Conferences. I would always rather listen than speak—but there is no clarion voice to listen to."[12]

A manuscript found after William Sangster's death illustrates the way God challenged him to face the leadership need. He was writing of his growing conviction that he should take more part in the leadership of the Methodist church in England.

> This is the will of God for me. I did not choose it. I sought to escape it. But it has come.
>
> Something else has come too. A sense of certainty that God does not want me only for a preacher. He wants me also for a leader—a leader in Methodism.
>
> I feel a commission to work under God for the revival of this branch of His Church—careless of my own reputation; indifferent to the comments of older and jealous men.
>
> I am thirty-six. If I am to serve God in this way, I must no longer shrink from the task—but *do* it.
>
> I have examined my heart for ambition. I am certain it is not there. I hate the criticism I shall evoke and the painful chatter of people. Obscurity, quiet browsing among books, and the service of simple people is my taste—but by the will of God, this is my task.
>
> God help me. . . .
>
> Bewildered and unbelieving, I heard the voice of God say to me, "I want to sound the note through you." O God, did ever an apostle shrink from his task more? I dare not say "No" but, like Jonah, I would fain run away.[13]

What are some of the organizational qualities a leader should develop? Oswald Sanders suggests tact, diplomacy, and executive ability. He states, "tact is defined as 'intuitive perception, especially a quick and fine perception of what is fit and proper or right.' Diplomacy is dexterity and skill in managing affairs of any kind. . . . It involves the ability to place oneself in the position of the persons involved and to accurately assess how they would feel and react."[14]

A real leader is one who has learned to use his leisure time. David Livingstone was one who used time wisely. He worked in a cotton mill in his native Dunbarton from six in the morning until eight at night. He started this work when he was only ten years of age. Before he was sixteen years old, he had so utilized his "leisure" time that he had mastered Latin and could read Horace and Virgil with ease. By the time he was twenty-seven, he had completed a medical course and also a course of study in theology. John Wesley and F. B. Meyer also used their time wisely. They divided their days into five minute periods and endeavored to make each period constructive.

Attitudes Which Should Be Avoided by Leaders

The first attitude to be avoided is putting an undue stress on short-range goals and looking for immediate, tangible results. Action is often mistaken for participation. A second attitude to avoid is lingering over each bit of minutia until it is exactly right. Certain tasks demand such close care, but others merit less concern. A third attitude to avoid is insisting that every item be dealt with by an expert. Responsibility for problem solving is often avoided by delegating everything to expert or specialist. The fourth attitude to avoid is regarding organizational activity as a form of sacrifice and demanding rewards in the form of prestige, rank, or praise.

In *Spiritual Leadership,* Oswald Sanders names some "peculiar perils of leadership" to be avoided: pride, egotism, jealousy, popularity, infallibility, over-elation, and depression.[15]

Attitudes Which Should be Developed by Leaders

R. E. Thompson suggests these tests of our attitudes as an indication of our capacity for leadership:

Do other people's failures annoy us or challenge us?
Do we use people or cultivate people?
Do we direct people or develop people?
Do we criticize or encourage?
Do we shun the problem person or seek him out?[16]

Motivation and Leadership

It has been suggested that there are several factors which tend to provide motivation for leaders. The first is a sense that one grows as he does something important. Men motivated to leadership recognize that the value of a life is computed by its donation, not by its duration. The next is what is termed as the developing of a trust level. The leader has the feeling that others have confidence in him and are trusting him. A third factor is the development of a support system. When leaders feel that they have adequate backing from others, they are stirred to advance. Charles Spurgeon was asked for the secret of his great ability to minister to his congregation. He is reported to have said that the secret rested in the fact that while he was preaching, five hundred were praying for him. A congregation can help make a preacher and leader. Leadership training also tends to provide motivation; when leaders are interested in their project and have the necessary skills to carry it out, they will be more highly motivated to perform. There are three elements to good motivation. They are "precept and example, encouragement, and appreciation."[17]

Creating a Climate for Leadership

Creating a climate for warm cooperation is one of the keys to the functioning of a leader. The leader has the responsibility for structuring a context in which positive interpersonal relations can be carried out among members of the group and between the group and its leader.

Renis Likert, in his book *New Patterns of Management,* describes five conditions which should be present to ensure effective supervisory behavior. The whole organizational climate and the behavior of the supervisor has to be seen by those within the organization as maintaining the personal worth of the members and supporting their values. Each member must feel a sense of group loyalty and effective interaction. The supervisor must have a contagious enthusaism about the goals of the group. He must deal competently with the problems or make sure that technical knowledge is provided where needed. The leader must maintain good linking connections with his superiors and bring back information from those superiors to the group with which he is working.[18]

Kenneth Gangel gives nine functions of a leader which are also principles to establish warm cooperation. These are as follows:

Understand people's needs.

Know when and how to listen.

Employ personal policies which help people. . . . God puts an enormous value on human beings. . . . But we often treat people as though they were robots existing for no purpose other than to carry out the goals of the organization in the way that we tell them to.

Avoid passing the buck.

Avoid manipulating people.

Genuinely care about how people feel. . . . The effective leader is sensitive to the feelings of his subordinates though he might not always agree with them.

Never give orders which you know will not be followed.

Never blame or praise a group member publicly.

Use punishment in only the most extreme cases.[19]

Leadership and Decision Making

There are at least three types of decisions. The first might be called the *cyclical* decisions. These are the ones which reoccur with regularity. *Confrontation* decisions are those which are forced upon us by circumstances or events. *Innovation* decisions occur only when we seek them out. This third kind of decision is not prevalent, because most church leaders become so involved in the first two kinds that there is no time left for it. The innovation decision can be stimulated by setting goals which will take us beyond the realm of expected procedures. It can help us plan for tomorrow and thus prepare for new methods and activities to serve our purposes.

A typical decision-making procedure might consist of four steps. The first would be the brainstorming phase, in which a random number of ideas are advanced. The next step evaluates these ideas in terms of Scripture, purpose, and operational constraints. In step three, the data is collected for the purpose of determining plausible alternatives. The final step involves summarizing data into a cost-effectiveness breakdown so that we can compare alternatives. The amount of time spent on each step depends upon the importance of the decision.

A good decision-maker must know how much effort a decision is worth and when he should stop deliberating and decide. A decision may cost more to make than its consequences are worth. The most powerful factor in the decision-making process in an organization is precedent—"We have always done it this way." The power of precedent is seen especially in older and larger congregations.

Chester Barnard, in *The Functions of an Executive*, tells us that there are at least four bits of advice we should heed in determining whether or not we should make a decision. We should avoid deciding questions which are not now pertinent. If decisions cannot be carried out, then we should not worry about making them. We should not make decisions which are premature. And finally, we should avoid making decisions which others should make.[20]

Schein, in his discussion of process organization, describes in a very forceful way the methods by which many decisions are proposed. There first is "the plop"—someone makes a speech, no one listens, and nothing is decided. There is a lot of talking but no listening. The next is "the lost question." This occurs when the speaker rambles and gets off the subject so that no one really knows what he is talking about. The third is "the terrible question," from which everyone runs away because it is too threatening. The question is put off as long as possible. The next is "the authoritarian approach," by which the boss lines everyone up and tells them what is going to happen. "The railroad approach" refers to decisions made by the minority: the foundational work is done beforehand, someone is appointed to make the motion and someone to second it, and someone calls for the question. This type of approach takes only three people and the cooperation of the moderator. The next approach involves decision making by the majority. The final method is to arrive at a consensus through give and take on both sides.

When we speak of consensus, we are referring to a collective opinion, or concord. It is a general agreement, or accord. After a discussion, in which everyone has had an opportunity to make his point, a proposal comes to a vote. Though some in the group may not go along wholeheartedly with the proposal, they may feel that they can live with it and that it is flexible enough to be modified by action and discussion. Therefore, for the sake of consensus, they will vote in favor of it.

Consensus promotes unity in the group and encourages creativity. It focuses on the goal toward which the group is working. It draws out commitment necessary to follow through on a decision. A consensus is a shared conviction that a particular decision is the right one.

Whenever possible, the ones who are to carry out decisions should be involved in making them. There must be good communication between all parties involved in a decision. Sometimes decisions are not implemented, because when they were made, no one had the responsibility for executing them. A board will sometimes make a decision which may be theoretically sound but not practically feasible. This decision may never be implemented. The decision must be accepted by the people involved; if it is merely forced upon them, it may never be carried out.

J. Oswald Sanders, in *Spiritual Leadership*, includes the following paragraph and poem, which sum up in a rather pointed fashion the challenge of leadership.

> The young man of leadership caliber will work while others waste time, study while others sleep, pray while others play. There will be no place for loose or slovenly habits in word or thought, deed or dress. He will observe a soldierly discipline in diet and deportment. so that he might wage a good warfare. He will without reluctance undertake the unpleasant task which others avoid, or the hidden duty which others evade because it evokes no applause or wins no appreciation. A Spirit-filled leader will not shrink from facing up to difficult situations or persons, or from grasping the nettle when that is necessary. He will kindly and courageously administer rebuke when that is called for; or he will exercise necessary discipline when the interests of the Lord's work demand it. He will not procrastinate in writing the difficult letter. His letter-basket will not conceal the evidences of his failure to grapple with urgent problems. His prayer will be:
>
> God, harden me against myself,
> The coward with pathetic voice
> Who craves for ease and rest and joy.

Myself, arch-traitor to myself,
My hollowest friend,
My deadliest foe,
My clog, whatever road I go.

—Amy Carmichael

Additional Reading

Drucker, Peter F. *The Effective Executive*. New York: Harper & Row, 1966.

Gangel, Kenneth O. *Competent to Lead*. Chicago: Moody, 1974.

———. *Leadership for Church Education*. Chicago: Moody, 1970.

Haney, David. *The Idea of the Laity*. Grand Rapids: Zondervan, 1973.

Kraemer, Hendrik. *A Theology of the Laity*. Philadelphia: Westminster, 1959.

Neil, S. C., and Weber, H. R., eds. *The Layman in Christian History*. Philadelphia: Westminister, 1963.

Sanders, J. Oswald. *Spirtual Leadership*. Chicago: Moody, 1967.

Schaller, Lyle. *The Pastor and the People: Building a New Partnership for Effective Ministry*. Nashville: Abingdon, 1973.

CHAPTER 6

Improving the Effectiveness of Boards and Committees

"Not all board meetings are dull; some of them are cancelled." We should observe, however, that people do not join boards to have fun. It should also be observed that the main function of a board is to solve problems, and these have a tendency to be tedious and complicated.

Most of the affairs of American life are controlled or influenced by boards and committees. The normal activities of life may not seem, on the surface, to be governed by a board or committee, but when examined more closely, they often reflect the fact that somewhere, around a conference table, a group of people have come together and made decisions. Growth has led to delegation of responsibility. Years ago everybody decided everything. In recent years, those organizations which have grown and expanded have abandoned direct control of all activities by all the people and have vested authority in a central group.

A board is always related to some institution or group of people determined to carry on a useful function. The goal of a board must be the same as the goal of the institution or larger group. The board's relationship to the parent group is one both of control and assistance. The board may have ultimate power, or its authority may be sharply limited, but it always has some responsibility to make policies and see that they are carried out. Unless a board accepts responsibility for both control and assistance, its proper functioning is impaired. A board is made up of individuals, each with his particular personality, ideas, prejudices, and habits. To think of a board only as a group of people is to fail to understand it. In effective board operations, individual personalities must be blended together into a functioning group which has its own spirit, tone, and quality. It must be able to achieve consensus or to define a majority opinion which reflects the wishes of as many of its members as possible. A board must work with an executive and staff who have rights and responsibilities of their own. The central value of a board is that it provides an opportunity for the use of collective wisdom. As a whole, it explains and interprets present activities and builds support for further advances in the program. A board provides for continuity of policy. It endures, though its membership changes.

There are four outstanding hindrances to effective board activity. The first is the tendency to forget the individual. It is the responsibility of the leader and the group to safeguard and encourage recognition of each member. The second hindrance is the tendency to expect too much from board activity. This attitude may later give an excuse to some to return to traditionalism and say, "We tried it once, and it didn't work." The third hindrance to effectiveness is wasting time. This will be most likely to take place if the purpose and problems are not made clear. The fourth hindrance is improper planning for the meetings.

There are several steps which can be taken in order to make board meetings more interesting and productive. The first is the proper development of an agenda. If the meeting is not important enough for a prepared agenda, it is not important enough to be held. The agenda should be prepared far enough in advance so that it can be circulated prior to the meeting. This gives the members an opportunity to prepare for the meeting. The patterns and procedures of board meetings should be reduced to routine as far as possible. Such matters as time, place, and frequency of meetings should not have to be decided each time. The board meeting should be the culmination of a long period of preparation. The reports given at the meetings should be short and well outlined. Whenever possible, these reports should be printed and distributed. As much time as possible should be reserved in the meeting for discussion. This discussion should focus on the issues and have a progression from one point to the next. There should be as much informality as possible in the meeting. Boards with good social relationships among the members are more likely to have good board meetings. Candy or light refreshments can be made available during the meeting. The meetings should be kept brief. There is a time to begin, and there should also be a specific time to close.

Church Officers

The church officer serves as a representative of the congregation. His plans and activities should take their wishes and needs into consideration. God holds church officers responsible for the purity and discipline of the congregation. An officer who compromises the biblical standards for church purity and discipline is failing in his most important task.

Effectiveness as a church officer demands that the officer remain spiritually alert. It is imperative that he be controlled by the Holy Spirit. It is also imperative that he study and assimilate the Word of God. His information must be kept up to date. He should have a job description and should study it carefully to determine priorities. The job descriptions for church officers should be made available to all of the church staff and to as many of the church members as possible. The members of the church family should know the areas of responsibility and the limits of accountability of each officer.

It is important to know about the lines of authority and the methods of communication which are operative. The church officer must know about the church plant. This will involve him in making a tour of it and taking special note of the equipment available, where it is stored, and who is responsibile for it. He must know the church program in terms of both particulars and generalities. It is important to know the church membership both as individuals and families.

An officer's effectiveness demands a careful evaluation of relationships to groups and individuals within the church. The church officer should relate very positively to the pastor; he should be the pastor's ally in prayer and be active in supporting him in other ways. It is taken for granted that he will be available to the pastor for advice and encouragement. He should also show respect and loyalty to the pastor. The church officer should protect the pastor's time and energy and bring to his attention matters of meaningful criticism as well as positive encouragement. He should do all within his power to promote spiritual harmony.

The church officer should help church committees see their tasks as being spiritually significant. This will encourage the committee and motivate committee members to be diligent and faithful in service. The church officer should not be afraid to initiate new ideas and actions, to disagree if necessary, and to encourage others to participate.

Church Boards

Church boards play a pivotal role in the total success of the church. They are often directly responsible for evangelism; spiritual growth; the fulfilling of physical, emotional and spiritual needs of the members; guiding in the provision and use of physical resources; and the maintenance of an effective organizational framework. These are weighty responsibilities.

A board is an organized group of people who collectively assist an organization which is usually administered by a qualified executive and staff. The *controlling* board usually possesses direct legal responsibility for the work of the organization. The *auxiliary* board is created to carry out certain agreed-upon responsibilities. This board is usually appointed by the controlling board. The *associational* board is the chief mechanism of continuing responsibility for a voluntary membership group. Its basic responsibility is to its own membership. There are also *legislative*, *judicial*, and *executive* boards.

When a board is to be appointed or elected, care should be taken to put down in concrete terms the type of people needed as members. One factor to be considered is the matter of representation from the various groups. The matters of sex and age may also be determining factors. The selecting group must consider the special capabilities needed. In some cases the location of residence will be important. The experience of the prospective board member in board processes should be taken into consideration. There are times when individuals have a desire to learn and to serve but do not have previous experience. These individuals should not be overlooked. When no individuals qualified by either experience or desire are available, it is better to leave the position unfilled.

The behavior of any group is determined by its background, leader, members, and pattern of personal relationships. Every group has a behavior peculiar to itself. The more individuals there are on a board, the more chances there are for the development of group problems.

Boards and committees limited in size are usually most effective in accomplishing their work. The board should be large enough to carry out its responsibilities but small enough to act as a deliberate body. When a board becomes too large it often creates an inner "board."

In a church directed by one major board, the church board is normally elected by the congregation and supervises all of the committee work of its constituency. Each committee in the church will probably be represented by at least one member on this board. The board should make certain that the church is effectively organized by the proper assignment of responsibilites to members. These responsibilities should be coordinated to form an efficient unit. The board should continually evaluate the church program in relation to changing conditions in and outside of the church. It should have a good grasp of the goals of the board and of the church as a whole.

There are several characteristics of a mature board. Such a board will have the ability to combine and maintain group and individual goals. There will be a continual development of leadership for efficient functioning. The old members will help train the younger ones. The procedures of the group will remain flexible enough to perform specific tasks which may arise. The board will provide opportunity for its members to give frank opinions, thus providing a means of examining group operation.

A short, outlined summary of each board meeting should be included in the church bulletin. All important decisions of the board should be made known to the church and should be presented as the decisions of the board and not of the chairman or the minister. The discussions carried on at the board meetings should be kept confidential and should not be shared even with the board member's family.

Tenure is usually a matter decided by the organization. Tenure is also decided in part by the member himself. The answers to the following questions will help him decide whether or not the time has come for him to leave the board.

Am I still strongly interested in the program?
Am I providing effective support and assistance for the program?
Do I have confidence in the effectiveness of the board?
Am I as well qualified to serve as one who might take my place?
Is my membership likely to strengthen the caliber and unity of the board?
Is my service on this board as significant as any other service to which I might devote the same amount of time?
Has God shown me in some way that He wants me to continue in this aspect of service?[1]

Lengthy tenure has its disadvantages as well as advantages. The main problem is that it reduces the number of new people who can have place on the board. This means that the breadth of representation may narrow, and cliques may determine policies. Brief tenure is sometimes a way of eliminating dead wood. It will also provide a constant supply of fresh ideas. Most boards have definite terms for their members with a provision for possible overlapping.

Cyril O. Houle, in *The Effective Board*, has listed several suggestions for a board. This list was assembled through a synthesis of literature and discussions with more than seven hundred board members. Some of the suggestions included:

1. Keep the goals of the program in focus and make sure that the work is in harmony with these goals.
2. Be sure that changing conditions are reflected in the program.
3. Work effectively with the executive and with the staff.
4. Be sure that the work is properly organized and that there is a proper assignment of responsibilities.
5. Make sure that board policies are established and followed.
6. Serve as arbiter in conflicts between staff members.
7. Use the special knowledge and contacts of the board members in the improvement of the church program.
8. Make certain that the board is well integrated within its immediate and broader environments.

9. Accept responsibility for securing adequate financial resources.
10. Make certain that the board's basic moral and legal responsibilities are met.
11. Abide by its own rules.
12. Do everything possible to keep board membership able, broadly representative, and active.[2]

Strictly speaking, a board exists only when it is meeting. Everyone knows, however, that actually it has a continuous life. That which goes on between meetings is very important. An effective group spirit on the board attracts members, makes them want to work with one another, and gives them a sense of pride in the program and the board. This type of spirit results from a strong belief in the program, a sense of progress in accomplishing goals, a conviction of the importance of the board, and good interaction among the members of the board.

Houle also lists the following qualities which are essential for the maintenance of an effective group spirit on a board.

> Every board member accepts every other board member with a due appreciation of his strengths and weaknesses.
>
> Everyone concerned with a particular decision actually helps make it.
>
> The contribution of each person or group is recognized.
>
> The attitude of the board is forward-looking. There is a confident expectation of growth and development.
>
> There is a clear definition of responsibilities so that each person knows what is expected of him.
>
> The members of the board can communicate easily with one another.
>
> There is a recognition of the fact that the whole board is more important than any of its parts.
>
> There is a capacity to resolve dissent or discord and to keep it in perspective in terms of larger purposes.

> There is an acceptance of and conformity to a code of behavior involving courtesy, self-discipline, and responsibility.
>
> In case of internal conflict, the board has the capacity to examine the situation objectively, identify the sources of difficulty, and remedy them.
>
> The board members must share a clear understanding of and commitment to the cause which the organization serves.[3]

The best way to motivate Christians is to teach them what they are as Christians. When a layman comes to believe that he is as much a part of the church as is the pastor, though he has a different function, he will then be motivated to serve. He should recognize that he is a colaborer with Jesus Christ (1 Co 3:9).

Enthusiasm is contagious. If we are enthusiastic and motivated, we will infect others with our attitude. We can motivate others by recognizing those who are doing an effective work. Every opportunity for service must be shown to be important. Motivation will be increased when we delegate authority equivalent to the responsibility given.

Spiritual motivation is important. Unfortunately many church board meetings are not characterized by spiritual discussions; many of the items discussed can only be remotely termed spiritual. The tone of the conversation is not always uplifting. We should remember to acknowledge God's presence in all board and committee meetings.

The primary task of the chairman of the board is that of helping diverse personalities merge into an effective whole. It is his task to lead, restrain, and blend in proper proportion the more capable and vocal members with the less experienced and silent ones. The chairman must coordinate and motivate the board as a unit toward the solution of problems. In discussion, he should encourage each member to participate. He should seek opinions from the members and be willing to express his own. Many are hesitant to share their opinions because the other members of the group are judgmental.

A good chairman will be on the alert to clarify the issue discussed by making sure that all members always understand what is being said. Verbal summaries should be provided throughout the discussion so that the members will be aware of the direction in which the group is going. The chairman should be sensitive to any attitudes and actions within or outside of the board meeting which might prove destructive. The basic leadership function consists of binding the group together through the ministry of the Holy Spirit in the love of Christ. A chairman must harmonize in the disagreements, compromise where compromise is feasible (*compromise* is not a bad word in this context), and keep communication between members open and relaxed.

The appointment of committees is one of the most interesting and creative tasks of the chairman. He should hold in mind two primary qualifications: competence and interest. The ideal is to find both qualities in the same individual. It is often helpful if a board chairman appoints as a member of each committee someone who has good potential for replacing him as chairman.

When a problem arises, the chairman should ask one or more of the following three questions: Am I myself the problem? Can the board solve the problem itself? Whom do we get to help us out of the difficulty?

People are selected for board membership chiefly in three ways. They are invited to join by those who are already on the board; they are appointed by some outside authority; they are elected by the people.

A church board or committee is no better than its members. Board members must constantly make judgments and discriminations. By doing this, they gradually achieve understanding and sophistication. Participation in a board provides a means of growth for the board member. It becomes a source of leadership for the organization.

The education of a new board member begins at the moment of invitation. One of the causes of later lethargy on the part of the board members is the poor handling of this initial interview. The invitation to join a board should never be hurried or casual. The interview should present a clear outline of the work of the board, its major problems, and the general responsibility of each board member. The interviewer should not ask for a volunteer; he should seek the will of God in this whole matter, and when God has laid a name upon his heart, he should then approach the individual. The one interviewed should be given time to pray about his possible involvement before giving a response.

Immediately after being selected, the new board member should receive a welcome and an offer of assistance from both the chairman of the board and the executive of the organization. Sometimes this welcome is supplemented by a conference in which information is supplied and questions are answered. In some cases, a social occasion is arranged so that the new member can become acquainted with the entire board.

Some boards have a board manual which they give to the new members. The board manual is a document, preferably a loose-leaf notebook, which belongs to the board but which is given to each member holding office. During his tenure, the board member is responsible for keeping it up to date. It should contain at least the following items: a statement of the purposes of the organization; the constitution; the by-laws; an annual schedule of plans and work; a list of members, with address and telephone numbers; a list of committees, with functions; an organizational chart; and the current budget.

Board members usually have only a limited amount of time to give to board activities. It is important that the time be devoted to the important rather than to the trivial. Emphasis should be placed upon policy-making decisions rather than routine decisions. A major concern should be performance rather than a discussion of organizational minutiae.

Board of Elders

It should be noted that there are two classes of elders. There are elders who both teach and rule, and there are elders who rule but do not ordinarily teach (1 Ti. 5:17). A minister would be properly termed a teaching elder. A congregation will normally have associated with their pastor a small group of men who join in the rule of the congregation. These men are properly termed elders, though custom lately has been to designate them as deacons.

First Peter 5:2 divides the responsibilities of the elder into two classes: "Feed the flock of God which is among you, taking the oversight thereof." (cf. Ac 20:28; 2 Ti 4:5). This does not represent all of the elder's duties, but it does represent his duties toward the flock. "Feeding" and "oversight" may also be termed as education and administration. These involve discipline and rulership.

As overseer, an elder's first duty is to rule (1 Ti 5:17). His second duty is to officiate as the leader and presiding officer in the general functions of the church, such as the observance of the ordinances. As overseer, he must superintend all discipline in the church.

The next duty of the elder, or overseer, is teaching. Educational responsibilities may be carried out by reading (1 Ti 4:13), teaching doctrine (1 Ti 4:11), and preaching (2 Ti 4:1-2).

Not only does the teaching elder, or minister, have responsibilities toward the congregation, but the congregation has responsibilities toward him as well. The first of these is obedience in matters of faith (Heb 13:17). The next duty is submission in matters of practice and polity (Heb 13:17). The third duty is support and teamwork in the pastor's program (Mt 28:19-20; Eph 4:11; 2 Co. 5:17-21). The congregation owes the pastor sincere respect and honor for his office's sake. They owe him sincere love and esteem. The congregation has the duty of caring for the minister's material needs (1 Co 9:1-4; Gal 6:6-7; Phil 4). The congregation is to test the minister on his faithfulness to the broad outline of Christian truth (Rev 2:2).

There are certain responsibilities that should rest and may be rightly imposed upon elders. They should pray for and care for the entire membership. They should visit the membership through some organized plan. (See chapter 12, "Expanding the Outreach of the Church," for a description of the zone plan). The elder should call upon his assigned members each quarter and bring back a report on each member to the chairman of the board. They should set a fine Christian example and meet the qualifications for elders as given in the Scripture (1 Ti 3:1-7; Titus 1:5-10).

The number of members on the board of elders should be adapted to the size of the church. A small church may have two elders plus one for each twenty-five or fifty members. A large church should have one for each fifty members.

A decision must be made by the church as to the length of term of office for the elders. Three-year terms are normally recommended, allowing one year to pass before reelection is possible, although this may not be wise in a small church where manpower is limited. One good system is to have a revolving election, in which one-third of the deacons pass from office each year, leaving two-thirds of the board as experienced members.

Board of Deacons

There are several significant facts which should be noted in connection with the institution of the office of deacon. The office was instituted to meet a definite need in a growing church (Ac 6:2-4). It was instituted by the combined authority of the apostles and the church (Ac 6:3-5). It was instituted by the leadership of the Holy Ghost (Ac 2:4).

The qualifications for the office of deacon are set forth in 1 Timothy 3:8-13. Most of these qualifications apply both to the elders and to the deacons. Deacons are "not doubletongued, not given to much wine, and not greedy of filthy lucre." They hold "the mystery of the faith in a pure conscience." They must be shown to be blameless. Their wives must be "grave, not slanderers, sober, faithful in all things." He must be the husband of one wife and must rule his children and own household well.

In our day it is generally the responsibility of the deacons to hold the church property in trust and to care for it. Some states have special requirements for these officers and list them as church trustees. It is wise to write to the department of corporation at the state legislature for information regarding this matter. Deacons should maintain oversight of the church property. It is their responsibility to sign all legal documents concerning property. At times these legal documents will also concern employees. Deacons employ and recommend the salary for many of the personnel in the church. It is this group which appoints a house committee to tend various rooms within the church and determine who shall use the rooms. They must arrange for adequate insurance on property and employees. It is also wise for them to provide health and accident insurance for the pastor.

This group may act as a finance committee, or they or the church may appoint a separate committee to serve in this capacity.

Three-year terms of service are recommended for the deacons, with one-third of the board passing from office each year. The church may want one year to elapse before deacons are eligible for reelection. The decisions of the deacons should be given to the church as the decisions of the board and not just of the chairman and certainly not as the decisions of the pastor.

Committees

Many negative things have been said about committees. They have been identified as groups of people who keep minutes and waste hours. They have also been referred to as groups of people who individually can do nothing but who collectively decide that nothing can be done. Some have said that if you want to kill an idea, refer it to a committee, and the committee will have a commital service for it.

In spite of all the negatives, there are some advantages connected with committee work. Committees provide the opportunity to make investigations and clarify policy. They carry out functions which are essential but which do not require the time of the full board. Committees sometimes speed up decisions. They provide opportunity for discussion of confidential matters not appropriate for discussion with the whole board.

There are two general models for committees. The first is the *crisis committee.* This committee is established for a problem-solving purpose. The second is the *consultative committee.* This committee is formed to provide helpful suggestions and information for the church and for the pastor.

There are three types of committees. The *standing* committee remains in existence indefinitely in order to be responsible for a certain category of problems or actions. The *special* committee is appointed to handle a particular situation or problem; it goes out of existence when the task is completed. The *coordinate* committees are those which provide general direction and guidance for the work of the board. The executive committee and the finance committee are two examples of a coordinate committee.

A committee has only those powers which are delegated to it by the board. Ordinarily the board should approve in advance or ratify afterward all the actions and decisions of a committee.

The committee should be composed of the most qualified people available. Avoid putting inactive people on committees as a means of motivating them to do something. The minister should be an ex officio member of all church committees. It may also be wise in some cases to have the chairman of the church as an ex officio member.

There are certain principles which should be followed in establishing church committees. The purpose of the committee should be clearly defined. It will help to name the committee according to the task or tasks it will be performing. The morale of committee members is largely determined by how effectively they accomplish their tasks. Expectations and concerns of the committee members and those of the organization they represent are the ground out of which the goals and tasks of the committee grow. They are also the motivational base from which the members work on these tasks. First, then, discern the expectations and concerns of the committee members. Set goals, the accomplishment of which will fulfill these expectations and eliminate the concerns. Outline as specifically as possible the steps necessary to achieve these goals. If there are multiple goals, set priorities. What resources, human and material, are needed to achieve these goals? What resources does the committee have available? If additional resources are needed, how can they be secured? Set specific schedules and methods of evaluating the committee's progress toward its goals.

Each committee should keep a record of its meetings. One copy should be kept by the committee, one sent to the pastor, and one sent to the church board. Committee reports should be given to the church in writing, in accordance with the stipulations of the church constitution. If at all possible, make public the workings of each group and the decisions and data they produce. Such a process contributes to openness and trust within the committee and among the larger group of people they represent. Nothing destroys trust more quickly than secrecy.

When a special committee has completed the task for which it was called into action, it should be officially disbanded. Committees should be appointed annually. It is recommended that committee appointments be rotated and that committees be kept small in size.

No committee should be established unless its duties are clear and it is definitely needed.

It is imperative that lines of communication be established and maintained between the church board and the church committees. Many churches have found it advisable to have each committee of the church include one member of the board. The board meeting can then serve as a unifying agent, coordinating committee information and activities. This type of arrangement will help to prevent any committee from becoming a "little church" within the church.

The key to a good committee meeting is the committee chairman. He should be primarily an enabler or facilitator of the committee work and not the dictator or controller. He should feel free to express his opinions, but it is not wise for him to start the discussion by giving his opinions first. His primary responsibility is to see that others have the opportunity to give their input, that they are heard, and that the group moves toward the accomplishment of its tasks.

The time of meeting should be settled in consultation with the members, and reminders should be sent to them before the scheduled time of meeting. A record of attendance should be kept and a follow-up made of absentees.

A written agenda should be prepared by the chairman well in advance. He can then add to this as the time of the meeting approaches. It is his responsibility to guide the committee through the agenda before other material is brought up. People easily stray from the agenda. Sometimes these sideroads are helpful and necessary, but many times they are not. The leader should be aware of each detour, remind the group of what it is doing, and check to see if the group wants to move in that direction or go back to the original agenda item.

It is important to make careful plans for the meeting. There are physical factors which the chairman should check such as the temperature of the room, the lighting, and the seating arrangement. The seating should be arranged so that the chairman is visible to all members. Audiovisuals and printed materials are standard equipment in effective committee meetings. If they are to be used, they should be ready well in advance of the meeting.

The chairman should create a relaxed atmosphere, encouraging contributions from everyone but having them made one at a time.

The committee should ask itself: How is the climate of our group? Is there openness? Do we feel free to express our ideas and opinions? How are we communicating with one another? Do we really listen to the others in the group, or are we focused only on what we have to say? Can the committee handle conflict and disagreement constructively, not repressing or avoiding it but allowing differences to be openly expressed? How are decisions made? Do all the members feel a part of the decision-making process, or at least that their opinions are taken seriously?

It is wise to summarize the progress being made by the committee from time to time. This will serve to keep before the committee members the agreements which have already been reached. It might be wise to have someone record on a blackboard the points of progress as they are made by the committee. Most groups fail to evaluate their work and life together. It is helpful at the end of each meeting for members to evaluate how they worked together and what they accomplished. Such a simple assessment can make the committee more conscious of how it is functioning and how it can work more effectively in the future. When a decision is reached, make certain that someone is designated to carry it out and report back to the group. Make a note so that provision will be made in the agenda of the next meeting for the report.

Always decide upon and announce the time of the next meeting before adjournment. Commend the committee members publicly for their good work.

Making Decisions in Committees

Every committee must make decisions—some simple, some complex. Most committees waste time because they do not know how to make decisions. In some cases a committee does not even know whether there is a decision to be made. The first step, then, is to clarify whether there is a decision to be made and what it is, or whether the group is merely discussing issues, brainstorming, or socializing. A committee does not need to make decisions all the time. It does, however, need to understand when it is in a decision-making process and when it is not. Once it is clear that there is a decision to be made, the committee should decide whether they are the appropriate group to make such a decision. They should also ask if all the resource people necessary to a good decision are available.

To make good decisions, a committee needs to gather as much relevant data as possible. The mistake most committees make is to wait until the meeting to gather data. As a result, too much time is spent with various members sharing their ideas or data or discussing the issue without adequate facts. Many a committee gets lost down this path and spends far too much time trying to find its way back through a morass of opinions. If information has not been gathered before the meeting, the decision should be postponed, if possible, and assignments given to collect the relevant data.

Too often, those who have information about or who will be affected by the decision are not given a chance to be heard. This results in a poor decision or one that will ultimately be ineffective because it is not supported by those who are affected by it. Avoiding this is particularly important in voluntary organizations where members may freely choose whether or not to comply with decisions which are made. If members feel they have been heard and their viewpoint has been valued, they will be more likely to support decisions even when they do not conform exactly to their wishes.

Some are always anxious to put decisions to a vote. Others feel people should be willing to compromise on issues. Both processes may be necessary from time to time, but the ideal way to handle decisions is to explore beforehand as many creative alternatives as possible in search of the solution that accomplishes the most for all parties. That is true consensus making. More persons are likely to own and support such a decision.

Decisions which do not reflect the true feelings or desires of those involved in them have a tendency to become ineffective. Those in leadership positions must constantly be aware of this possibility, even when decisions seem solid or have been voted in and written down. Nothing is permanent; new circumstances or data that did not surface when the decision was first made may necessitate reconsideration. In many cases, the original decision will be reaffirmed; but it is worthwhile to recycle the decision so that this reaffirmation and increased ownership can take place. Again, this is particularly true in a voluntary organization.

Additional Reading

Asguith, Glenn H. *Church Officers at Work.* Valley Forge: Judson, 1951.

Gangel, Kenneth O. *Competent to Lead.* Chicago: Moody, 1974.

Girard, Robert C. *Brethren, Hang Loose.* Grand Rapids: Zondervan, 1972.

Green, Hollis L. *Why Churches Die.* Minneapolis: Bethany Fellowship, 1972.

McGavran, Donald A., and Arn, Winfield C. *How to Grow a Church.* Glendale, Calif.: Regal, 1973.

Miles, Matthew B. *Learning to Work in Groups.* New York: Teachers College Press, 1967.

Schaller, Lyle. *The Decision-Makers.* Nashville: Abingdon, 1974.

———. *Hey, That's Our Church.* Nashville: Abingdon, 1975.

Thomas, Donald F. *The Deacon in a Changing Church.* Valley Forge: Judson, 1969.

CHAPTER 7

Mobilizing the Laity

Lay leadership is a critical factor in the survival and growth of the church. The contemporary church, with its great number of boards and committees, cannot revolve around the leadership of just one person. The minister can be a coordinator and resource person, but the making and carrying out of decisions must have a broader base. There is a widespread unrest and dissatisfaction in today's church due to the fact that the bulk of the membership, the laity, has traditionally been regarded as inferior to the clergy. But such division of church membership into two classes is quite removed from the intent of Scripture. The recovery of the laity will have a positive effect upon the recovery of the church.

The most vital periods in the history of the Christian Church have been those in which laymen have realized and earnestly sought to discharge their responsibility to propagate the Christian faith.

According to apostolic practice, the ministry was carried out by laymen deputed by the apostles to serve the Christian community and to the spread of the Kingdom of God. The early Church grew because laymen told others the Good News. The early churches were started by laymen.

The church is to be the salt of the earth, and it can only fulfill its function when the laity is alert and active. Unless the laymen fulfill their function as witnesses, there will be vast areas of our society in which no Christian witness is borne. It has been said that the laity is the greatest undeveloped resource of Protestant churches today. The laity can minister to one another within the fellowship of the church, strengthen the church to become a redemptive community, and go forth with a penetrating Christian influence into the world.

One of the significant reasons for the impact of the early Church upon the inhospitable world was the fact that it became the most sacred duty of a new convert to diffuse among his friends and relations the inestimable blessing that he had received.

Clement of Rome has been given credit for first using the term *layman.* In a letter written about 95 A.D., he stated, "The layman is bound by the lay ordinances." He implied in his writings that the layman was a full participant in the life and work of the church. Not much was written about the work of the laymen during the Dark Ages. Francis of Assisi, born in 1209, was used by the Spirit of God to launch a movement to release the layman in Christian witness and aid to the poor and needy. On October 31, 1517, Martin Luther nailed ninety-five theses to the door of the castle church at Wittenberg. It was at this time that he gave outward evidence of joining Saint Francis in Italy, John Wycliffe in England, John Huss in Bohemia, and a multitude of others who felt that there were needed changes in the church and that the laymen should be heard.

The origin of the word *laic* (singular) and *laity* (collective) is secular, dating back to the time of the Byzantine Empire. Some also feel that it can be traced to the biblical word *laos.* There are many ways of defining the word, irrespective of its origin. It has been defined as those who do not possess the professional theological knowledge of the clergy. A sociological definition denotes those who earn their living in a secular occupation rather than in the service of the church. Both of these definitions are negative. A scriptural definition emphasizes the positive, noting that the laity is the people of God. Rather than speaking of a theology of the laity, we should speak of a theology of the whole Church as the people of God. Both the ordained and the lay ministry are ministries in and to the world. Such a statement, when taken seriously, will broaden the scope of activity of the ordained and will establish the importance of the labors of the laity. We must learn to look at the laity as people of potential rather than people with problems. The people of God in the local church must listen to the people of God in the world and also to the non-Christian neighbor in the world.

Actually, the lay ministry—the ministry of the people of God—is the only ministry. Those who make up the Church are distinguished by their knowledge of God and their use of His power to do His will. The New Testament knew no distinction between clergy and laity other than in function. All Christians are God's laity, and all are God's clergy. There is a great temptation to put the ministers in a class by themselves. When this is done we violate the doctrine of the priesthood of all believers and the Reformation doctrine of vocation. Though the minister is to carry out certain activities, this does not mean that the layman is any less a minister than he. The great power of the church in the future is not going to come from the theological seminaries but from the lay people who recognize and use the gifts given to them by the Holy Spirit.

The Laity and the Church

Laymen are often disillusioned, dissatisfied, and disoriented, because they cannot figure out how to become vitally involved in a church which appears to be merely struggling to survive rather than seeking to fulfill a God-given mission.

There has been a widely prevailing and grave misconception among laymen of what it means to be a church member. Many regard the church as a society in which a few speak and many listen. Others have the impression that the church is a society where a few speak and work while the majority listen and make financial contributions.

Lyle Schaller observes that in most congregations, the adult membership can be divided into four categories. The first includes those who have deep roots in the congregation. The next includes those who have a strong commitment to the congregation because of its present ministry and program. The third group has a strong commitment to the congregation because of both heritage and contemporary goals. The fourth group is inactive.[1]

The concept of the centrality of the minister has led many churches to feel that the key to their success or failure rests in him. But the conception of the minister as a little king of a little kingdom is an affront to the faith and intelligence of the members of the church. It brings constant frustration to individuals and groups within the church who would like to become active. They come to feel that the church is ruled by the clergy and that the talents of the laity are not needed or wanted. A layman in this kind of situation either fades into the background or moves on to some other place for possible service.

When we think of *church* we normally think of buildings, clergy, seminaries, and social responsibility. We should think of more than these, however. The church, like a family, can exist without these things. The church or family is not primarily an institution; it is people living together. The Church is the people of God living the life of Christ.

The spirit of clericalism is to despise the laity. The spirit of anti-clericalism is to react to clericalism. The abuses which grew out of this led Quakers and Christian Brethren to dispense with an ordained ministry.

The dualism of clergy and laity tends to departmentalize the work. An emphasis on service seems to be what we need; we are called to serve and not to rule. The church's first duty Godward is to worship, and the church's first duty manward is to witness.

During the last twenty-five years there has been a discovery of the laity. The church has traditionally regarded the laity as those to be served, protected, and nurtured. But in these more recent years, the church is seeing the laity as an entity which should assume a major responsibility for the life and work of the church.

There are many influences which hinder laymen from participating in the work of the church. One is the prevailing secularism of our time, which generates an atmosphere of unbelief in the supernatural. This has held the laymen back from identifying with the work of the church. Multitudes of laymen are merely nominal Christians because they lack a personal, continuing experience with Christ. Many have become slaves of their environment and find themselves so heavily engaged in business and the general flurry of activity that they have no time to think about serving as a layman within a church.

Some have such strong ties with altruistic organizations outside the church that there is little time, energy, or finance left to invest in the work of the church. The average church member contributes between 1.5 and 2.5 percent of his total income specifically to the Lord's work. Many services formerly carried out by the church are now the responsibility of other agencies. As a result, some who were involved with the church in these services shifted their allegiance to the new agencies.

The development of specialization within the church has led many laymen to feel that they should leave church work to those who are better trained. We now tend to hire others to carry our rightful load of church responsibility. When specialization leads to alienation, then our problems are compounded.

Many churches do not have a program calculated to kindle the interest and call forth the participation of strong men. In some cases this problem has been in the church leadership, which has failed as leaders to open doors for service and guide laymen toward these doors.

The ordained have too often been thermostats, controlling the "temperature" of their congregations. This is unfortunate. In many cases, spiritual temperature would rise rather rapidly if the ordained "thermostat" were either removed or turned higher. The people in the pew should have more freedom in the local congregation. They should be allowed to be more than assistants or maintenance men for the church.

Out of the Reformation came Luther's basic concepts of the church and the laity. He emphasized that before God, all Christians have the same standing. Each Christian is a priest and needs no mediator save Christ. Each Christian, not only the priest, has a duty to pass on the Gospel which he has received. The phrase *the priesthood of all believers* took on special significance. This was not meant to emphasize individuals to the exclusion of the organized church but to emphasize that every man was a priest to every other man. The Reformers proposed a return to the biblical concept of the church as a single, unified body in which all are saints and priests. The layman, in medieval worship, had been a spectator; the Reformation made him a participant again.

The vital truth of the priesthood of all believers has sometimes been lost or badly obscured. Its recovery has meant restoration of life within the Christian community. Among the vital results of the recognition of the priesthood of all believers are the following:

1. It removes the misconception that the ministry has a special

knowledge of divine things and an experience of Christ different from that of the laity.
2. It leaves no ground for doubt that the layman, as well as the minister, has an acute consciousness that God Himself has given him his work.
3. It places upon the entire membership of the Christian community responsibility for the expansion of Christ's Kingdom.
4. It ensures the full impact of the Christian community upon the non-Christian world.

It has been suggested that there are three basic reasons for the inactivity of the layman: (1) he does not understand what the church is, what his role in the church is, and what the functions of the church are; (2) he suffers from an inferiority complex; and (3) he has never been given a real challenge.

There are other factors which contribute to the lack of lay involvement in the church:

1. The sharp distinction between the clergy and laity has encouraged laymen to let the clergy shoulder the responsibility for the church work.
2. The church loses so many at the transition time between boyhood and manhood that the number of available men is not as large as it should be.
3. The church has, through the years, conveyed the impression that it is apathetic, lacking in vitality and world-conquering power; this deters rather than attracts men.
4. The seeming pettiness of the church program and life is repellent to men who are accustomed to dealing with real issues.
5. The feminine majority of attendants and workers in most churches causes men to feel uncomfortable.
6. Many of the services once offered by the church have now been turned over to community agencies, thus encouraging men to feel that the church has lost some of its usefulness.

Women and the Church

There are many reasons why women are not busy in the church.

Sometimes they have not been asked to do anything. Some of them are engaged in secular work. Some feel that this is a man's world, and therefore they feel inferior. There is the lack of commitment to Christ on the part of some. In some cases women feel that all of the work of the church should be given to specialists. In some churches there are clans or cliques which seem to do everything. The needs of the family sometimes conflict with the needs of the church. To some women, the seeming pettiness of some church activity is repulsive.

The spirit of united involvement is healthy and points to progressive productivity. Work motivated by love for Christ is contagious, permeating, and begets more of its kind.

The organization of a women's fellowship with a strong emphasis on missions and evangelism, can direct church women to paths of service. There may be small fellowship groups within a large church, but these should unite for general meetings at least twice each year. The pastor should be interested in the organizations but should not run them even by remote control. He should be a resource man, ready to help when called. He should visit the meetings occasionally, but not stay for the entire meeting unless he is the invited guest. The pastor may want to invite the officers and their husbands to the parsonage for a time of fellowship. The pastor's wife should not take an official part in the organization and should be especially careful not to be her husband's mouthpiece.

The Laity and Spiritual Gifts

Every believer is indwelt and baptized by the Holy Spirit at the moment of conversion. The believer is commanded to be continually filled with the Holy Spirit. This Spirit-filled life is the normal life intended for every Christian. The Holy Spirit empowers the church for ministry. In His sovereignty and omniscience, He gives a variety of gifts to the church so that each believer may use his gifts for building up the family of God. We should rejoice in the love, joy, peace, and power which the Holy Spirit has given us. We should not blaspheme against the Holy Spirit by attributing His work to the devil, nor should we quench the Holy Spirit by trying to restrict Him to our own traditional patterns. The contemporary Christian church should not feel threatened by the Holy Spirit but should recognize that He is the indespensible One. Apart from the ministry of the Holy Spirit, there can be no true and lasting revitalization of the church.

Every Christian desiring to be useful and effective in Christian service should ask himself, What are my spiritual gifts? There are a number of tests which may be applied to determine this. First of all, there should be a desire for a particular gift. The next step is to use the gift. Gifts will be discovered while in operation. As service is performed, the results will indicate whether or not a particular gift is actually present. Another test is whether or not others recognize in our service the presence of a gift. Once a gift is discovered, we should strive to develop it. Individuals should be placed in positions of service in which they can exercise their spiritual gifts.

The church can never make a desperately needed impact upon the world until individual Christians begin to utilize, in the power of the resurrected Lord, the gifts God has given them. Little progress can be made so long as church members feel that a minister can be hired to exercise all the gifts while the laymen merely listen to him and pay him. And church leaders must avoid exploiting the talents of the congregation rather than helping them find their spiritual gifts. The value of our Christian life will be determined by the degree to which we make use of what God has given to us. God chooses His workers on the basis of what they can become rather than on the basis of what they are.

Two chapters we should study in connection with the subject of spiritual gifts are 1 Corinthians 12 and Ephesians 4. They describe how God provides spiritual enablement beyond our natural ability and thus makes provision for the progress of His work.

In Ephesians 4:12-13, Paul reveals the purposes of spiritual gifts: "To prepare God's people for works of service, so that the body of Christ may be built up until we all reach unity in the faith and in the knowledge of the Son of God and become mature, attaining the full measure of perfection found in Christ" (NIV). Spiritual gifts are for the perfecting, or mending, of the saints. Spiritual gifts make the believer complete in order that he may serve. The ultimate purpose of the gifts is the building up of the body of Christ.

A spiritual gift is given for benefit in the realm of the Spirit and is given to those who are indwelt by the Spirit. It may be exercised through the channel of a natural talent and leave others spiritually refreshed and strengthened. Though a spiritual gift differs from a natural talent, God does not allow our natural abilities to go to waste; He endows us with spiritual gifts in order that the natural abilities may be used effectively in His service. Someone may be an effective teacher in the public school but not in teaching Bible in the church. If that person were given the gift of teaching, then his teaching ability could be used effectively to further the ministry of Christ. Spiritual gifts are divine enablements given to every Christian for service to the body of Christ. The results are due to the power of divine grace operating through the Holy Spirit.

The body is a unit, though it is composed of many parts. There is a law of dependence working between these parts; each part has its individual function and each part is important. There is also a law of compensation working between the parts. If one part suffers, all parts suffer. If one part is honored, all parts are honored. John Wooden, of coaching fame, has said that there are three principles for developing a winning team. The first of these is to get the individuals in condition. The next is to teach them the basics, and the third is to get the individuals to work together as a team.

God gives the gifts. He does not give all the gifts to all the believers. We are not to envy or despise the function of others.

Laymen and Their Organization

Various types of organization have been developed for the laity in the church. One is the church-officer type of organization, in which the church officers sponsor, once a quarter, a meeting of all the men of the church for fellowship, inspiration, instruction, and enlistment. Another is the men's-Bible-class type of organization, in which the members of the class, in a monthly or quarterly meeting, enlist every man in the church to carry out the work. Sometimes an organization of men is formed specifically to carry out the purposes of the church. Where two or more churches are associated, with a small number of men in each, these may join together for monthly meetings. There is also a key-man type of organization, in which a church or church board appoints someone to direct the men's work.

We might list three basic purposes of a men's organization within a church. The first purpose is to evangelize, to seek the unsaved and help to bring them to a saving knowledge of Jesus Christ. The second objective is to educate. This involves training leaders and instilling an appreciative understanding of the whole work of the church. The third objective is to energize and encourage the men to practice stewardship of time, talent, and treasure. They should also be encouraged to promote needed projects for the cause of Christ.

Some possible goals of a layman's organization might include:

1. To promote intimate spiritual fellowship
2. To foster the spirit and practice of Christian worship
3. To cultivate loyalty to the church
4. To study fields, history, work, and problems of the church
5. To further the social service and missionary program of the church
6. To facilitate union with similar bodies of laymen

The programs of the organization must fit the purpose of the organization. They must be well planned and executed. The programs should use the members of the organization, since one purpose of a lay organization is to develop its members for service for Christ. Use guest speakers wisely and sparingly. There are some topics which can best be presented by a guest speaker who is a specialist in a particular field of interest.

The programs must be well balanced. If possible, they should include a good meal, announcements and introductions, an entertainment feature, a devotional, and the consideration of an appropriate topic. Minimize business items. All programs should begin and end on time. The programs should lead to action. Information, inspiration, and fellowship are all good in themselves, but they should result in men becoming more active in achieving the purposes of the organization.

Be sure that the regular meetings are for men only if it is a men's organization. The number of special meetings should not be overdone, though four which have been found helpful are a father-son banquet, father-daughter banquet, sweethearts' night, and family night.

Projects can normally be discovered by exploring such areas as buildings and grounds, the church program, and the community needs. There are often tasks which church members or family groups would like to do. Some of these projects might involve work with boys; the men might start hobby clubs, organize special excursions, develop a big-brother plan, plan a father and son banquet, or send boys to youth camp. There might be projects connected with the advertising field, such as setting up Christ-honoring highway signs or planning for radio and television spot announcements. Laymen might develop a visitation corps. There are often servicemen's centers which need volunteer help. This is a good opportunity to witness as well as work. They might fund scholarships to help worthy young people in school. Laymen can also become involved in mission projects, literature projects, church improvements, and youth-center activities. They might develop a tape ministry for shut-ins, a family-altar crusade, or a senior-citizen recreation program.

Attendance at the monthly men's meeting is normally not the result of any one thing but of a chain of activities. One link in this chain is the program of the meeting. This will probably have the largest drawing power. If it is interesting and informative, the men will come back. Adequate publicity, clearly written and properly distributed, can bolster a sagging program or can arouse the curiosity of men who can be brought out in no other way.

A good program takes time to prepare. Plan everything down to the finest detail well in advance.

Too much levity is a danger. The quickest way to breed boredom is for the president to allow the meeting to get out of hand.

Make a guest feel at ease, and you have made a friend. Let a stranger know that he is welcome, and it is not difficult to persuade him to return. A guest should be properly introduced to the group sometime during the meeting. A telephone call or a postcard sent the day following the meeting lets him know that his attendance was appreciated.

A good meal will bring out the crowds. Wholesome food, well cooked and in quantity, produces a feeling of well-being and leaves those present in a receptive frame of mind.

A typical house meeting might have the following agenda:

1. Prayer
2. Bible study
3. Roll call. Go over the list of members and arrange for helping any who may have needs.
4. Service of the neighborhood. See if there is someone in need in the neighborhood whom you can help.
5. Chat-and-chew time. Discuss some subject of national or local concern while having light refreshments.
6. Farewell prayers of intercession for those who have needs

Certain aspects of Christian service especially appeal to men. Worship experiences help them disentangle themselves from the immediate affairs and provide a spiritual perspective. The layman has a part to play in the worship of the church beyond being a passive, silent observer. Worship brings blessing not as something he watches but as something he does. Clergymen have been slow to release their hold upon leading the worship service, but laymen have also been hesitant to participate. One reason for this hesitancy may be the language used in worship. The clergyman has developed a theological jargon unknown to and often unappreciated by the layman.

There are other church-related activities that are beneficial to laymen. Bible studies are appreciated as helps in solving life's pressing problems. Personal involvement in witnessing provides an opportunity for them to share their experience of Christ with other men, and visiting gives them an opportunity to make new contacts and broaden their circle of friends. Opportunities to give financial support add a new dimension of meaning to their daily employment.

The Laity and Its Development

In the past, the duty of the laity has been to attend, to listen, to contribute money, and to be instructed. But the laity needs to be given increased responsibility; they should be given an opportunity to make decisions and take action.

The church should develop a training program for the laity so they can carry out the duty of witnessing to the world. Dr. John Stott, of London, has developed in his church a training school which meets one evening a week from October to February. Twelve lectures are given on the theory and practice of evangelism. Lecture summaries are provided and are kept in notebooks. A written and an oral examination are given at the close of the course. When all has been completed, a commissioning service is held. Most of these commissioned workers spend their first year in house-to-house visitation. They visit the elderly and sick, children and young people, members of the congregation and strangers.

Dynamic literature is another means of interesting, enlisting, and building up laymen. Books, pamphlets, and mimeographed material can provide both instruction and inspiration.

Particular attention should be called to laymen's retreats as a means of challenging men to a broader ministry for Christ. Shorter work weeks and the early retirements have made retreats even more practical now than in the past. Retreats have proven such an effective means of inspiring and motivating men that a more appropriate term than *retreats* might be *charges*.

One of the most productive methods of liberating the hidden powers of laymen is encouraging the formation of small groups of kindred spirits with an unselfish or service objective. Men feel most comfortable serving in groups of their own social, cultural, and economic peers; they hesitate to cross barriers.

Older people should be invited to share in carrying out the ministry of the church. We should plan programs which will open for them new and meaningful roles in life. Instead of being objects of ministry, they should be challenged to become partners in ministry.

We can only develop leadership among laymen as we get to know them, observe them, know what they need, and discover the potential in the adult-education group. We must keep in mind the fact that we want something to happen to them as well as to get the work done.

One of the first tasks of a congregation is to discover where God is at work in its community. The congregation must listen to, converse with, and learn to love the world beyond its doors. As citizens in society, the laity are called to enter into the common tasks of community life.

There are several guidelines for Christians who would like to participate in Christ's ministry in the neighborhood. The Christian should enter into community organizations and perhaps even politics. Since the focus of his concern will be the needs of the people, he should seek to discover what their immediate and ultimate needs are. He should engage in loving service in the name of Christ and not out of selfish motives.

We can point individuals to Christ both verbally and nonverbally. When doors of spoken witness are closed, there is still the door of intercession; this also is the work of the Christian.

Christians must engage in dialogue. They must learn to listen to the world as well as to speak. They must discover the meaning of the world's pain and the nature of its longing. As laymen become involved in the life of the world around them, they will discover their mission.

Additional Reading

Ayres, Francis O. *The Ministry of the Laity*. Philadelphia: Westminster, 1962.

Haney, David. *The Idea of the Laity*. Grand Rapids: Zondervan, 1973.

Kraemer, Hendrik. *A Theology of the Laity*. Philadelphia: Westminster, 1959.

Neill, S. C., and Weber, H. R., eds. *The Layman in Christian History*. Philadelphia: Westminster, 1963.

Schaller, Lyle. *The Pastor and the People: Building a New Partnership for Effective Ministry*. Nashville: Abingdon, 1973.

Schindler-Rainman, Eva, and Lippitt, Ronald. *The Volunteer Community*. Washington, D. C.: Center for a Voluntary Society, 1971.

Walker, Daniel D. *Enemy in the Pew?* New York: Harper & Row, 1967.

CHAPTER 8

Managing Conflict Creatively

Change in the local church is no longer an option, it is a necessity. Modern man feels a gap between the world of the church and the outside world. The world is changing rapidly and the present-day church, with its rigidity of form, cannot cope with that changing world. We must be ready to face a changing world with a changing church.

Growth means change. In the local congregation, change results from confrontation with situations that demand decisions. There may be changes in structure, behaviors, assumptions, or values. The church is often faced with such changes as cutting off organizations, changing church habits, removing a church official, or getting new societies into its organization. Larry Richards, in *A New Face for the Church*, wisely observes that the success of change in a church depends on the personal spiritual growth of the church members and on their sense of freedom to take part openly and honestly in the change process.[1]

If we are going to take seriously the updating of the local church, we must be willing to grapple with change including its theological, psychological, and sociological aspects. We must be sensitive as to how to effect change with a minimum of damage. We must pay attention to people in the midst of these changes. We must accept them as they are and expect responsible behavior from them.

Conflict is an inevitable part of growth and life, but conflict need not be destructive. We do not therefore desire to learn how to eliminate or avoid it but how to manage it creatively and constructively. Conflict is increasing. We might give two reasons for this. The first would be the increase in the number of people, and the second would be the increase in communication.

Conflict is usually centered on our value system and our emotional involvement with it. Value conflict always involves priorities. We are forced to assign some things more importance than others.

Each person's self-esteem is at stake in conflict. In his dealing with conflict, the individual would do well to ask, How do I feel in conflict? What do I do in a conflict situation? What would I like to be able to do in the midst of conflict? Some will discover they feel embarrassed, revengeful, fearful, angry, confused, hurt, or excited. Some run away from conflict, and some rise up to fight.

Conflict and Change

There are four methods of getting things done. The first is *coercion*, using force to produce desired results. The second is *co-optation*, bringing opposing individuals into the supporting group. *Cooperation* brings two groups together to work for the common good. The fourth method is *conflict*, drawing the battle lines.

The advocate of change must be aware that there are many sources of conflict within the process of change. Conflict may arise over the anticipated consequences of change. Conflict often arises over the definition of purpose. Authority and leadership styles often spark conflict. Conflict sometimes arises over the question of allies, such as whether the liberals will cooperate with the conservatives. Conflict sometimes is rooted in personality differences or differences in philosophy. Conflict is produced not only by change but by resistance to change.

Conflict that accompanies change frequently provides a far more fertile climate for creativity than does rigid orderliness. Conflict can be constructive to personal growth. It may lead to significant social progress. It may contribute to the solidarity of the group. It may nurture greater fellowship between embattled groups.

It is wise to anticipate conflict since it is an inevitable part of the process of change. When conflict is anticipated, we can often keep it from becoming such a diversion that it halts the planning process.

One must be able to distinguish between surface symptoms and real problems. It will help to set limits for permissible conflict. There are several signs of restiveness which, when recognized, can alert us to possible conflict. Voting patterns will often indicate the rise of opposition to the leadership. There may be direct protests of policy or decision. The change in attendance at meetings may be an indicator of conflict. Fluctuations in financial support will often point to unrest and coming conflict. Members sometimes withdraw support as an indication of dissatisfaction which may in time lead to conflict. The formation of factions may be a prelude to a fight. An issue which has remained unsolved for a long period of time may trigger conflict.

When conflict is anticipated we can often prevent polarization, which can immobilize an organization. It either halts or diverts the process of intentional change. There are several steps which can be taken in avoiding polarization. The following ten rules have been used by church leaders in an effort to prevent polarization.

1. Keep the channels of communication open.
2. Depersonalize dissent. Termination of communication often comes when an individual takes the criticism of his proposal or program as a personal attack.
3. Try to look inside the other person's frame of reference.
4. Open the door to creative and meaningful participation by every person.
5. Keep opening new opportunities for people to invest themselves in service and ministry.
6. Seek agreement on short-term or intermediate goals.
7. Recognize the diversity of ministries.
8. Build a sense of mutual trust within the organization.
9. Establish a grievance committee.
10. Recognize the events and factors that produce a paralyzing effect.[2]

It has been suggested that the twin objectives of change agents are to minimize resistences and maximize resources.

Kinds of Conflict

All conflict falls into one or more of the following categories. The first category is *intrapersonal* conflict. This is conflict which occurs within us. It takes one of two forms; we see a problem either as someone else's fault or as our fault. We either project it upon someone else and thus get rid of it, or take it on ourselves and become depressed. In intrapersonal conflict, the purposive self rises against its inner and outer environment. It often arises as we try to fulfill our needs and wants. Conflict develops situations in which we cannot simultaneously fulfill needs, values, and tasks in the way we desire.

The second category is *interpersonal* conflict, conflict between and among individuals. It involves transactions with others. Conflict between people is unpleasant and frustrating, because those involved feel their needs, wants, and values are in jeopardy. A disagreement over a single issue can threaten the esteem of a pastor or church leader. Some feel that interpersonal conflict is to be desired within an organization, as an indication that the organization is neither aleep nor dead. The early Church grew rapidly when its members were under the threat of death by the Roman emperors.

The resolution of conflict between individuals is never an easy task. Sometimes the best approach is to ignore it rather than to try to settle it. When we take this route, however, we run the risk of having the conflict come out into the open later, with even greater force. It seems that interpersonal conflict is best handled by confrontation. If the confrontation is to be successful, it must come of a true desire to resolve the conflict and restore the fellowship of love. Unfortunately, even our best efforts to solve conflict on a one-to-one basis do not always succeed; sometimes a third party should be brought in to help settle the conflict (Mt 18:15-17).

Intragroup conflict is the third kind of conflict. This is sometimes referred to as individual-organization conflict. This conflict is within a group and among its members. Conflict in a group often arises from unclear goals, distrustful relationships, uneven power distribution, and poor communication. It blocks a group's productivity, drains off energy, creates low morale, makes for poor cohesiveness, and produces competitive subgroups. The individual has his goals, and the organization has its goals. Very often an organization tries to impose its goals upon the individual although they differ from his. The key to avoiding this type of conflict is having a variety of goals.

The fourth type of conflict is *intergroup* conflict. We tend to identify positively with the group of which we are a member, and we perceive other groups with disinterest or antagonism. Conflicts may occur between groups which differ or ones which are similar. It may occur between groups within an organization or groups outside an organization.

Intergroup conflict may involve a contest for power extending over a long period of time. The participants may have established the means of conflict well in advance. The conflict may be unspecialized and limited in scope. The object of the conflict is rewards found within the situation. If the conflict centers in a single redistribution of power, it is referred to as terminal in nature.

Styles of Conflict Management

Conflict always occurs in a context of interdependence. If the parties in conflict were not interdependent, in the sense that actions of one party have consequences for the other and vice versa, conflict could not occur. In his lectures, Robert Worley, of McCormick Seminary, describes the various conflict management styles which persons, groups, and organizations employ as attempts to deal with this interdependence.

Denial. Straightforward denial is a hopeful attempt to avoid the necessity of facing a conflict. "I just don't recognize this as a conflict." Denial by diversion evades direct responsibility. "But I didn't mean it that way."

Withdrawal. Isolating ourselves from the situation seldom works well, because it thwarts the actual interdependence within the system. We do not solve problems by running away from them.

Projection. Projection refuses responsibility for the conflict, placing the blame upon another or "circumstances beyond my control."

Avoidance through polarization. When the issues are too hot and the stakes are too high, some may try to polarize it so that it seems hopeless. This action usually results from a feeling that personal relationships are threatened or from a fear of being rejected.

Coercion. Some use various kinds of power to enforce compliance of the opposition in conflict.

Win-lose elimination. Submitting to the decision of a third party, a referee or arbitrator, eliminates one side of the conflict. It ends the power struggle but not the feelings.

Steps to Creative Conflict Management

Check the personal power base

If a person is to manage conflict, he must understand that he is a person of worth, that he has strengths, that he is able to accomplish what he sets out to do, and that he is able to accept both his strengths and limitations. In other words, he must be a person with a "power" base. If he does not have this self-image, his chances of managing conflict are limited, and he will tend to be victimized by conflict instead of using it for creative growth.

Check the mutual trust and acceptance

We move from the individual to those persons or groups seeking management of conflict situations. Unless there is at least some modicum of trust and acceptance of one another, the conflict is unlikely to be managed. Trust must be present and operative in the situation. Do the parties trust one another? Some trust is absolutely necessary, because without trust, you cannot accept; and if you cannot accept, then you cannot listen.

Discover the core conflict

After you have analyzed yourself and the trust and acceptance level, then you must ask, How do I determine the core of the conflict? Have I narrowed or focused this conflict? Sometimes we consider the extraneous manifestations of conflict as the central issue and core. We mislead ourselves and try to manage the symptoms instead of discovering the central issue of the conflict. That central issue is the core. The third step, then, is to determine the core of the conflict.

Paul Mickey and Robert Wilson, in their book, *Conflict Resolution,* suggest a process for analyzing a conflict situation. The first focus of their suggestions deals with discovering the core of the conflict.

> What are the factors causing the conflict?
> Are there underlying factors which are different from the apparent causes of controversy?
> Who are the protagonists?
> What were the critical points of decision which led to the present situation?[3]

Analyze the assumptions

Once the core has been determined, then you can, with the other party, look at the underlying assumptions. What does the other party assume about the conflict? What do you assume about the conflict? This kind of analysis will reveal to the parties in conflict the many things that they hold in common, and isolate those assumptions about which they disagree. Solutions will probably focus on the assumptions that they hold in common.

Own your feelings and perceptions ("I" statements)

If you try to manage conflict, you must deal with your own feelings and perceptions. Do not say, "I think everyone thinks that is wrong"; but rather, "I think these things are wrong." Be willing to risk being as honest and open as you can. Avoid hiding behind words like *they,* and *the group.*

Brainstorm creative alternatives

The two parties in a conflict have to attempt to let go of their own opinions and brainstorm to come up with as many different ways to manage the conflict as possible. Do not discuss suggested alternatives until you have come up with as many alternatives as you possibly can.

After you have selected the two or three alternatives both parties think they can use, then select the one alternative that you are going to try first. How do you elect that one? After both parties have examined the strengths they have, choose the alternative that uses both of the parties' personal strengths. Both parties will also have to determine the time available to them to manage the conflict.

After you have chosen the number one alternative, try to project the kinds of risks involved and the kind of results that might occur if you use this particular method to manage the conflict.

Commit, covenant, and evaluate

Once you have chosen a method and examined it in some detail, you must commit yourself to use that particular method. You covenant with one another to give it a try. Does the alternative chosen manage the conflict effectively?

Principles to Remember in Conflict management

We should seek to manage and use conflict creatively rather than to try to eliminate it. We should not assume that conflict is bad.

Acknowledge that different expectations and goals are always present and will be in conflict. There are three types of goals in every organization: (1) the goals of the individual; (2) the individual's goals for the organization; and (3) the organization's goals. These may be in conflict with one another. These must be made public in order to be managed.

It is more helpful to take a goal-oriented approach to conflict management to seek causes of the conflict. Look ahead rather than backward; do not just keep asking why you got into the conflict. We do not want to ignore history, but neither do we want to dwell on it.

Persons and organizations need an adequate psychological power base in order to be able to manage conflict. They need to have a valid self-perception.

An open, friendly climate in an organization is necessary for creative conflict management.

Creative communication is essential to managing conflict. This includes the communication of our own assumptions and perceptions. It is necessary that I recognize that the message I am sending is my understanding of the situation and not the ultimate evaluation of it.

Numerous assumptions are always present in a conflict and need to be verbalized and evaluated. If the assumptions prove true, then keep them; if they are not true, they should be removed. This is the filtering process.

One of the most essential elements in conflict management is the identification of what a person, group, or organization is trying to accomplish in a situation. Clarification of goals will make the conflict public, though it sometimes makes it more intense, as well.

It is not necessary to homogenize values or goals in order to be able to work together as individuals. Creative conflict management finds the places where values overlap and works on the things that you have in common rather than focusing on differences.

We should explore all the alternatives. There are always more alternatives than we see at first.

To be most effective, conflict-management processes must be institutionalized and not created for special occasions. They must be built into the organization.

Robert Worley, of McCormick Seminary, reminded his classes that a church cannot be spiritually healthy until differences are recognized and dealt with honestly, and ways are discovered whereby we can live with and love one another with our differences.

A church can never really get on target until it has gained the ability, with the guidance of the Holy Spirit, to deal openly with its differences. Conflict must be recognized as a fact of life and managed creatively and constructively.

Additional Reading

Bennis, Warren G.; Benne, Kenneth D.; and Chin, Robert. *The Planning of Change*. New York: Holt, Rinehard & Winston, 1969.

Come, Arnold B. *Agents of Reconciliation*. Philadelphia: Westminster, 1964.

Fray, Harold. *Conflict and Change in the Church*. Philadelphia: Pilgrim, 1969.

Gamson, William A. *Power and Discontent.* Homewood, Ill.: Dorsey, 1968.
Judson, Arnold S. *A Manager's Guide to Making Changes.* New York: John Wiley, 1966.
Leas, Speed, and Kittlaus, Paul. *Church Fights.* Philadelphia: Westminster, 1973.
Mickey, Paul A., and Wilson, Robert L. *Conflict Resolution.* Nashville: Abingdon, 1973.
Schaller, Lyle E. *The Change Agent.* Nashville: Abingdon, 1972.
———. *Community Organization: Conflict and Reconciliation.* Nashville: Abingdon, 1966.
Smith, Clagett, ed. *Conflict Resolution: Contributions of Behavioral Sciences.* Notre Dame, Ind.: U. of Notre Dame, 1971.
Tucker, Michael R. *The Church That Dared to Change.* Wheaton, Ill.: Tyndale, 1975.

CHAPTER 9

Strengthening Interpersonal Relationships

It is imperative that we become a people who understand who we are, who God is, and what God is doing in the world. We need some new approaches to church work and some new programs; but most of all, we need new people. We need people sensitive to and responsive to human need and who appreciate the preciousness of people. Friendship is more than just enjoying and taking delight in the presence of each other; it is also accepting responsibility for meeting the needs of each other.

Some groups have emphasized the vertical relationship, man's relationship to God, to the exclusion of the development of one's relationship to his fellowman, the horizontal relationship. Others emphasize the horizontal with little or no reference to the vertical. Ideally, we should be developing both kinds of relationships.

With this in mind, Dr. William Graham reads five Psalms a day, in order to find out how to communicate with God more effectively, and one chapter of Proverbs each day, in order to find out how better to communicate with his fellowmen.

The Carnegie Technological Institute has stated that 90 percent of all people who fail in their life's vocation, fail because they cannot get along with people.

The problems and sins of all people revolve around three basic relationships: one's relationship to self, to God, and to others.

We need to establish redemptive interpersonal relationships. Personality is formed through our relationships with others. It is deformed through personal relationships of a negative nature; it is reformed by the grace of God acting through creative relationships. Personality is transformed through the ministry of the Holy Spirit. It is essential that all within the fellowship of the church become aware of the fact that each person is a means through which their faith may be strengthened. Christian love personified speaks more clearly than the most excellent verbal description of the nature of love. Members must be given opportunity not only to study and to worship together but also to work together, to have fellowship together, and to come to know and care about each other.

Our society is becoming increasingly impersonal and mobile. This heightens people's feelings of restlessness and loneliness. It makes it all the more necessary for the church to provide deep, mutual concern among its members. We are always in danger of playing the numbers game, putting great emphasis upon how many but forgetting the importance of who. We cannot allow people to become lost in church. They must be known by name and not by number.

To get work done with people, much thought, time, and tolerance are required. Skills in developing human relationships are imperative. People at best are "almost fits"; they do not come in the proper size and shape for the tasks to be done in an organization. But God did not create people merely as resources for organizations.

The art of working with and getting along with people demands applying fundamental ideas of kindness and understanding. It leads us to conform where we cannot alter, and to maintain our serenity when friends and fellow workers seem perverse.

Some time ago, while on a speaking assignment in Indiana, I noted a sign on the wall behind the registration desk in a hotel. I stopped and copied it because of the insight it gave into developing an ability to get along with others.

The six most important words—"I admit I made a mistake."
The five most important words—"You did a good job."
The four most important words—"What is your opinion?"
The three most important words—"If you please."
The two most important words—"Thank you."
The least important word—"I."

Dr. Carl S. Winters, of Oak Park, Illinois, has formulated "Ten

Commandments of Human Relations." These have been given by him in lectures across the country.

1. Thou shalt love people, not just use them.
2. Thou shalt develop thine understanding.
3. Thou shalt compliment more than criticize.
4. Thou shalt not get angry.
5. Thou shalt not argue.
6. Thou shalt be kind.
7. Thou shalt have a sense of humor.
8. Thou shalt smile.
9. Thou shalt practice what thou preachest.
10. Thou shalt go to school to the Headmaster of the universe, the Master of men, the Secretary of human relations—namely, Jesus Christ.

It is profitable to study the techniques used by Jesus Christ in His dealings with individuals. One might begin such a study by surveying the thirty-four interviews in the gospel of John. Such passages as Luke 7:36-50; Luke 18:18-26; Luke 19:1-10; John 3:1-14; and John 4:1-30 also provide helpful insights.

Relationships Between Pastor and People

Pastors need special help in the area of interpersonal relations. Dr. Samuel Blizzard, of Pennsylvania State University, did some research on how a pastor spends his time. His research showed that a pastor spends an average of nine hours and fifty-seven minutes on the job, seven days a week. Three hours and fifty-seven minutes of this time each day involves administration. One hour and ten minutes is spent in organizational work. The ability to get along with people is one of the prime attributes of a good administrator and organizer.

The pastor must not change his chair into a throne. Many have an unduly exalted opinion of themselves. Only little men try to dominate rather than inspire. Wise men strive to enlist the goodwill of people rather than to strike fear into them. They do not fight to win a point but rather seek to win support by inspiring to get behind their plans.

Unfortunately much of the misery of preachers is self-imposed. Dr. Charles Koller has given four deadly assumptions which pastors often foster regarding others: (1) his predecessor was a moron; (2) his members are ignoramuses; (3) his deacons are obstructionists; and (4) his troubles are caused by "unspiritual" opponents.

Koller also lists some occupational diseases which plague the preacher. The first he calls wandering minds. The preacher with this disease is always looking for larger congregations. Next is the disease of ingrown eyeballs. The preacher thus afflicted puts self-interest above Kingdom interest. The third disease is the animated jawbone. This preacher is noted for denunciation rather than reconciliation. He is very belligerent in the pulpit. He is noted for his whip and not for his winsomeness. The fourth disease is that of itching palms. This characterizes the preacher who is constantly hinting for more of everything.

Sound pastoral administration is the sum total of mature imagination, mature perception, and mature judgment. It is especially in voluntary organizations that the great battle goes on between maturity and immaturity. Unfortunately, some have never learned the difference between childlikeness and childishness. Maturity means completeness of growth and development, physically, socially, intellectually, and spiritually. Only those who are spiritually mature can solve the problems of our day.

The term *mature* does not appear in the King James Version of the Scriptures. The general concept, however, is referred to in 1 Corinthians 2:6, 13:11; Ephesians 4:12-13; and Hebrews 6:1.

The mature individual must be willing to accept imperfections and to recognize the human capacity to make mistakes. We are not perfect at this point, but we are pressing on toward that end (Phil 3: 12-16).

The mature individual recognizes that it is wise to forego some present pleasures for the sake of lasting, future gains. He has adopted a new sense of values. He is willing to deny now in order to obtain later, as emphasized in Philippians 3:7-11.

The mature individual is willing to accept new ideas. He has laid aside his childish ways and is willing to expand his outlook. He is ready to broaden his associations. His activities evidence maturity of development. His attire is in accord with his development. He is willing and ready to exercise authority and control from within rather than relying upon outward authority.

The mature individual will act in love toward others (Eph 4:15; 1 Jn 4:21). He gets more satisfaction from giving than from receiving.

A good pastor will provide his helpers with four satisfactions: a feeling of self-esteem; a chance to develop; the stimulation of new experiences; and a sense of freedom.

A pastor will profit by developing patience, modesty, and enjoyment of his work. Impatience can tear holes in any plan; a pastor must be patient enough to see his suggestions pulled apart by a committee without being upset. He must be patient enough to wait for others to understand and accept an idea which already seems clear to him. He must be modest and refrain from trying to throw his weight around when actually there is not enough there to throw.

A pastor needs emotional stability. It is unwise to let his temperament rule. Someone has defined *temperamental* as 90 percent temper and 10 percent mental. A person, particularly one in a position of leadership, who is subject to moods and gives way to them becomes a troublemaker.

A pastor must build and operate a church of men and women who have individual skills and accomplishments. He must provide a climate in which these diverse people can function as a team. There must be a "conductor" at the podium to keep all the "instrumentalists" in time and in harmony. The spirit of teamwork will be maintained if you give every man enough responsibility to make him feel his own importance. Your staff have put their working days into your hands. They have the right to expect that you will study your profession and keep up-to-date. Whoever is under your power is under your protection.

Understanding People

Understanding people demands that we recognize first of all that all people are different, though we often are not aware in what respect, to what degree, or why. The second truth we must recognize is that we are all acting and reacting in different environments. It becomes imperative, therefore, that we look at each situation from the other person's point of view and not just from our own.

We should take every opportunity to see an individual in different settings. This will give us a chance to observe his friends and how he spends his leisure time. These are both important factors. A visit in the individual's home will broaden our understanding of him.

Remember that it is difficult to understand a person who is involved in a problem situation. We must extract the real problem from the problem situation and separate fact from fiction. Problems are complex, and they keep changing.

We should be ready to learn from other people. It was Ralph Waldo Emerson who said, "Every man I meet is superior in some way. In that I learn of him." We must focus on strengths and not on weaknesses. We must seek out people's abilities rather than their disabilities.

We should be open-minded when we first meet people. It is impossible to understand people if we prejudge them. It is important to discover why they do what they do. Very often, to know all is to forgive all.

Look charitably on the motives of people. The most unhappy person on earth is one who goes through life suspecting evil of everyone with whom he comes in contact.

In management, the "different" or "nonconforming" individual is viewed as a problem person. These individuals are found in the realm of church activity as well as in businesses, and too often they are automatically classified as problem people within the church. Such automatic classification is unwise. The individual who does not conform to the standards of the group in behavior, attitude, and dress is not necessarily a problem person who must be dealt with at once. A nonconforming person does not automatically threaten group unity and teamwork.

The real problem person is one who actually interferes with the progress of the work or hinders fellow employees in their work. He damages the image, reputation, and ministry of the church. Beware of acting as a psychiatrist when you are not one and trying to deal with the real problem-individual when you have neither the time nor the training.

Relationships Between Leader and Followers

Every organization must have a leader; no organization will run by itself. This leader must keep a jump ahead of his group. He must know how to inspire those who are working with him.

Security and maintenance, order, personal interaction, and bodily needs are not the key determinants of the motivation to perform effectively. Effective performance occurs as a person sees the opportunity to achieve meaningful goals, to be recognized or given status and position for his efforts, or to enjoy the success of a well-executed team effort. We are now finding that the traditional reward incentives have little or no motivational effect on performance; a person's salary is not sufficient incentive to do good work. Perhaps the most successful motivation is job enrichment. Job enrichment means that there is wide variety of tasks, which makes the job more challenging, more interesting, and more fulfilling for the person who performs it.

In church work, job enrichment means giving an individual greater latitude in decision making, more responsibility in the areas of planning and policy making, greater authority to spend money, and a greater influence in those activities of the church which concern them. Kenneth Kilinski and Jerry Wofford, in *Organization and Leadership in the Local Church*, state some of the implications of this action. It may take the form of a financial system that allows each Sunday school department or each youth group to have a budget that they may spend at their own discretion rather than going to their director for authorization.[1] It may mean that teachers and workers at the lowest organizational level will be able to choose material and supplemental aids without "watchdog" surveillance. It may mean that leaders anywhere in the church will have the freedom to choose their own personnel and create their own programs. It will invariably mean that the church or denominational leadership must loosen control and allow the local church greater freedom and responsibility.

A second approach motivating our church workers to effective performance is goal setting and review. The essential ingredients of this approach are the establishment of goals for future performance and the recognition of the successes in achieving these goals. Concrete and specific goals should be established by the person who is to carry them out.

Another suggestion for motivation is to begin where the individuals are and then challenge them to go forward. Help them see the value of internal motivation instead of prizes and other external motivation. Allow them to help you plan, and use their ideas whenever possible. Help them to see that results and changes are gradual and require steady work. Expose them to creative, enthusiastic people in their field. Encourage them to attend conferences and conventions. (The church would do well to help them with their expenses at this point.) Let them know that you understand their limitations, yet continue to press them toward high standards.

In leading others, it is important to make clear and logical assignments of responsibilities. A job description for each position will give guidelines for responsibility and accountability. Do not enlist helpers unless they are needed. It is important to praise every improvement and to remind workers that others are depending upon them and are interested in them. Make suggestions and ask questions rather than give orders. The leader must be sincere and enthusiastic. We must remember that in order to get strength, we must put up with weaknesses.

A good leader is principally concerned not with things but with people. No man has true authority unless he has a genuine interest in people. He is always on the lookout for individuals who can relieve him of details, fill in for him when he is away, and contribute toward constructive planning. People, not things, get the job done.

It is important to build a reputation as a helper of others. One of my colleagues said something which I have found thought provoking and helpful: "I would rather be a kingmaker than a king."

A leader must have confidence in his judgment. This confidence cannot be a bluff; it must be real to be effective. He must also be noted for self-control. This will enable him to adapt to shifting conditions and deal with unexpected crises. He must also be discreet, able to evaluate a project before challenging others to become involved in it. Courage is also needed. Many a good idea has been lost because the leader did not dare to promote it. Good ideas are also lost when a leader is unable to make a wise decision without dithering. A leader must learn to leave his emotions at home. Only his family should know of his temperamental upsets.

Negative attitudes are disastrous to the person desirous of improving his leadership ability. It is imperative to take a positive approach to situations and challenges.

A pastor should refrain from criticizing those who are serving with him. A barrage of criticism will destroy their peace of mind and will to do their best work. Criticism of the denominational leaders under whom the pastor works will also prove detrimental. This does not mean that he cannot give a fair evaluation of a denominational leader, but it should be given to the individual himself, in a constructive spirit. All men have faults and peculiarities. Those of leaders are often just more noticeable than those of the followers.

In most organizations there is a time when criticism must be given. When this time comes, focus on the act and not on the person. Everyone makes mistakes, but it is foolish to scold. Criticisms should begin with praise and honest appreciation of what the man does well, and then go on to point out how he could do better. Be specific about the nature of the error and be specific about the suggested remedy. Able men take pains to spare others humiliation, even when it is necessary to criticize their actions. It is best to criticize in private, thus allowing the one who has made the error to save face. If humor is used in the criticism, make sure it is friendly. Give the one being criticized a chance to ask questions. Assure him that you are trying to help and not hinder him. You are on his side.

The effective leader must have energy, enthusiasm, and a sense of responsibility. He needs intellectual power, lively imagination, knowledge of men, and a personality which makes other people eager to carry out his suggestions.

Be sure and develop a creative climate, a quality within the organization which makes it conducive to creative activity. Begin by generating excitement over new ideas. Make it clear that new ideas are important. Spotlight the areas where new ideas are especially needed. Let the people know that you are willing to help them develop new ideas. Remember that anyone in the organization can have new ideas. Do not eliminate anyone. Be ready and willing to applaud originality. Give credit where it is due.

In dealing with staff, it is better to try to convince and persuade rather than to domineer. Do not try to push people around. It is nice to be important, but it is more important to be nice.

Department heads should be consulted during the making of plans affecting their departments, and they should be given the authority needed to carry out their projects. Prime Minister Churchill told the House of Commons, "I am your servant, and you have the right to dismiss me when you please. What you have no right to do is ask me to bear responsibilities without the power of effective action."

In order for leaders and followers to get along well, there should be mutual respect, mutual approval, and mutual stimulation. When these are not present, strains appear. These may come because of a difference in standards, for instance, all may not agree as to what is ethical. Strain may develop if the leader is afraid a follower is trying to take his job away from him. However, it may be that the follower just cannot bring himself to accept directions from his leader. Search for the roots of the problems in relationships.

Not every disagreement can be settled to the satisfaction of both parties. When disagreements arise, it may be wise to agree to disagree and to go on from there. Sometimes there is really no tenable middle ground. By trying to force an agreement, you might gain outward consent but eventually lose the contest. There are times to concede and conciliate. Sometimes it is wise to retreat and wait for a more favorable time.

Avoid arguments. The only way to get the best of an argument is to avoid it. It is no use to win an argument and lose a person. Beware of the attitude which says: "In matters controversial, my attitude is fine. I always see two points of view—the one that's wrong, and mine."

No matter what gadgets may be provided or systems devised, the leader's function is still that of directing people. He must have a feeling for humanity. The leader achieves nothing on his own. His leadership brings out the best qualities and efforts in others. A leader discharges his duties by influencing people rather than by exerting power over them.

Careful Communication

A good leader should have both an active and a contemplative life. One great foe of many an executive is the assumption that he knows it all. He should continue to spend time thinking and learning. "Out of the abundance of the heart the mouth speaketh" (Mt 12:34). The enriched life demands an enriched mind. This enriched life will be evidenced in speech and selective listening.

Listening is important for three reasons: (1) no one knows the problems of the job and the implications of change as well as the man who has been doing the work; (2) only by listening can the supervisor detect a possible trouble spot before it develops; and (3) the worker likes to feel that the supervisor takes an interest in his viewpoint.

No one in a leadership position can do too much listening. It has been said that the average manager spends up to 70 percent of his time listening.[2] What is true of the manager must also be true of the pastor. Effective listening is an art. Try to avoid distractions. Concentration is not easy; you must work at it. Sometimes it is helpful to take notes on what you are hearing.

Poor listening sometimes has its source in the difference in speed between thinking and speaking. As one individual is speaking, the listener is thinking ahead and will often turn the speaker off in his own mind since he has already assumed what the speaker is going to say. This is probably one reason why preachers are generally poor at listening to sermons preached by others. One way to correct this problem is to use the time between thinking and speaking to evaluate what the speaker is saying. This will prevent your mind from going on a detour while waiting for the speaker to complete his message.

Dealing with people requires the communication of ideas. This is a two-way project. Think about the person to whom you are talking. Pay attention while he is talking. Never contradict him until you are certain you know exactly what he is saying. Do not assume that the way you use a word is the same way that the other individual uses the word. Ask for expressions of opinion, but do not take another's difference of opinion as an attack upon yourself. Separate principles from people. A group faces a real crisis when one member gets angry with another. If we approach questions with a gentle, tolerant attitude, we retain our poise under trying circumstances. Great men are not quick to take offence. Self-control is necessary to working with people successfully.

Every communication between a superior and his workers does two things: it conveys ideas, and it generates feelings. A good relationship between the leader and his workers demands that he pay attention to their suggestions and complaints.

It is important to know how to say no. In all cases, *no* by itself is not an answer which should be given to a request. The shortest would be "No, thank you." When you want to say no to a request, consider whether or not the request is justified. The reasons for the request may not be clear. Get the facts first, and then expand your response accordingly. It may be that the work situation demands that you turn down the request. Do not contradict others abruptly. Benjamin Franklin said, "I make it a rule to forbear all direct contradiction to the sentiment of others and all positive blunt assertions of my own."

When an individual says that he wants to leave his job, try to discern whether he actually wants to leave it or is actually seeking a chance to make his grievances known to someone. Pay attention to the reason he gives for leaving the position. Is it a final statement, or does it imply that he could be induced to stay under certain circumstances? There are some times when an individual's voluntary resignation is a relief to the organization. In such a case, accept the resignation with kindness and appreciation. If you would really like to have him remain, try to get him to discuss his position in order that you may understand the reasons behind the resignation. You may be able to eliminate or alleviate the source of dissatisfaction.

Do not broadcast your attitudes. There are times when negative feelings arise as we meet or work with individuals. You may have a tendency to publicize these negative feelings as a means of punishing the individual. Try rather to locate and objectify the reason for your negative feeling toward him. The reason may really be in yourself and not in him. Seek the wisdom of the Holy Spirit in this process of discernment, and pray for His help in your attempt to love the individual rather than loathe him. Look for his good qualities, and center your attention upon them.

Be more afraid of those who flatter you than of those who attack you. King George V of England had a motto on his study wall which read, "Teach me neither to proffer nor receive cheap praise."

Developing Personal Effectiveness

Auren Uris, in *The Executive Deskbook*, reminds us that there are four keys to personal effectiveness. The first is mental fitness. Personal efficiency, using energy wisely and economically, is the second. The third key is physical fitness; regular checkups and proper medical guidance will bring benefits. The fourth key is mastering one's profession. It is important to stay on top of developments in one's profession.[3]

There are several more specific suggestions which, when heeded, will assist in developing personal effectiveness. Smile and be pleasant. No man is ever fully dressed until he has a smile on his face. You will feel better if you smile. Williams James of Harvard said, "Action seems to follow feeling, but really action and feeling go together." The perennial pessimist poses problems to any group or organization. In some cases pessimism is curable. It may come as a result of overwork or a run-down physical condition. Correcting these conditions may cure the outlook. It may be wise for a pessimist to work in an area where his negativism will not spread and where it can be controlled.

Take the initiative to be friendly. Go to the people rather than waiting for them to come to you. Be kind to people you meet on the way up the ladder of success, for they may be the same ones you will meet on the way down the ladder. There is a difference between friendliness and friendship. Friendliness implies a warm and friendly attitude. Friendship involves intimacy and special considerations. Show friendliness to all, but avoid favoritism. Beware of accepting friendly overtures from cliques. Friendliness with a person means that you have, over and above your general merit, some particular merit to that person.

One mark of a good leader is his ability to carry out his responsibilities with ease. The man in a hurry indicates that what he is tackling is too big for him. Rushing wears on the body and on the nerves.

No one who aspires to getting along well with people can afford to ignore courtesy, being considerate of others in little ways. Courtesy is a quality that will lift one above the crowd. Courtesy and etiquette are closely allied. John Wesley said to his lay preachers, "Act as if you were brought up in court." True etiquette, hospitality, courtesy, and good manners come from the heart; it is not an artificial cloak. The purpose of etiquette is to glorify God and to promote a fruitful witness. There are two reasons for social rules: the first is to help other people, and the second is to smooth out the social machinery. For the Christian, poise, ease, and gracious rapport are to the glory of God.

There are several general principles of etiquette. Etiquette has the ingredients of convention (custom), courtesy (politeness plus kindness), culture (improving through education and discipline), and common sense (punctuality, orderliness, dependability, and loyalty). Common sense should be used in every situation. Good manners are based entirely upon kindness. Be yourself. Be sincere. Cultivate the attitude of gratitude. Never be too busy to say please and thank you. How you say and do things is an important as what you say and do. Do not be afraid to admit when you are wrong. Always keep a sense of humor.

The practice of etiquette covers a wide scope. Two very important areas are those of introductions and table manners. Cleanliness of body and clothes is also included within the scope of etiquette. The matters pertaining to conversational etiquette and calling etiquette should be given attention.

Everything we are bears testimony. Study your Bible and an up-to-date book of etiquette. The pattern of etiquette is to be found in the Lord Jesus, and the root of etiquette is established in 1 Corinthians 13. Christians are God's gentlemen.

Additional Reading

Bell, A. Donald. *How to Get Along with People in the Church.* Grand Rapids: Zondervan, 1970.

Collins, Gary. *Effective Counseling.* Carol Stream, Ill.: Creation House, 1972.

Jefferson, Charles. *The Minister as Shepherd.* Fort Washington, Pa.:, CLC, 1973.
King, Guy H. *What to Do with Yourselves.* Fort Washington, Pa.:, CLC, 1956.
Lee, Irving J. *Language Habits in Human Affairs.* New York: Harper, 1941.
Pentecost, J. Dwight. *Man's Problems—God's Answers.* Chicago: Moody, 1974.
Sweeting, George. *How to Solve Conflicts.* Chicago: Moody, 1973.
———. *Love Is the Greatest.* Chicago: Moody, 1974.

CHAPTER 10

Organizing Church Finances

Church effectiveness in all areas, including the financial, is founded upon commitment to Jesus Christ and to His Church. Beyond commitment, there is intention. All members should be given an opportunity to express their intentions, including the hopes and fears which arise from their commitment. The leaders should then do some planning in an attempt to bring to reality the hopes of the members. This planning will lead to budgeting, which includes a mobilization of time, energy, skills, and money. This stewardship process is the concern of this chapter.

A steward is a dispenser of another's goods. In Bible times, a well-to-do householder had a steward to manage his affairs, his property, his farm, his accounts, and his slaves. It was required of a steward that he be found faithful (1 Co 4:2).

All Christian people are God's stewards and have been entrusted with goods. These goods are not just for their own blessing but for the blessing of the household of faith.

God is the sovereign Owner and Lord of all. He owns all but gives gifts to mankind. These are gifts of creation and gifts of redemption. Man is totally responsible for his use of these gifts. The parables of the talents and the pounds illustrate the responsibility resting upon Christians to improve and use the opportunities and gifts which God has given. Material items such as money are neither good nor bad in themselves. We have been charged with the responsible management of them. If the time comes when a material gift becomes the center of our life, then a Christ-centered life is impossible; the gift, and not Christ, is our master. God holds His people ultimately accountable for their use of money. There will be a judgment not only of the believer's work but also of his management of the resources committed to his care. God is the Owner to whom man is responsible and accountable.

Stewardship is a broad, bold, strong, and cutting word. Stewardship is an honest response to God, to self, and to the world. It is the process of using life in the grand manner of a willing servant of Jesus Christ. We may not have much choice of what we get, but we do have a choice of what we give. Our stewardship publicizes our priorities.

The General Board of Lay Activities of the Methodist Church in a pamphlet entitled *Christian Stewardship* defines stewardship as man's grateful and obedient response to God's redeeming love, expressed by the use of all resources for the fulfillment of Christ's mission in the world. The following additional definitions provide guidance for reflection.

> Christian stewardship is the practice of handling the affairs or property of God, according to the wishes of God, as revealed to us through His Son, Jesus Christ.
>
> Christian stewardship is the inevitable, spontaneous response of the Christian to God's mercy for us as expressed in the life, death, and resurrection of Jesus Christ.
>
> Christian stewardship is the practical expression of one's experience with God.
>
> Christian stewardship is the practical implementation of the fundamental concepts of our Christian faith.
>
> Christian stewardship is man's response to God's love.
>
> Christian stewardship concerns our attitudes toward, and use of, everything that God has placed at our disposal during our stay in earth. This includes our body, mind, abilities, health, time, home, friends, church, country, opportunities to learn and to work, material resources of the earth, money, all that money can buy, and even life itself.

One method of providing an opportunity for the expression of stewardship intention is to hold small meetings either in the homes of the church families or in the church itself. Ten to fifteen minutes can be spent in introductions and getting acquainted. This is important so that all will feel free to speak. Three to five minutes can then be used to clarify the purpose of the meeting. This purpose is to gather information from the membership so that goals may be established and a budget formulated on the basis of the goals. It is an attempt to discover what the members enjoy about the church, what they are concerned about, and what they would be most interested in doing. The next sixty minutes can be spent in the actual gathering of information. The following questions should bring forth some information:

What do you like most about what we are doing here at the church?
What additional hopes do you have for the life of our church?
What needs to happen here which is not now happening?
What specific changes would you like to see in our church?
In what specific ways do you think the congregation should be ministering to the community?
What should and can be your involvement in the life and ministry of this church?

The responses to these questions should be collected and categorized. A summary may then be presented to the group either verbally or in writing at a later date. This list will provide a first step toward making the eventual church budget one which majors in ministry rather than in money.

A Church Budget

A conventional church budget can be transformed into a program or planning budget. We could put some rather realistic price tags on Sunday services, midweek services, and calls. One public school teacher spent considerable time in a personal project of trying to determine how much each class he taught was actually costing the taxpayer. He then divided that figure by the number of students in his classes. At the beginning of the year, he told the students how much was being invested in each class hour and challenged them to remind him when they felt they were being shortchanged. It would be interesting to determine the cost of various aspects of ministry. Giving might be increased if the givers were aware of our attempt at objectivity. It might be wise to have major sections in the budget identified as congregational care, evangelism, mission, and witness. We need to move from a program of pledging the budget to one of Christian stewardship. We need to compare the proportion of the budget expenditures which are for financing current program activities and those which are for increasing the future capability of the organization. We should be heading toward fulfilling our purpose and mission. A glance at the budget will tell much about the priorities of the budget makers. Check the list of general purposes included in the church constitution and the objectives chosen by the church. Analyze the budget in terms of these purposes and objectives. Does the financial report identify our purposes and objectives?

Beware of the dream budget formulated the last minute before the annual meeting by one individual to whom the task was assigned. Without careful planning and input by the various groups, only a dream sheet will result rather than a workable budget. Some churches can be thousands of dollars behind in raising their budget and yet be able to pay their bills. This type of budget actually serves no constructive purpose.

A budget is a statement of purpose and a diagram of expectations. It is a plan which specifies goals, puts price tags on the goals, and shows how to reach those goals. It is a precedent for future decisions and a basis for evaluation.

The typical budget outlines the anticipated expenditures for the coming year but says little about what the church actually hopes to accomplish. Most Protestant churches allocate between 18% and 35% of their income to the care and operation of their property.[1] This has led someone to remind us of the fact that the church is property poor and that it should not build buildings without endowing them. It is encouraging to note that there is a comparatively low administrative cost in the church. The average is about 9%, compared to 67% in the federal government, 51% in the state governments, and 27% in city and county governments.

The members have a right to know what is included in the budget and the progress which is being made toward meeting the budget. The budget is normally formulated by a budget committee which consists of representatives from the major organizations in the church and the financial officers of the church. The church bulletin should include each week the amount needed by the budget for the past week and the amount received.

Open, public communication should be the basis of decision making in church organizations and especially in the formulation of the budget. The goal should be to seek unity in diversity. We should not view differences as obstacles.

There are dangers connected with designated giving. Popular items in the budget will be overpledged, and items which are necessary but not as popular will go wanting. It is more glamorous to designate money for the support of the missionary on the field than it is to provide transportation for him to reach the field. Administrative expenses are necessary but are not glamour items in the budget and therefore do not attract designations. It is preferable to have a budget formulated that all can support and then to contribute to that budget without designations. Many of the dangers connected with designated giving will be overcome if the financial officers, in agreement with church vote, specify that designated moneys for budgeted items go toward meeting the budgeted amount, with the understanding that if the budget amount is oversubscribed by designations, then the total amount will go to that project.

There are several advantages to a unified church budget. It provides an overview of the total financial picture. It is important that all sections of the budget be met rather than just one or two at the expense of others. A unified budget provides the church member with a detailed account of where all finanical gifts are going. The balance between the giving for missions, for instance, and the support of the local church is visible at a glance. There are some organizations within a church which insist upon supporting their own projects. If they fail in this support, however, the responsibility falls back upon the church. We advise, therefore, that these commitments be included within the printed budget as a self-supporting budget. The entire church will then know all commitments of these auxiliary organizations.

The budget should be divided into areas of concern. More members should be allocated for each area than are actually used, so that items may be added without altering the numbers of the entire budget. A unified budget helps to publicize the various activities sponsored by the church and gives the donors a feeling of personal involvement in them through financial support.

It is helpful to draw a circle representing one dollar given to the support of the budget. Divide the area within the circle into proportionate sections in accordance with the amount of the church budget going to each major area. This will visualize the percentage of each dollar going to the support of each budget item.

When organizations within the church pay their own way, there is a tendency to develop a self-centeredness which may, in time, short-circuit the blessing of giving. It is preferable that organizations have a part in supporting the total ministry of the church and that the church support the individual groups. In this way the church membership will have knowledge of the total ministry of the church and will tend to follow it with their concern and prayer.

Portions of an actual church budget are included in order for the reader to see in print the principles and specifics which have been noted. Ten categories are included in the general budget. Note that within each area, the officer who has the responsibility of vouchering the funds is designated by office and not by name. Within this budget you will note a number of items listed as "administrative." This category is more commonly known as "miscellaneous." It is not wise to have large miscellaneous listings in a budget, since too many items can be hidden within it. This budget points out the fact that this church makes no provision for the support of Christian schools, colleges, and seminaries.

Quarterly financial reports can be made to the church by using this same budget. Just put the remaining amount beside each item. The difference between that amount and the original figure tells at a glance the amount which has been expended from that fund to date.

It is wise to print on the budget the principles of finance which have been adopted by the church. When they are so noted, they can be carried from year to year and will not become lost in the books of minutes.

1975 BUDGET

ADMINISTRATIVE EXPENSES (1-20)		
(vouchered by executive committee)		
1. Part-time pastor	$6,120.00	
2. Pastor—housing	2,880.00	
3. Pastor—car expense	1,200.00	
4. Pastoral intern (travel)	975.00	
5. Honorarium	100.00	
6. Pulpit supply	400.00	
7. Custodian service	1,000.00	
8. Church office secretary	1,560.00	
9. Administrative	200.00	
Total (1-20)		$14,435.00
BUILDING AND GROUNDS (21-35)		
(vouchered by chairman)		
21. Building maintenance	$ 775.00	
22. Decorating	200.00	
23. New equipment	1,000.00	
24. Custodial supplies	500.00	
25. Insurance	955.00	
26. Telephone	500.00	
27. Gas & electricity (heat & light)	2,880.00	
28. Administrative	100.00	
Total (21-35)		$ 6,910.00
GENERAL OFFICE EXPENSE (36-45)		
(vouchered by executive committee)		
36. General printing	$ 200.00	
37. Mimeograph & Addressograph supplies	200.00	
38. Postage	300.00	
39. Equipment repair	50.00	
40. Office supplies	150.00	
Total (36-45)		$ 900.00
GENERAL PROGRAM EXPENSE (46-50)		
(vouchered by executive committee)		
46. Advertising	$ 100.00	
47. Bulletins	300.00	
48. Offering envelopes	85.00	
49. Books, Bibles	100.00	
50. Administrative	300.00	
Total (46-50)		$ 885.00

WORSHIP COMMITTEE (51-60)
(vouchered by chairman)

51.	Church instrument tuning and repair	$ 150.00	
52.	Church music	130.00	
53.	Guest musicians	220.00	
54.	Flowers (sanctuary)	85.00	
55.	Administrative	50.00	
	Total (51-60)		$ 635.00

EVANGELISM AND VISITATION COMMITTEE (61-70)
(vouchered by chairman)

61.	Flowers and gifts	$ 325.00	
62.	Communications	75.00	
63.	Benevolence	100.00	
64.	Administrative	65.00	
	Total (61-70)		$ 565.00

BIBLE SCHOOL (71-85)
(vouchered by Sunday school superintendent)

71.	Supplies and literature	$ 600.00	
72.	Equipment	150.00	
73.	Prizes—programs, films, promotion	125.00	
74.	Decorations	20.00	
75.	Postage	50.00	
76.	GCSSA annual dues	30.00	
77.	Christmas program refreshments	25.00	
78.	Sunday school picnic	60.00	
79.	Vacation Bible school	150.00	
80.	Administrative	50.00	
	Total (71-85)		$ 1,260.00

JUNIOR CHURCHES (86-90)
(vouchered by assistant Sunday school superintendent)

86.	Junior Church I (cradle)	$ 25.00	
87.	Junior Church II (preschool)	25.00	
88.	Junior Church III (pal-chum)	25.00	
	Total (86-90)		$ 75.00

TEENS AND COLLEGIANS (91-100)
(vouchered by senior youth sponsors)

91.	Retreats	$ 175.00
92.	Banquets	25.00
93.	Postage	50.00
94.	Films	75.00

95.	Games and props	100.00	
96.	Administrative	200.00	
	Total (91-100)		$ 625.00

AWANA CLUBS (101-120)
(vouchered by commander)

101.	Awards, uniforms, equipment	$ 700.00	
102.	Camp Awana—prizes and fees	105.00	
103.	Contest prizes	175.00	
104.	Retreats	60.00	
105.	Leadership development material	25.00	
106.	Charter and Olympic registration	60.00	
107.	Administration	150.00	
108.	Postage	30.00	
109.	Bus rental	120.00	
	Total (101-120)		$ 1,425.00
	TOTAL CURRENT EXPENSE BUDGET		$27,715.00

MISSIONARY BUDGET (121-180)

FOREIGN MISSIONS
(vouchered by chairman)

121.	Sudan Interior Mission:	
	Dr. & Mrs. Burt Long	$1,100.00
122.	Association of Baptists for World Evangelism:	
	Mr. & Mrs. Frank Jenista	1,652.00
123.	Slavic Gospel Association:	
	Mr. & Mrs. Peter Deyneka, Jr.	332.00
	Mr. & Mrs. Jack Koziol	1,320.00
	Mr. & Mrs. Andrew Semenchuk	332.00
124.	The Evangelical Alliance Mission:	
	Rev. & Mrs. Jack MacDonald	484.00
125.	The New Tribes Mission:	
	Miss Nancy Dillin	1,320.00
	Mr. & Mrs. Paul Dye	1,320.00
	Mr. & Mrs. Larry Johnson	660.00
	Mr. & Mrs. Richard Perik	1,320.00
126.	Far Eastern Gospel Crusade:	
	Rev. & Mrs. Phil Armstrong	400.00
	Mr. & Mrs. Gene Taylor	660.00
127.	Wycliffe Bible Translators:	
	Mr. & Mrs. George Insley	1,848.00
	Mr. & Mrs. Al Meehan	1,124.00

Mrs. Ann Williams	440.00	
128. Tlapaneco Missions in Mexico:		
Mr. Hubel Lemley	500.00	
Total (121-150)		$14,812.00

HOME MISSIONS (151-180)
(vouchered by chairman)

151. International Students, Inc.:		
Mr. & Mrs. Phil Smick	$ 600.00	
152. Campus Crusade for Christ:		
Rev. & Mrs. Jesse James	500.00	
Mr. & Mrs. Alan Mokry	500.00	
Mr. & Mrs. Richard Swanson	500.00	
153. Light Bearers Association:		
Rev. & Mrs. Paul Munsen	396.00	
Total (151-180)		$ 2,556.00
TOTAL BASIC MISSIONARY SUPPORT		$17,368.00
Conference & Misc. Expense	800.00	
TOTAL MISSION BUDGET		$18,168.00

Note: It has been resolved, by the church board, that only those individuals affiliated with recognized mission boards will be supported by this church.

1975 BUDGET TOTALS

TOTAL CURRENT EXPENSE BUDGET	$27,715.00
TOTAL MISSIONARY BUDGET	18,168.00
TOTAL BUDGET FOR 1975	$45,883.00

SELF-SUPPORTING BUDGET

AUXILIARY ORGANIZATIONS

All organizations not included within the church constitution and budget, meeting within the church building and/or having the church name in their title are defined as auxiliary organizations.

Ladies Missionary Fellowship

Treasurer's balance August 31, 1974	$ 97.37
Proposed budget—1975:	
Speakers	$ 25.00
Light & heat	25.00
Equipment repair	10.00
Postage	5.00
New projects	40.00
Proposed Expenses	$105.00

PRINCIPLES OF FINANCE

Note No. 1: Various organizations represented within the church budget contribute their offerings to the general church treasury, thus offsetting much of the budgeted expense.

Note No. 2: No free-will offerings will be taken in connection with any church service without prior approval of the church board.

Note No. 3: We are all supporting all of the items in the budget by giving His tithes and our offerings to our one treasury.

Note No. 4: Items not listed in the budget should be requested of the treasurer, who will then review them with the finance committee. This should be done prior to any financial commitment.

Note No. 5: The budget committee (church board) forms the budget on the basis of the recommendation of the finance committee.

CHURCH CASH FLOW

All churches, regardless of their denominational affiliation, should have their fiscal year agree with the calendar year. If a fiscal year of a church begins in June, experience has shown that the income for the months of June, July, and August will be below the average monthly sums needed for the year. This means that the church will be unable at the beginning of the year to pay all bills in full. This will tend to limit the program and will create a negative outlook on the part of the boards and congregation. When a church begins their fiscal year January 1, they will receive more than one twelfth of their income each month for almost the first half of the year.

It is essential that a church establish a cash-flow chart. This cash-flow chart should cover both anticipated income and anticipated expenditures. This will enable the church to pay its bills each month as they are received.

Each church has an individual pattern of income and expense which can be rather accurately anticipated. Consider the income and expense from previous years, and allow for anticipated major program changes. The special gift income, loose offerings, and Sunday school giving will follow in general the pattern of previous years, month by month. Total the anticipated income and decrease the estimate by one percent as a safety factor. You can

CASH-FLOW CHART
(six months)

INCOME	Jan.	Feb.	March	April	May	June	TOTAL
Pledges							
Loose Offering							
Special Gifts							
Church School							
Total							
Total to Date							
EXPENSES (Budget Areas) Administration							
Building & Grounds							
Evangelism							
Youth							
Bible School							
Worship							
Building Fund							
Missions							
Total							
Total to Date							

then assume that the church should not plan to spend more money each month than the total of anticipated income. In this way, you can determine which expenses should be postponed until a later month in the year. When you have adjusted the planned expense program month by month you can then anticipate paying all bills each month as they are received.

Church Finance Principles and Assumptions

Lyle Schaller, in *The Pastor and the People*, has an interesting list of financial principles which he discusses in connection with his work in a Lutheran parish. The first principle is that the budget should be presented to members in terms of needs which they will understand. The one presenting the budget should avoid abstractions. A second principle is to listen to people rather than merely to exhort them to give. The next principle is that the local church tends to reflect each member's perception of need; the quality of internal communication; and the degree of the member's involvement in the life, program, and ministry of that congregation. It does this far more than it reflects the financial capability, commitment, or loyalty of each member. The fourth principle states that people respond to real needs when they become aware of them. The next reminds us that a few years ago, people would contribute to the church simply out of loyalty, whereas today they want to know how the money is going to be used. Next, we are reminded that two-way communication is superior to one-way communication, which means that feedback is beneficial. Another principle is that we must increase the volume and quality of our communication with the people on financial matters to match the progress which has been developed in communication in other areas. When talking to people about church finances, we should begin with discussing their needs, not with trying to encourage them to feel an interest in solving our financial problem. We are not trying to push a product but to meet the needs of the people. The longer a local church delays beginning to plan for its finances, the fewer the options open and the lower the chances of a satisfactory outcome from the planning efforts. Financial programs are limited by the traditions, values, attitudes, and practices of each local church.[2]

Some additional principles might include the encouragement to reduce the financial machinery to a minimum but to keep accurate records. The needs of the church should be presented directly to the church; people enjoy giving to what they can see. The money raised should be expended only when the bills have been checked by authorized personnel in the church. The financial records should be audited on a regular basis.

It is important that the people be kept aware of the fact that church giving should be on a biblical basis. Giving should be associated with the worship services of the church. Scripture verses can be included in the order of service or in the church bulletin to guide the thinking of the people at this point. Some of the verses which might be used are: Leviticus 27:30; Psalms 24:1; 50:14; 76:11; 96:8; Proverbs 3:9-10; 11:25; Malachi 3:10; Matthew 6:9-10; Luke 6:38; Acts 20:35b; 1 Corinthians 16:2; 2 Corinthians 8:7, 9; 9:7-8.

Raising Church Finances

Tithing should be encouraged as a method of church financing. The tither experiences a blessing both spiritually and materially. Scripture encourages the practice and promises blessing in connection with it.

The every-member canvass is used by some churches as a means for raising church finances. Every home is visited by an official of the church with the object of encouraging church attendance and support. The canvassers should be equipped with financial and program information in order to be able to answer questions, and they can leave printed material with those whom they visit. Pledge cards can also be left to be returned directly to the church by those making a pledge. This gives individuals time for careful and prayerful consideration and assures the privacy of the pledge.

The Belmont Plan is followed in some churches. Under this plan, a certain period of time is set aside during which the people practice tithing. When the people practice tithing they will experience its benefits and, hopefully, will continue.

"Joash Chests" or other honor systems are used for fund raising. The chest is given a prominent place in the church, and the pledges or gifts are placed in the chest on a specified date.

Some churches become involved in commercial ventures for raising church finances. However, such procedures often raise more problems than they solve.

Some churches use professional fund-raisers to help meet special financial obligations. A few of these professional fund-raisers are the Campaign Associates, Chase Associates, Kirby-Smith Associates, and the Broadway Plan. This method of church financing is not as popular as it was a few years ago; many churches have experienced problems with it.

Faith-promise pledges are used in many churches. This is not tithing. The parishioner meets with the Lord and promises, by faith, that he will give a stated amount of money for some special work of the Lord. This method of finance is usually reserved for mission projects or some special project, such as the establishment of a new church. The amount to be given should usually be stated in terms of a weekly commitment rather than a yearly one.

Special projects can often be handled through memorial gifts. These memorial gifts might provide for mission needs, music personnel and equipment, educational projects, evangelism projects, staff support, property, and equipment. Publish a list of needs which might be met by memorial gifts, and put a financial estimate beside each item. Not only memorial gifts but also general gifts related to special individuals or events may be encouraged. A Sunday could be designated for public recognition of the memorial gifts given during the year. These should also be recorded for permanent church record. Emphasize that this giving should be beyond the regular giving and not in place of it.

Responsibilities of Church Finance Personnel

The finance committee oversees the financial affairs of the church. It supervises and approves the collection and expenditure of all church funds. Committee members may delegate authority to approve expenditures which are made in accordance with the budget allocations. They approve the procedures and systems of accounts used by the treasurer and financial secretary. It is their responsibility to insure proper safeguards for all church moneys. They establish procedures for the annual development of the church program and budget. Periodic reports are to be made to the boards and church membership when needed. It is this committee which develops and recommends canvasses for pledges and ways of meeting unforseen financial needs.

The program-and-budget committee leads the congregation in identifying the purposes and objectives of the church. It evaluates and coordinates the program proposals of the several departments and organizations and tries to determine the potential of the congregation. This is the committee which presents the program and budget to the congregation for consideration, discussion, and approval.

The treasurer is under the finance committee; he receives, records, and deposits all moneys of the church. He expends the church money in accordance with the authority delegated to him. The treasurer should render a monthly report of the status of the treasury and of the expenditures made against the budget. He should arrange for an audit of the church financial records each year. It is his responsibility to arrange for bonding for himself, which will be paid for by the church. He should provide the program-and-budget committee with historical data which will aid them in the formulation of the budget.

The financial secretary is under the supervision of the finance committee and is responsible for maintaining a record of all remitted pledges, contributions, and offerings. A separate account should be kept for each contributor. At least once a year reports should be rendered to all contributors on record. All information concerning individual contributions and contributors is to be guarded.

More churches are hiring church administrators in search of increased efficiency in administration.[3] Some of the general areas of responsibility of the church administrator include finance, insurance, management, public relations, purchasing, contracts, administration, development, and taxes.

Some churches have found it profitable to have life trustees in addition to the regular trustees. The life trustees facilitate twenty-year planning for buildings, equipment, and endowments for local churches.

INCREASING CHURCH FINANCES

People support financially what they help create and carry out. One of the best ways of increasing giving is to have the people become involved in as many parts of the financial program as possible. One of the best ways to promote commitment and involvement in the church is through small groups in homes which will clarify the values and goals of the church. A lay-directed church maximizes financial income of that church. The ladies should be involved more in church finances. They have 84 percent of the estate money pass through their hands each year.

The largest increases in financial giving are often from an emphasis on designated special gifts and memorials.

Experience has shown that the monthly reporting system increases recorded giving by at least 12 percent. This means that the church contacts the giver twelve times a year, which serves as a reminder to him. When mailing the monthly report of the individual's giving, include a stewardship education leaflet which describes the program of the month. Giving should be associated with the programed services of the church. It is also profitable to include a report of the monthly expenditures. A fourth enclosure might be a personally signed mimeographed communication outlining some of the major program plans for the coming month. This financial mailing is more a report than a solicitation of funds. To plead for money is to advertize failure.

Dramatize the needs when communicating financial matters to the congregation. This involves using pictures and outlines and putting financial figures in terms which can be understood and appreciated by the people.

Twelve major themes and emphases can be selected for the year. An educational leaflet can be prepared for each month and mailed to the members showing where part of the budget is to be used that month. A sheet noting the income and expense for the month should also be enclosed so that the people feel that they are insiders and have been given all the financial information.

One church sought to increase church giving by diagraming the present giving, thus encouraging the donors to aim higher.

ANALYSIS OF GIVING

Nine Months Ended September 30, 1974

Number of Families in Group	Percentage of Families in Group to Total	Giving Level of Group	Percentage of Group Contributions to Total	Average Amount Given By Group Per Month
67	24.1%	$10 to $25 per month	5.4%	1,113
75	27.0%	$25 to $50 per month	13.0%	2,660
53	19.1%	$50 to $75 per month	15.6%	3,197
21	7.5%	$75 to $100 per month	8.8%	1,807
22	7.9%	$100 to $125 per month	12.0%	2,464
40	14.4%	$125 per month and over	45.3%	9,303

Scale: 0, 10, 20, 30, 40, 50, 60, 70, 80, 90, 100%

Note: Of our families (giving units), fifty-three, or 19.1% of our families, gave $50 to $75 per month, which accounted for 8.8% of our support and averages $1,807 per month. For the first nine months of 1974, there were 278 families giving at least $10 per month. It is this group which is considered as giving units and is reflected in this graph. In addition, 120 additional families contributed under $10 per month and provided under $500 per month in church support.

Controlling Expenditures

A church in financial difficulty must increase income and control expenditures. When these steps are not taken, deficit spending results, and this can continue for only a limited time. A church should meet its financial obligations on time and thus maintain a good Christian testimony.

Churches have found it profitable to employ some of the following suggestion in their attempt to keep expenditures within a reasonable boundary.

It is imperative that an authorization control system be employed in connection with the church budget. It is preferable to have a controller for each segment of the budget rather than one for the entire budget. Designate the controllers by office rather than by name. You then will have one person who is responsible if a particular portion of your budget goes beyond its allocation.

Make all of the budget information available to those who authorize purchases and to the ones who determine purchases for the various areas of church work. They must see the importance of doing their part to solve the financial problem.

When a financial crisis comes in the middle of the year, figure the amount of money needed to meet the financial needs of the church for each of the remaining months of the year. Consider the cost of necessities at this point rather than the amount allocated in the budget. The expenses must be cut back until the church is financially stable.

Establish a purchase-requisition system for the church. Insist that purchase orders be obtained for all purchases and that a purchase of over fifty dollars must have two signatures.

Some churches have published a list of some of the bills owed by the church and have suggested that members select certain of these bills for payment. This might be a means of meeting a crisis but is generally not a good procedure to employ.

Telephone expenses are often large. To help alleviate this, pay phones can be installed. Check the telephone rate system which is now in operation in the church to make sure it is the most economical. Beware of having telephones available for general church use.

You may want to install locks to prevent unauthorized telephone calls.

The cost of light is often more expensive than people realize. Locks could be put on some of the switches in the church. Individuals should be assigned to turn off the lights. Smaller light bulbs can be installed. Urge people to turn off lights in rooms as they leave. Signs can be posted on light switches reminding the people of light conservation.

Heat conservation is another important factor. Are there unused rooms being heated? Can the heat be lowered at times during the week with no disastrous effects? Check the window and door seals to make certain that heat is not escaping. Put locked shields on the thermostats so that unauthorized individuals cannot change them.

Evaluate the cost of various procedures and programs being sponsored by the church. How expensive is the bulletin? Can you restrict the purchase of new choir music for a period of time? In some cases, library purchases could be curtailed for a time.

There are several activities which are very fine, providing there is money for them. Suppers, breakfasts, farewells, and receptions enhance the friendly climate of the church. But during the conservation period, these should be kept within the limitations of the budget, and whenever possible be held without the expenditure of church funds. Friendliness does not always have to be funded.

Certain activities drain money from the general church giving. We must remember that there is just one set of pocketbooks. Money which is contributed to pay-as-you-go church activities will not be given for budget support. Love gifts also drain from general support. Curtail offerings taken during church services for special features and speakers which are not part of the church budget. When such offerings are taken, they should have the permission of the stewardship committee and go toward the budgeted expenses.

Each committee and organization within the church should check its program and determine to hold down expenditures for a short time until word comes from the stewardship committee that the church is in a satisfactory financial condition.

Remember that there are two sides to the coin. Not only must we control expenditures, but we must strive to increase income. Emphasize stewardship and tithing education in all branches of church work. Inform the congregation week by week of the financial condition and needs of the church. Demonstrate to the congregation that the church officials are really concerned about the financial situation and are spending the Lord's money with care. Develop a friendly and positive climate within the church so that the people will want to support the work. Call upon the church family to pray regarding the raising and spending of the Lord's money.

Additional Reading

Banker, John C. *Personal Finances for Ministers*. Philadelphia: Westminster, 1968.

Beall, Delouise. *Christian Stewardship*. Grand Rapids: Zondervan, 1955.

Schaller, Lyle E. *Parish Planning*. Nashville: Abingdon, 1971.

———. *The Pastor and The People*. Nashville: Abingdon, 1973.

CHAPTER 11

Establishing Small Groups for Ministry

More than one hundred metaphors are used in the New Testament to describe the Church. One of the prominent metaphors, the one used in 1 Corinthians 12, is that of a body. Within a body there are many 'cells'. These can represent groups of various types which react to one another and which work together. It is in these smaller cells within the body that individuals have their friendships. It may be ideal, but it is certainly not realistic to expect individuals to relate in close fashion to the church body as a whole.

The development of effective small groups within the local church may be one of the most important keys to church revitalization. Much can be accomplished within a small-group situation which might otherwise be impossible. There is nothing really new about small fellowship groups. There are several types of small groups which we already have in the church. There are the Sunday school classes, which are basically study groups. There are several organizational groups, such as the men's and women's fellowship organizations. Some churches have divided their membership into membership groups, each of which is under the guidance of one of the church elders. Many churches have prayer-and-share groups.

The most productive eras in the history of Christianity have been characterized by small-group activity. The apostles were a small group. In the Middle Ages various religious orders were developed. John Wesley organized class meetings.

Small groups within a church can serve many constructive purposes. They can be a key element in the educational program, taking the form of church school classes and adult education seminars. The traditional church school class can be divided into small discussion units where people have an opportunity to get to know one another and to share. The fellowship-group concept is enriching the activities of church boards and committees by motivating members to share personal concerns and discuss questions of faith. Many churches are providing small groups for Bible study. Discussion groups can often provide a foundation for the promotion of social concerns.

Dialogical preaching can be structured to provide opportunity for small-group discussion. Groups can meet following the message to discuss what has been said. Groups often meet before the message to study the scripture passage which will be used

Some churches have organized groups which concentrate on the personal growth of their members. In such groups, the members minister to each other. They encourage openness, freedom, and sharing.

Small, mission task-groups provide a rather fresh approach to church organization. Each group carries out in the community or church a task which it feels called of God to accomplish. People appreciate having the opportunity to use their gifts and be involved in the decision making connected with the task.

A group is several persons working in a face-to-face situation on a task that requires their cooperation. The two main concerns of any group are the achievement of a task and the relationship of the members to one another. People may live close together but actually be miles apart. The task-oriented small group is composed of three or four people working together to do a specified job or to reach a common goal.

Groups may be established on a short-term or a long-term basis. Research has revealed that changing groups is often the most effective way of changing individuals. Building groups involves getting individuals who are opposed on some issues to work together on other matters on which they agree.

Group action is based upon group consensus achieved through the participation of all members according to their ability to contribute. When people are involved in the development of plans, they are more willing to give time and effort to seeing the plans carried through. A group will be productive to the degree that there emerges in the group a sense of common purpose. There is increasing evidence that providing opportunity for the sharing of personal feelings can greatly enhance the working effectiveness of a group. Members of a group who know one another well work with less friction.

Group Purposes

A group purpose is like an iceberg; there is more beneath the surface than is visible to the eye. The group leader realizes that the expressed purpose is not the whole story, but it does give him something on which to work. When working with groups, it is always in order to ask such questions as, What is our purpose? Are we getting anywhere?

When purposes have been stated, they should not be treated as though they were static. As a group moves forward, the purposes need to be restated and redefined. The leader should make certain that everyone in the group understands what the purposes are at all times. A restating of the purposes from time to time will help to keep the group members abreast of one another as the project develops. A restating and reworking of the statement of purposes will help the members verbalize their real feelings about the purposes. The reworking of the statement of the purposes will help the participants reevaluate their own purposes and motives and thus grow and mature themselves.

Each group within a church should see its specific goals in light of the overall purposes of the church. Both the church and the group should have short-term and long-term goals.

If the group is to mature and be productive, it must have a clear understanding of its purposes and goals. There must be an atmosphere of freedom so that the members can express their opinions. There must be a high degree of intercommunication. It is important to arrange for channels of communication between groups. If this is not done, then the body will become fragmented and will have isolated cells rather than a cohesive unity. The group must provide for a satisfactory integration of individual values, needs, and goals with those of the group. As goals or purposes are established for a group, there are three concerns which should be evident: concern for the individual, concern for the fellowship, and concern for the Kingdom.

Groups might be identified in terms of their purposes. Findley Edge in his book, *The Greening of the Church*, lists six types of groups. They are Bible study groups, prayer groups, witnessing groups, vocational groups, mission groups, and searching groups.[1]

The basic purpose of the searching group is to probe for a deeper meaning in life and religion. It is a search to discover a deeper reality of God in life. It is in this group where one might share his frustrations, questions, and doubts. The group should be small, probably having no more than six or ten members. Edge has a list of five disciplines necessary for each group: attendance, prayer, study, confidentiality, and sharing.

Dr. John Stott, of All Souls Church in London, has fellowship groups. These seek to give expression to the common life which its members already enjoy and to deepen and enrich it. Each group engages in intercessory prayer. Each group adopts one or two church missionaries and corresponds with them. Group members often move out into the community and help people in need. They are able to share what is on their heart and pray for one another in the group since they are vitally concerned for one another.

There are some groups which have problem solving as their purpose. In most respects, groups are superior to individuals in problem solving. This is especially true when the problem to be solved is complex in nature. Groups generate a variety of ideas in contrast to problem solving by an individual. This means that they are able to generate a greater number of alternative solutions. Groups are considered to be superior in the quality of their solutions, but they are not as rapid in arriving at the conclusion.

Synectics is the process of solving problems through small groups. There are four phases in this process. The first phase is that of defining the problem. There needs to be a common agreement among the members of the group as to what is the central problem and what are the subsidiary concerns. The next phase is that of developing possible solutions. The group needs to create as many alternative solutions to the problem as possible. The leader should not move into an evaluating or sifting process until all of the alternatives have been advanced. The third phase is that of evaluating solutions. This includes the weighing and sifting of proposals of the group without the names of those who advanced them in the earlier phase. The final phase of the process is that of putting the decision into action.

Group Formation

Group formation and participation is a complex process. A group is an aggregate of people with a wide variety of individual goals, values, skills, and blocks to group participation. These individuals must mold themselves into a productive group. It is difficult to describe the complex process of formation. There are, however, certain essentials common to the development of all groups. One is a basic drive, or motivation, expressed through individual interests. Interests held in common must also be highlighted in this process of group formation.

Any new group should establish in writing principles which will provide guidance for the group. The purpose for the group's organization and meetings should be understood. The size of the group must be determined. It has been suggested that less than eight or more than fifteen may diminish the chances for success. The composition of the group is an important factor. There may be sociological, cultural, economic, geographical, educational, age, and spiritual factors to consider. The time factor for the meetings must be cleared. It is important to clarify the level of interaction. One group may be a discussion group and another may be a decision making group designed to focus on business matters. The leadership factor is significant. Some groups may have an expert as a leader, another may have a chairman, and a third may have a shared leadership. The group will want to predetermine some matters pertaining to group discipline. These matters may involve regularity of attendance, preparation for the meetings, and prayer for the meetings. If the group asks little of its members, then little may be expected in return. Personal involvement and responsibility are important.

Alvin Lindgren, in his book *Foundations for Purposeful Church Administration*, has an extended discussion of what he calls the "Neighborhood Family Group Plan."[2] The parish is divided into geographical segments, with a leader selected for each segment. These leaders should then be called together and instructed in the purpose of the plan and some of the helpful procedures to follow. The purpose of the plan is to discover and meet the needs of the individual and the family. When there is a lack of real fellowship in the church, a large group of inactive members, or limited lay participation in leadership, this plan may prove useful. It will help in providing members with knowledge of the church program.

The leaders should catch the vision of the ways in which this group can foster fellowship, assist the pastor in getting acquainted with all the families of the church, discover those in need of pastoral care, welcome new members, and assimilate new members. This neighborhood group plan provides an opportunity for those members of a church living in a neighborhood to come to know one another and to unite in a common loyalty to the church. It provides the laymen with an opportunity to express their faith in active service.

Classification of Groups

One of the most useful ways of thinking about small groups in the church is to use the social scientist's distinction between *task-centered*, or work groups, and *personality-centered*, or relational groups. This second group has as its primary concern the recognizing and the meeting of the individual needs of its members.

Edgar H. Schein, in *Organizational Psychology* identifies two kinds of groups. *Formal* groups are often permanent and center in management. They are created to fulfill specific goals and carry out specific tasks. *Informal* groups arise spontaneously, from simple interaction of people. The rotation of members would tend to break up these informal groups.[3]

Charles H. Cooley identified primary and secondary groups. In the primary group, members have warm, intimate, and personal ties with one another. Their solidarity is a matter of sentiment rather than calculation. In the secondary group the characteristics are the opposite or complement of those in the primary group. Relations among the members are impersonal, rational, contractual, and formal. Secondary groups are typically large.[4]

Gordon Lippitt categorizes three types of groups on the basis of their member activity. There is the interacting group, coacting group, and the counteracting group. The interacting group is one in which the performance of the task by each member depends upon the successful completion of the tasks of the other members. In the coacting group, the members work together on a task. In the counteracting group, each individual is working to achieve his own ends at the expense of the others.[5]

Seifer and Clinebell, in *Personal Growth and Social Change*, list five types of groups: task-oriented, study, supportive or inspirational, growth, and counseling groups.[6]

Beal, Bohlen and Raudabaugh, in their work, *Leadership and Dynamic Group Action*, make reference to three additional types of groups. There is the *democratic* group, in which decisions are made by the group as a whole, with each member participating on the basis of his skills and interests. The *laissez-faire* group is characterized by its lack of organization. The great defect of such a group is its inability to accomplish any purpose. It is easy for individuals to get control of such a group and convert it into an autocracy. The *autocratic* group is under the domination of an individual or a power clique.[7]

There is a rather extensive variety seen in the five approaches to classifying groups. It should be noted that a group might fit into more than one classification. These classifications provide identifying labels for individual groups.

The Group Leader

It is the task of the group leader, in most instances, to free the group from emotional dependence upon him, allowing it to grow to a state in which each member shares responsibility for the life of the group. The authoritarian leader evokes either rubber stamping by the group, or hostile opposition. The laissez-faire leader is passive. The democratic leader is the one who senses that he needs the group and the group needs him to function effectively. The democratic leader helps the group define its task and discover its needs. He seeks to relate to persons within the group and encourages each to contribute his best to the group. The leader is a resource person for the group. He helps the group evaluate its work and conserve its gains.

Gordon Lippitt adds some additional leadership functions. The leader is to help the group accept new ideas and new members without conflict, to learn to accept discipline in working toward long-range objectives, and to learn to profit from failure. He is to help the group create new task forces or subgroups as needed, and to learn to terminate them when it is wise to do so. The leader will help the group develop methods of evaluation so that the group becomes conscious of its own procedures in order to improve its problem solving capacity.[8]

The trait approach to leadership assumes that leaders are born and not made. Leadership is inherent within the individual, and he is destined to be a leader. The more satisfactory explanation of leadership is that it is the result of the individual traits which are inherited. These are combined with training; the purposes of the group; and way the persons in the group talk, work, and relate to one another.

It has been suggested that there are two phases in the process of leadership emerging within a group. The first phase consists of eliminating those who are clearly unsuitable, whether because they do not take part or because they are uniformed or unskilled at the task. The second phase consists of intensified competition.

Ernest and Nancy Bormann, in *Effective Committees and Groups in the Church*, suggest seven steps to natural leadership. The first is to avoid being a manipulator. The one who will be the leader must show that he is sincerely and completely dedicated to the welfare of the group and is not just involved in manipulating the group for his own ends. The natural leader must be willing to pay the price of leadership. He must want to help the group enough to do the work. He must promote and take an active interest in the group's work. The natural leader must do his homework so that he will know what is going on. Natural leaders are those who are willing to make personal sacrifices. They are not primarily concerned about getting credit for their own work. They are more concerned about being king makers than about being kings. The one who emerges as a natural leader carries out the procedures which tend to develop group cohesiveness.[9]

A functional view of leadership and group behavior has some clear consequences for one's beliefs about how people learn to be more effective as either leaders or members in groups. The functional view is that leadership is learnable and is shared by many members, instead of being only a matter of one person's behavior. It emphasizes that leadership can be improved and is not fixed by heredity or childhood experiences. This functional view leads, then, to an emphasis upon training and growth of persons.

Group Members

There are responsibilities resting upon the members of the group. They should make certain that they understand the purposes of the group. They should analyze their own motives for joining the group. It is important that they try to understand the viewpoint of the other members of the group. One's point of view is extremely important. The member should raise honest questions regarding group procedures and problems. It is necessary that the member learn to accept and handle verbal opposition and avoid taking it as a personal affront. Members should express their opinions openly and honestly and encourage the others in the group to do the same. It is important that the members of the group be willing to share the responsibilities of the group. The work should not be left just to the leader. The member must be willing to share not only in the successes of the group but also in its failures. Group loyalty is an important feature.

The group member most useful to the group is the person who can sense which style of behavior is most needed by the group and then act accordingly. Each individual within a group should ask himself, What do I do most often? How do I see myself? It is helpful to check perception with others who see us in group settings. Once we know our most frequent pattern, then we can begin to experiment deliberately with new roles and thus expand our usefulness to the group.

1. The *initiator-contributor* suggests or proposes to the group new ideas or changed ways of regarding group problems or goals.
2. The *information seeker* asks for clarification of suggestions made in terms of their factual adequacy.
3. The *opinion seeker* asks for a clarification of the values pertinent to what the group is undertaking.
4. The *information giver* offers facts or generalizations which are "authoritative" or relates his own experiences pertinent to the group problem.
5. The *opinion giver* states his belief or opinion pertaining to suggestions which have been made. His emphasis is upon what he feels the group's view should be of pertinent values.
6. The *clarifier* interprets ideas or suggestions. He defines terms and indicates alternatives.
7. The *elaborator* gives examples and makes generalizations indicating how a proposal might work out if adopted.
8. The *summarizer* pulls together the related ideas and restates the suggestions which the group has made.
9. The *encourager* praises, agrees with, and accepts the contributions of others.
10. The *harmonizer* mediates the differences between members. He reduces tension by getting people to explore their differences.
11. The *compromiser* admits his error, yields status, and disciplines himself to maintain harmony.
12. The *expediter* attempts to keep the communication channels open.
13. The *standard-setter* expresses standards for the group to attempt to achieve in its functioning.
14. The *supporter* goes along with the movement of the group, accepts the ideas of others, and serves as an interested audience.[10]

Group Dynamics

Every group has several dynamics, or forces, that operate to hold the group together and determine the quality of its life. The more concrete the tasks of a group, the easier it is to measure the group's effectiveness. Groups have a strong impact upon the performance behavior of their members. They apply pressure toward conformity, and they influence the performance level.

Robert Leslie, in his book, *Sharing Groups in the Church,* presents several very practical suggestions for guiding a sharing group. These are not rules but guidelines. The personal-sharing group is always conscious of the presence of others. Each member recognizes that the needs of others should be met even as his own needs must be met. As a second guideline, the group should strive for communication rather than socialization. The focus should be on the present, without ignoring the past. Personal sharing is preferred over diagnostic probing. No leader can really encourage sharing until he is willing to share himself. Attacks should be discouraged, but observations should be welcomed. No group is an end in itself. Action is expected outside the group and shared.

Cohesiveness, the ability of the group members to stick together, is one of the keys to successful work groups. Another term which is often used is *group loyalty*. The more cohesive the group, the more efficient is the communication within the group. The morale of the group is likely to be tied to the cohesiveness. In cohesive groups, the members take the initiative and help one another.

The more cohesive the group, the more effect it has on all aspects of individual behavior, including performance. Cohesion depends more on goal commitment, wanting to belong to the group, and respect for others, than whether or not each member of the group agrees with the others.

Cohesiveness is dynamic. It fluctuates from day to day. A congregation which is highly cohesive this year, with a large hardworking membership, may suffer reverses so that in the next year it is in trouble.

Ernest and Nancy Bormann list seven steps to greater cohesiveness in a work group. The first is to identify with the group. The leader refers to himself as a part of the group. The members work as a group and not as individuals. They will very often identify their group by insignias, mascots, or nicknames. The second step is to build a group tradition. The next two steps are to stress teamwork and to recognize good work. Long-range and short-range goals should be established. Group rewards should be offered. The final step is to treat members as people, not machines.[11]

Group climate is one of the dynamics. The group may have a cold and unfriendly emotional tone or one that is warm and friendly. Group climate can help or hinder the group as it proceeds toward its goal. The pattern of participation should be noted. Groups often tend to drift from the matter actually being discussed to one which may arise momentarily. This is sometimes done to avoid an unpleasant task.

Leadership competition is a common group dynamic. If the leader offers a measure of freedom to the group, or if his leadership position is not very well established, others in the group may seek to establish themselves as leaders, thus promoting a competitive situation.

Group members sometimes come to a meeting with a concern which is not the real purpose of the group meeting. This will often be a form of hidden agenda and will sidetrack the accomplishment of the primary purpose of the gathering. Group members tend to develop a trust level near the beginning of their group meeting which will govern, to some degree, the amount of sharing and freedom which will prevail.

Groups must socialize as well as work. Do not ignore the social dimension of your work group. Let the members get acquainted at the beginning of the meeting, and encourage them to stay after the meeting to relax and have fellowship.

Group Problems

If good intentions could make organizations flourish, most of our volunteer and charitable organizations—churches included—would function smoothly. Difficulties arise, however, when people work together, no matter how well-intentioned they are. When a third party makes a team into a work group, then social dimensions begin to multiply.

The presence of problems within a group should be recognized as being rather common. When problems are recognized, the easy but unprofitable approach is to walk away from the situation and disband. The more constructive approach is to analyze the situation and seek to correct the problem.

One common problem in group activity is in the area of its leadership. The leader will often insist upon dominating the group rather than allowing its members to share in its operation. The group leader should communicate love and acceptance to his group. He should learn to let go of the reins of leadership by encouraging the members to take an increased share in the responsibility and leadership. The leader is responsible for developing honest fellowship within the group. Domination of the group does not promote such authentic fellowship. He has the responsibility of creating a climate in which members feel free to minister to one another. Domination by the leader will often lead to apathy on the part of the members of the group, due to their low involvement.

Groups will sometimes face the problem of dealing only with the superficial. They deal only with the surface matters since the trust level is low and the members try to protect themselves from one another. Actual decisions are often made by groups in such a way that their members will not be threatened or involved to any noticeable degree.

One common problem in small groups is the existence of a powerful clique. This clique will often meet apart from the group, make unilateral decisions, and then railroad decisions through the group.

Some groups have the problem of not really meeting the needs of the group members who are involved. Many of these problems center in the area of poor interpersonal relationships.

Hindrances to Group Effectiveness

The leader plays a very important role in a group. If he tries to dominate the group, however, such action will block constructive action on the part of the group as a whole. If he lectures at each meeting, group participation will be excluded. If one or two are allowed to dominate the discussion, the group will lose interest. If the leader attempts to answer all questions himself and thus not encourage the members to express themselves, effectiveness will be impeded. If the leader complains about the small number attending and pays no attention to the needs and interests of those who do attend, interest will wane.

If the discussions are kept on a theoretical plane rather than on the practical, the group will lose interest. When a group is too large, they will not be able to know one another, and will not have an opportunity to participate. When a long business session precedes the small group meeting, the participants get restless and lose enthusiasm for what is to come.

There are additional blocks to participation within a group. Individuals may be ignorant of the real goals of the group, or they may disapprove of the methods used to attain the goals. An individual may be hesitant to become involved with a group when he is not sure of the group's expectations of its members.

Dangers Connected with Groups

Without coordinated planning, groups in the church may come to feel that they are ends in themselves and lose their sense of perspective in relation to the church. There is the temptation to spiritual pride, wherein they will see themselves as the spiritual elite. The small group may become a clique or closed circle. This will soon become obvious to others, and dissension will arise. In some cases there will be the tendency for a small group to take over most of the leadership positions in the church, posing great problems.

When small groups deal with deep, personal problems, they may have a harmful effect on one or more members of the group. It is one thing to be able to diagnose and disclose difficulty; it is another thing to be able to prescribe wisely for its correction. Many small groups can do the first but not the second.

Group Meetings

Meetings are essential to effective communication within the modern organization. Meetings provide channels for communication, build cohesiveness, identify the work of the group, and give a chance to develop a tradition. Meetings and discussions are techniques for solving problems and developing policy. Admittedly, some meetings are held for no good reason. Such meetings should be abolished. Be sure you need a meeting before you schedule one.

There are at least five types of meetings. The *ritualistic* meeting aids the cohesiveness of the organization. The meeting is important to the social interaction of the congregation. The *briefing* meeting provides members with information so they can carry through on plans already laid. The *instructional* meeting is used to teach people in order to make them more proficient in their tasks. The *consultative* meeting is one in which the individual responsible for a decision asks the others for advice. The *decision-making* meeting is one of the most difficult yet most useful meetings. Members who help make and who are responsible for decisions are usually more fully committed and work harder to implement the action.

When planning for a meeting, determine the purpose of the meeting, and make sure the purpose is well known to those participating in it. The agenda made for the meeting should be such that the purpose will be accomplished. In this connection, decide what plans can be made at this meeting and, roughly, how they can be developed. Be sure to plan the little details of the meeting. Evaluate each meeting to determine whether it accomplished what you needed to accomplish. The results of the meeting should be publicized and implemented.

Evaluation of Group Meetings

The leader of a group should make evaluative notes soon after a meeting, while he is still able to reconstruct what went on. There are eight items which might be considered.

1. The situation in which the meeting was held
2. The atmosphere of the meeting
3. The sequence, or movement, of the meeting
4. The accomplishments of the meeting
5. Things that contributed to the accomplishments
6. Things that interfered with accomplishments
7. My role as a leader
8. Plans for the next meeting[12]

Some groups have improved their performances by having each member fill out an evaluation form after each of several meetings. These should not be signed by the individuals who fill them out. Four questions which might be asked are:

1. Was the purpose of the meeting clear to you?
2. Did you have adequate opportunity to make your contributions to the deliberations?
3. How productive was the meeting in comparison with those of other groups you have been in?
4. What suggestions do you have for improving the next meeting?

Types of Church Groups

There are social groups in the church which may be open or closed to membership. Some operate formally and some informally within the church. They are generally formed by a common age factor or common concern. There are contact groups which meet periodically giving individuals an opportunity to meet others in an unstructured setting. There are interest groups which have a common theological, social, hobby, or intellectual interest. There is a growing interest in Bible study groups.[13] There are work and service groups which are task oriented and work together to complete a specified task.

There is a great variety in types of groups and in the purposes of formation. Churches should make a realistic survey of the groups which they already have. Survey the needs of the constituency to see whether or not the present groups are meeting the needs. Some groups may be so close to death that they should be allowed to die. Others may just need a new injection of life. Build on what you have, first, and then develop new groups as needs, demands, and resources of personnel permit. Man's good and God's glory is the target. Keep on target!

Additional Reading

Bormann, Ernest G., and Bormann, Nancy. *Effective Committees and Groups in the Church.* Minneapolis: Augsburg, 1973.

Casteel, John L. *The Creative Role of Interpersonal Groups in the Church Today.* New York: Association, 1968.

Clemmons, William, and Hester, Harvey. *Growth Through Groups.* Nashville: Broadman, 1974.

Howard, Walden. *Groups That Work.* Grand Rapids: Zondervan, 1967.

Larson, Bruce, et al. *Groups that Work: The Missing Ingredient*. Grand Rapids: Zondervan, 1968.
Leslie, Robert C. *Sharing Groups in the Church*. Nashville: Abingdon, 1971.
Luft, Joseph. *Group Processes: An Introduction to Group Dynamics*. Palo Alto, Calif.: National, 1963.
Meissner, W. W., S. J. *Group Dynamics in the Religious Life*. Notre Dame, Ind.: U. of Notre Dame, 1965.
Miles, Matthew B. *Learning to Work in Groups*. New York: Bureau of Pub. 1959.
Olmsted, Michael S. *The Small Group*. New York: Random House, 1959.
Raines, Robert A. *New Life in the Church*. New York: Harper & Row, 1961.
Reid, Clyde. *Groups Alive — Church Alive*. New York: Harper & Row, 1969.
Richards, Larry O. *Sixty-nine Ways to Start a Study Group and Keep It Growing*. Grand Rapids; Zondervan, 1973.
Schein, Edgar H., and Bennis, Warren G. *Personal and Organizational Change Through Group Methods*. New York: Wiley, 1967.

CHAPTER 12

Expanding the Outreach of the Church

Contemporary church outreach can be an exciting study. The aids and challenges posed by new modes of transportation, easy communication, sociological shifts, financial pressures, and cultural barriers demand attention. Yesterday's methods are not adequate for today's problems.

We must remember that we are co-laborers together with Jesus Christ (1 Co. 3:9). We cannot face these challenges alone. Salvation is free, but discipleship is costly. Lip praise is easy, but life partnership with the One we praise demands our best. God worked alone at creation, in providence, and in the atonement; but He works with us in outreach.

Outreach, as other church emphases, should not begin with a plan or program but with a clear sense of purpose. This sense of purpose must be acknowledged by the organizers and those who are to participate. It is imperative that we know why we are doing what we are doing. Many church programs have collapsed because this purpose orientation has been neglected.

There are several questions which, when answered, will provide some clarification of purpose:

1. Why should the church reach out to the community?
2. Why should the community be interested in the church?
3. What are some of the hindrances to church outreach?
4. What qualities should one possess as equipment for reaching out?

5. Where are some of the places that we should go in order to reach individuals?
6. Where and with whom should we start the outreach program?
7. What agencies outside the church can help us in the outreach program?
8. What are the limits of the members' responsibility for reaching out?

As these questions are posed and discussed, it will become evident that clear answers cannot be given until there is some common understanding about the meaning of some concepts. There is often a difference between the dictionary meaning and the meaning which we attach to the concept from a Christian perspective. Some terms you may need to define would include: *making a visit; church; religious, or religion; worship; and Christian.*

Churches grow in at least three ways. *Biological* growth takes place within the church family. *Transfer* growth takes place when people move from one area to another. Unfortunately, some are lost to the church during this transfer process. *Conversion* growth is the result of people coming to know Jesus Christ as Saviour and Lord and then uniting with a local church to become vitally involved in Christian service. It has been said that if we want the church to grow, we should choose more of the leaders from among the new converts. The outreach of the church and church growth are inseparable.

Branch Churches

This concept of the branch church stresses growth through division. Before a branch church is established, there must be a clear realization of the need for one. One need may be in the church considering expansion. When a local church is too large for the pastor to know the people and to minister to their needs, then the church should consider establishing a branch church rather than expanding at its one location. The second basis of need may be in an unchurched area where born again people live and have need for a local testimony.

The people, not just the pastor, must be motivated to begin the work. This motivation can be stimulated by providing education as to the ministry and concept of the local church. Motivation can also come from reviewing the needs of the new area. The pastor's enthusiasm will also provide motivation.

Make a study of the new area, noting the population trend, types of industry, present churches and their ministry, and the kinds of residents. Be interested in denominational preferences, present memberships, and whether residents are transient or permanent.

The choice of a proper site is important. The church should be located on a sizable lot which will allow for expansion and for parking. It should be near a main thoroughfare but not on it. A corner lot is preferred.

The mother church may provide for all of the financial needs up until organization and incorporation, but from that point onward the local church should establish its own financial policies. It is important that the new church not feel that the mother church is ready to provide all financial supplies. The local group will be motivated and have their interest increased when they invest in their project.

The mother church will probably guide the entire operation until the time of incorporation. They will assist in writing the new constitution but will not try to domineer the organization. The mother church provides help but lets the branch church operate on its own. Make certain that the policies between the mother church and the branch church are written out so there will not be a misunderstanding.

The planning and building of the new church is a complicated process. The future needs offer the greatest challenge to the capability of the building committee. The building committee must answer the following questions:

1. What is the group's philosophy of the local church?
2. How large should a church become?
3. Should we locate on a main street or on a side street?
4. How far does our neighborhood extend?
5. How far will our outreach be effective?
6. What is the community's economic situation now?

7. What will our neighborhood be like ten or twenty years from now?
8. How much land should we have to meet our present and future needs?
9. What about the land around the church site?
10. What are the plans for future highways, home construction, and business expansion?
11. Is there an estimate of the time which will be required for the completion of the project?

Newspapers

Newspapers attempt to give news to their readers, and there is little which means more to newspaper editors than local news. It has been observed that it is the public, not the editors, who determine what is news.

Ralph Stoody has identified several ingredients which add news value. People are more interested in what happens in their own community than they are in what happens thousands of miles away. Things happening now are important. Important names are newsworthy. Extremes or variations from the normal catch attention. Events which interest large numbers of people are newsworthy. Readers are interested in catastrophes, accidents, conflicts, cruelty, crimes, floods, fires, and tornadoes. People are interested in reading about struggles against the unknown. Attention is drawn to basic needs and concerns such as children, romance, marriage, travel, health, and self-improvement.[1]

Stoody goes on to list according to topic, some suggestions for church news stories.

THE MINISTER—His call, appointment, installation, reception, retirement, speaking engagements, denominational duties, hobbies, vacations, travels, attendance at conventions, pastors' schools and retreats, civic recognitions, community service, interchurch participation, counseling programs, articles, pamphlets, or books written.

ORGANIZATIONS—Staff changes, annual meetings, meetings of governing boards, elections of officers, adoption of budget, reports of financial progress or membership growth, choirs, ushers' clubs, church school teacher elections, teacher installations, graduation ceremonies, leadership training, vacation church schools, curriculum changes, mission, Bible and stewardship study groups, outings, men's clubs, women's organizations, youth fellowships, Boy Scouts, Girl Scouts, conferences and conventions.

UNUSUAL PUBLIC SERVICES—New Year's Eve, February patriotic days, Ash Wednesday, Lenton missions, Holy Week, Maundy Thursday, Good Friday, Easter, Whitsunday (Pentecost), Commemorative days, Children's Day, Mother's and Father's days, Independence Day, Labor Sunday, World Communion, Veteran's Day. Thanksgiving, Harvest Festivals, Advent Sundays, Christmas Eve, Christmas Day, Student Recognition Day, Evangelistic Services, Founder's Day, Layman's Sunday, Temperance Sunday, Rallies, Pageants, Oratorios, and dramatic programs.

PROPERTY—Bequests, new church plans, landscaping, new education wings, new parsonages, renovations, redecoration, new furnishings, organs, carillons, memorial windows, new recreational facilities indoor or outdoor, new kitchens or kitchen modernization, and nursery.

SERVICE ACTIVITIES—Children's and teen-age programs, recreation, assistance to displaced families, young marrieds, baby sitters, get-acquainted and fellowship projects, child study groups, audio-visual utilization, panel programs, forums, drama and choral groups, work programs, paint-up and cleanup crews, and every-member canvasses.[2]

In writing your church news story, it is important to follow an established pattern. Your first sentence or two is called the "lead." This lead must answer the following five questions:

Who is it about?
What happened?
Where did it happen?
When did it happen?
Why did it happen?

The body of the article will expand on the answers to the questions set forth in the lead. The paragraphs following the lead are arranged according to the degree of their importance. Make the paragraphs short; most newspaper paragraphs do not contain more than three sentences. Use action words, and keep adjectives to a minimum. Stick to the facts, and avoid editorializing, giving your own opinions.

When you supply news items to more than one paper, be sure they are different. The copy should be typewritten, double-spaced, on one side of the sheet. Always identify the source of the article with your name and telephone number in the upper left-hand corner of the page. Be sure to give the date when it should be released. Start your article about one-third of the way down the page. If the article carries over to a second page, put the word *more* at the bottom of the first page.

It is important that your facts be correct. As someone suggested, it would be devastating to identify someone as coming from Penn State and staying at the Park Central when actually he had come from the state penitentiary and was sleeping in Central Park.[3]

Radio, Television, and Telephone

A minister making use of radio or television should prepare himself in the skillful use of their techniques. Studio personnel do not appreciate last-minute arrivals, unrehearsed programs, disregard for the basic rules of the station, and bad production technique.

Both of these communication media reach vast audiences including the churched and the unchurched. They have an open acceptance in the home.

Before going on the air, a program must be considered in terms of its major thrust, its format, and the time of the broadcast. It seems that few will come to a knowledge of Christ as Saviour directly and solely through the use of radio and television. It might be wise to have as the main thrust of a program motivating the unchurched to get under the preaching of the Gospel.

Various types of formats might be considered. A one-minute spot might be used to invite listeners to attend the local church. Religious drama is popular with both unchurched and churched people. Christian music is accepted and enjoyed by most people.

Christian truth can be conveyed through the use of comments made between music selections. Bible-study talks are used for biblical and doctrinal instruction. Take care that these are relevant to the lives of the listeners. A discussion or debate gives an opportunity to present the application of biblical truth to daily living.

The question should be raised as to whether or not it is wise to broadcast a church service live from the auditorium. Such a broadcast raises many problems, including the timing of the broadcast and the minister's task of speaking to the seen and the unseen audiences at the same time. It would appear that this type of broadcast would be the least popular and effective.

The best broadcast times for radio are early-morning hours on weekdays or late-night hours. The evening is best for television, but any time other than Sunday morning is good. The smallest audience of the week is on Sunday morning.

Introductions to programs are especially important. What is said in the first twenty seconds will often determine the size of the listening audience. Those speaking should use a pleasant voice and speak in a conversational manner. Manuscripts should be used but should be worded so that they sound like normal conversation. In preparing the manuscript, you might record the message on tape and then have a secretary type it, using the same wording. One feature which separates oral and written style is the use of contractions. Written style disparages their use, but oral style encourages their use. Avoid excessive use of theological terms. The use of professionally recorded music is to be preferred over poor local talent.

The telephone is an instrument of church outreach which has often been overlooked. A telephone call can provide a quick reminder of responsibilities. It provides an opportunity for those without transportation to share in contacting individuals who are or should be involved. In a smaller community, the telephone directory could serve as a visitation file.

Visitation

The importance of visitation can be seen by surveying the purposes of this type of ministry. Some of its purposes include providing comfort, securing recruits, inquiring after absentees, welcoming new arrivals in the community, and establishing more personal relationships. Through visitation, the pastor can become more aware of the topics and concerns relevant to his particular congregation. This will tend to improve his preaching. Counsel and correction, as well as comfort, can be provided through visitation. One of the major purposes of visitation is to listen to the ones within the parish. Avoid the tendency to talk too much and listen too little.

Visitation tends to increase attendance, foster lasting friendships, and afford opportunities for evangelism. When the clergy is involved in visitation, bridges of cooperation will be established with the laity. Visitation establishes ties between the church, the home, and family. It provides a systematic means of reaching those in need. It affords an opportunity for Christian service for the visitors. Spiritual growth is fostered in the lives of those involved in reaching others.

There are basically three types of visitation. *Absentee visitation* is directed toward those who attend church services but who may or may not be Christians. This type of visitation provides contact and counsel. *Prospect visitation* is concerned with those who are not attending the church but could and should be. This type of visitation manifests concern. *Evangelistic visitation* proclaims the Gospel of Jesus Christ. But it is not soul winning, since the actual drawing of people to Christ for salvation is the ministry of the Holy Spirit.

Visitation is important in making contact with newcomers. We must be willing to go out and call upon people and get acquainted with them if we really expect them to come to our church. We must recognize that as we reach out to the newcomers, there may be changes which we will have to make. People will not come unless we are willing to open up and be receptive to them. When we are willing to let the Holy Spirit bring about some changes in our own modes of thinking, then we will see a greater ingathering of new people.

Visitation establishes contacts with people so they can become aware of the opportunities for identifying with interest and service groups within the church. It becomes evident that each person is a means through which the faith of others may be strengthened.

The visitation program maintains contact with the senior saints. This group of God's people have special needs. They need group contact with people of their own age and temperament. They need to have a renewal of hope. They need to have regular, personal contact with someone with whom they can develop a friendship that will demonstrate the love of God.

Many churches are making elaborate provisions for youth activities, and they hire specially trained personnel for this work. Likewise, someone should plan special programs and activities for the senior saints. The individual designated by the church to arrange such programs could also plan for the visitation of this segment of the church family.

Visitation does not come easily to everyone. There are many human hindrances. Some of these may be selfishness, love of ease, procrastination, pressure of other duties, fear of contacting or conveying disease, natural timidity, and the dread of coming face to face with spiritual perplexities. Visitation requires self-sacrifice, sympathy, tact, and spiritual insight. It must always be undertaken in a prayerful frame of mind.

It is easier to send five dollars to someone so they can reach an individual in a foreign land, than it is for us to contact someone in our own community for Christ. Many of our churches need to face the question of whether or not they are really reaching their community for Christ. If this is our aim, then we should make an effort first of all to get to know the community. Many urban centers are doing studies of their communities both for welfare and industrial purposes. Using the material which they have compiled will save the church much time and effort. Information regarding a community can be obtained also from the chamber of commerce, school boards, welfare and social agencies, city planning commissions, urban renewal agencies, the census bureau, and the public library.

Some churches have used the "zone plan" to organize visitation. Obtain a map of the community being served by your church. Locate on the map the homes of the members. Take note of any natural geographical divisions. If the elders are to be responsible for this visitation, identify the location of each of their homes. As far as possible, have each elder responsible for visitation in the area in which he lives. The location of the homes of the elders as well as the natural geographical divisions will be important factors in dividing the community into areas of responsibility. The ones responsible for visitation in each section will keep in contact with the members, visit newcomers, and be on the alert for special human needs within their section. The zone plan can be used as a means of assisting the minister in his pastoral responsibilities.

The zone leader serves as a shepherd and as an evangelist. As a shepherd, he will visit each home within his zone often enough to maintain a bond of friendship. He will learn of such news as illness, death, promotion, birth, anniversaries, and moves in the families. This information will be forwarded to the pastor. As an evangelist, he will be on the lookout for potential Christians within his zone. He will be especially concerned about the unchurched families. He will keep a watchful eye open for ways of helping people not only find Christ as Saviour but mature in their Christian life.

One church, in setting up such a program, urged that special attention be given to the aged and the shut-ins. Transportation was to be provided for those needing it. The pastor was to be notified of any illness, trouble, or sorrow in the zone.

When planning an every-home survey, one of the first steps is to determine the area to be covered. This will normally be established on a radius from the church. Then obtain a map of the area and divide it into zones. Each zone should have a committee member as the captain for that zone. The ones selected for surveying should not be argumentative but should be intelligent, tactful, dependable, courteous, and accurate. The zone captains are responsible for apportioning their zones and calling meetings of their surveyors. Each one canvassing must know the area of his responsibility and must be given his necessary materials. After his visit, the caller should fill out a card, recording the date and address of his visit, and any results of the visit. The zone captain collects the cards and returns them to the committee for collation and analysis.

GENERAL VISITATION

Many methods have been used in promoting a visitation program within a church. It is important that the project be owned by the group as a whole and that it not be just the private project of an individual. The church staff, church boards, Sunday school workers, and the entire membership should be sold on the project. It is helpful to have a commissioning service not only for the sake of the ones doing the visiting but also to call attention to the project. Some churches hold a banquet at the beginning, midway through, and at the close of the project. These banquets provide opportunities for instructing participants, reflecting upon results, and stimulating interest. Posters will keep visitation before the eyes of the people. Slogans dealing with visitation and statistics of needs and victories will provide profitable material for the church bulletins and newspapers.

A regular time should be established for the visitation. No calling should be done on Saturday, which is usually a cleaning day. Do not call after nine o'clock at night. It is unwise to say to the visitors that they should just visit when they can. There should be an attempt made at being specific. They may call once a week or once every two weeks. They may call on the same day each week. They may call between certain hours on certain days.

Assignments should be made by areas and also by age groups. Allocation by age groups will establish points of interest and contact between the visitors and the visited. Visitors should be sent out two by two. In most cases, it is not wise for husband and wife to go together.

After extending an invitation to visit the church, visitors may return to the church to report, evaluate, and record their results. The complete information should be made available to the secretary for filing. The leaders should be alert at this time to give commendation to the workers for achievement.

The basic purpose of this whole program is visitation and not the establishing of another organization. The mechanics should be kept to a minimum. Two leaders can normally handle the administrative work. One, the director, should be a born-again, consecrated individual of unquestionable loyalty. He should have a good understanding of the various aspects of the total church program. He should be a good visitor himself, so that he can help others improve their procedures. Through doing visitation work himself, he will gain an acquaintance with problems to be encountered and some corrective procedures to follow. Those who work with him will regard him as a co-laborer rather than a slave master. He must be able to work with people and to inspire them to greater service.

A visitation secretary will also be needed. The secretary will prepare information cards for the visitors and keep files of the information gleaned by them. This person must be outstanding in dependability.

The accumulation of information files provides data for arranging calls. There can be a prospect file, in which the names of all visitors to the church who sign visitors cards will be included. A future file will have the names of those who need a follow-up call. A file should be kept of those who are ill and those who are in the hospital. There may be a general calling file where cards are kept, listing those who may be visited on the church's regular calling night. A master card should be made on every person or family, with a record of every call made. This will include the names of the callers, the dates of the calls, and the results. A responsibility file might be established to include the names of family members of those enrolled in the Sunday school, friends of present members, and prospects within the community.

It is profitable for the visitor to have a visitation packet. This might be a plastic case containing a Bible or New Testament and Psalms. The case would also include an identification card to present at the hospital, the information cards to be filled out, and some literature to leave with the one visited. This literature should be varied for different age groups and life situations. A record book of names might be included.

Additional material might include doorknob hangers to use in case the people are away. Illustrated church and Sunday school brochures should be available, providing time schedules, for services. Such simple things as a flashlight, breath sweeteners, and a pencil should be included also.

Visitors make several types of contacts. One is the casual contact. Many times some of the most effective contacts are those made without prior planning. The visitor should keep his eyes open at all times for opportunities to make personal contacts on behalf of Christ. The planned visit is the one which, though planned, is unannounced. It is imperative in this type of call that the visitor be ready to adapt the length of the call to the circumstances at hand. The next type of visit is the one made by appointment. This will save much time and may well enhance the productivity of the call. All parties involved can be better prepared for such a visit.

Some pastors announce in the bulletin and from the pulpit the streets where visitation will proceed during the following week. Although this does not provide for planned visits, it does limit the scope. Postcards or telephone calls can be used to make definite appointments.

If definite appointments are not made, the visitor may get caught playing the game of hide and seek. The visitor may call when no one is at home and leave a calling card with a greeting to the neighbor. The individual will return home later and find the calling card which was left. The individual may then call the visitor and express regret that he was away and appreciation for the visitor's concern. But no one really meets anyone in this situation. We tell ourselves that we are reaching out to people, but actually we never really contact them.

During the visit, the visitor should take an interest in the things about the home, the health of the members of the family, the work they are doing, the schooling of the children, and recent happenings in connection with the members of the family. Interest, but not undue curiosity, should be shown in the personal problems of every member of the family. There may be something of special interest about the neighborhood, the landscaping of the home, or structure of the home which can serve as a beginning point for conversation. Begin the conversation in the realm of the secular, and then proceed into the realm of the spiritual.

How can one lead the conversation indirectly so that it will go into a productive area of concern? One of the best ways is through the use of questions. Remember that one of your primary tasks is to get them to talk so that you can listen. Plan your questions ahead of time, but be willing to adapt your line of questioning to the circumstances. Do not appear nosey, but let them sense that you have a sincere desire to get to know them better.

When you come to a discussion of spiritual matters, it might be wise to begin by discussing relationships with the church and then proceed to the discussion of the personal relationship of the family members to Christ. In conversation, avoid arguing. Be positive in your discussion of the church, pastor, and Sunday school. Do not condemn, but be honest in evaluation of the subject under discussion.

When calling on a home which could be classified as irreligious, do not offend the family by a harsh forcing of the Gospel. If you do, you will not have an opportunity to return for further discussion. Do not introduce the subject of religion by reproving them of sin unless the offence is an open scandal.

It is wise to ask permission to read a few verses of Scripture and have prayer. The prayer should be short. Remember the members of the family, both those present and those which are absent, in your prayer.

Your conversation should revolve around three centers of interest: the home, the nearby church, and Christ. Remember that the most important thing in calling is not what you say but how you relate to people.

If you are not invited to enter the home, make the best of the conversation at the door. Sometimes you may invite yourself in, if it seems wise and appropriate. You should take your rubbers off outside, but keep your overcoat on. When invited to remove your overcoat, suggest that you merely take it off and keep it with you rather than having it put away in a closet. If you allow it to be placed in a closet, you may be delayed in terminating your visit.

If the radio or television is on when you call, ask if this is one of their favorite programs. If it is, then either volunteer to remain and watch it with them or ask for another time to return for your visit. If you take this latter course, try to make the date for your return visit definite.

It is imperative that as a visitor you adapt yourself to each home in which you call. Make yourself a part of that home while you are there, but at the same time guard your own individuality. While visiting in the home, do not reveal deterimental, negative reactions through voice, countenance, or manner.

Give evidence of the fact that you consider visitation a privilege and that you have a sincere desire to do God's will in this as well as in every enterprise. Realize that you are representing Jesus Christ to the person you are visiting. Focus on the needs of the one being visited and be willing to leave your own problems behind.

Special attention should be given to the initial part of the contact. The contact should be preceded by prayer and carried through in a spirit of prayer. Wear a sincere smile and give a hearty greeting. It is important to have the name of the one being visited memorized. Speak clearly and distinctly, and be mentally alert. If you radiate confidence, this will help to put the contact at ease. Be enthusiastic about having the opportunity to visit.

It is important to be neatly dressed and clean. Such mundane matters as body deordorants and breath sweeteners should be given attention.

PASTORAL VISITATION

Dr. Ralph Sockman used to say that a pastor has a twofold task, namely, preparing the people for the Word and preparing the Word for the people. The pastor's visits are for the purpose of continuing the discussion about the Word of God presented in the pulpit the previous Sunday and continuing the next Sunday. The routine call is the one made by the pastor on a parishioner for no other reason than that the person is a member of his church. In a small church, the pastor should call at least once each year in the homes of all of his members. Since the pastor does all the talking in the pulpit, he should do most of the listening in the home.

The pastor will often be tempted to neglect pastoral calling. Calling will take persistence and determination. If the pastor desires to learn to love people, then he must try to become a part of their lives. A regular, full-time pastor should make about one thousand calls a year. It has been suggested that the pastor spend twenty hours each week in meetings, twenty hours in his study, and twenty hours in calling.

There are at least three types of pastoral calls. There are *routine* calls in which the church's message and fellowship are carried regularly to individuals and families. *Crucial* calls are made when Christian resources are needed by those experiencing crises or distress. *Casual* contacts involve meeting individuals in unstructured settings.

The new pastor should not begin his ministry in a new church with a problem-centered approach or a program-centered approach, but with a person-centered approach. Persons cannot be understood apart from their social and group relations; therefore, the pastor must make contact with his people. The minister is establishing his relationship with people in everything he does. It is not just confined to the impact his personality makes in his "on duty" hours.

"Nickels and noses" have often summarized the purposes for pastoral calling. This is unfortunate. The pastor should perceive that calling will give him an opportunity to minister to the needs of persons. He will get to know the persons and families involved. He can convey God's love and the church's concern. He can also establish a bridge for more effective pastoral care in the future.

HOSPITAL VISITATION

The expanding concept of health describes illness as caused by the interplay of four factors: physical, spiritual, mental, and social. Those who are kept at home through infirmity or who are in the hospital because of a short- or long-term illness will especially appreciate a call from the pastor or someone serving the church in visitation. A radio ministry, a shower of cards and letters, and gifts of plants are appreciated but cannot fully take the place of a personal call.

The visitor will want to take some preparatory steps. He should read literature pertaining to a hospital-visitation ministry. He also needs to develop a Christian attitude toward sickness and pain. It is imperative at this point that the testimony of Scripture be well known and applied. The following Scripture passages are useful in hospital visitation and also serve to give the visitor a healthy mental and scriptural attitude.

Exodus 15:23-26
Exodus 23:20-25
Job 23:10
Psalm 23
Psalm 34:18
Psalm 46:1
Psalm 50:15
Psalm 55:22
Psalm 103
Psalm 119:67, 71
Isaiah 53:4
Matthew 8:16-17
Matthew 11:28-29
Mark 1:41
Mark 6:56
Luke 13:16
John 14:1, 27
Romans 8:28-29
2 Corinthians 12:9
Philippians 3:14
Philippians 4:6-7
11, 13
Hebrews 9:53
Hebrews 12:3-11
James 5:14-18
1 Peter 5:7

It will be profitable to cultivate professional relationships with the doctors. This will aid in the interchange of information. Whenever possible, the visitor should establish rapport with the one he is visiting before making the hospital call. The congregation should be encouraged to notify the pastor or visitation committee when they know of illness within the parish.

The time of the call is important. Normally it is wise to call at other than the regular calling hours for the family. This reserves time for them. An official church visitor is usually given permission by the hospital to call at other times, but permission should be gained from the hospital for such off-hour visits. Time the visit so that you will not interfere with the hospital routine. This is especially true when visiting in the obstetric unit. It is also best to avoid visiting at mealtime, in the very early morning hours, or immediately following an operation. The visitor should call during the evening before an operation.

When it comes time to make the call in the patient's room, the visitor should check with the person at the reception desk. A calling card can be left at that time and the number of the patient's room obtained. The visitor will also be informed of any hospital rules pertaining to his visit.

Before entering the patient's room, the visitor should check with the head nurse on the floor where he is calling. She can give information about the health of the patient and can also protect the privacy of the visit. A visitor should not enter a room without first checking.

The patient is going to receive the visitor's undivided attention during the call. He should stand where the patient can see him and talk with him easily. This will not normally be at the foot of the bed. A visitor listens to the patient in order to detect any feelings of fear, resentment, guilt, or loneliness. This will give him some guidance as to help which he may provide. He should make good use of his resources of encouragement and reassurance, including Scripture, prayer, poetry, and his own positive statements of faith and conviction. He may leave some devotional material with every patient to read later.

A visitor should always pray for spiritual guidance before entering a sickroom. Whether or not he prays audibly with the patient will depend upon his leading by the Holy Spirit and the patient's circumstances, spiritual background, and present mood. It is better to suggest prayer than to ask whether or not it is wanted. The prayer should be short and should reflect hope and faith.

Special types of calls should be given special consideration. If a patient has a contagious disease, the visitor must be sure that he makes that call the last one on his list for that day. He may carry a vial of mercuric chloride with him for use in a washing solution following the visit.

When calling on a new mother, a visitor must be sensitive to her feelings; let her set the mood of the visit. Be sure that you do not project your feelings about parenthood onto her. Watch for opportunities to provide counseling help. The visit should be short.

Calls in connection with an operation have two areas of concern. The preoperative calls should be especially reassuring and comforting. Try to converse about spiritual matters naturally rather than forcing the issue. Promise that you will pray for the patient at the time of the operation, and be sure that the promise is kept. Be sure and call the evening prior to the operation.

During the operation, your concern is with the family. You can help allay their fears during the waiting period by finding out information for them. Delays do occur and are especially hard at this time. If something unusual has transpired during operation, wait for the doctor to convey the information to the family. There may well be a period of depression. Be prepared to help them in this regard. Make the calls especially short, but make them often during this period.

When the patient has had a heart attack or stroke, the visitor should recognize that very often he will have a fear of life as well as a fear of death. The counseling should be directed toward the alleviation of these fears. The most active pastoral care will take place after the first two critical weeks following the attack.

The visit with a terminal patient poses special challenges. The patient probably will express changing reactions. He may be depressed because of the loss of relationship, of comfort and pleasures, and of himself. He may deny the end. He will experience grief which may express itself in guilt, anger, hostility, or idealization of his family. The patient should be allowed to express his feelings. The visitor should provide support and encouragement. Be especially alert to present the way of salvation if the patient is not a believer. Minister to the family as well as to the patient, helping them understand the feelings of the patient.

There are a few special suggestions for a visit with people passing through a time of grief. Encourage the reliving of memories, since this helps a person work through his grief. Allow grief to be expressed. Do not discourage weeping. Anger and hostility are often expressed in grief and may be directed toward you or toward God. Be prepared to recognize them for what they are. Accept the expression of guilt, and encourage confession and forgiveness. Help the person to face his loss realistically.

There are some general suggestions regarding the visitation which should be added as a conclusion to this section. Some may seem rather mundane, but they are significant. The visitor should, as far as possible, avoid talking about himself. Any conversation in the patient's room is important. There should be no whispering to doctors and nurses, no sharing of information regarding the diagnosis, no questioning of the patient about his illness, no expressing of medical opinions about remedies and doctors, and no conversation which would upset the patient. The visitor should not jar, sit on, or lean on the hospital bed. He should not be hesitant to have a spiritual ministry when there are others in the room who may hear. This ministry may be especially appreciated by those who otherwise might have no pastoral care.

EVANGELISTIC VISITATION

There are five essential elements in an effective program of visitation evangelism. First, the visitor must have a faith to proclaim and know how to articulate it. Second, the visitor has to believe and express confidence in the Church as the body of Jesus Christ. Third, he must have and express concern for the person he is visiting. Fourth, he must be able to share his own experience of faith. Fifth, he has to be able and willing to help the person he is visiting make a response to the challenge of the Christian Gospel.

The church cannot face the task of evangelism in the same way that the church of the first century faced it. We are living in a different day. The New Testament church faced a world that was unfamiliar with the Gospel. Today's world has the Gospel presented on radio, television screen, and printed page. In the first century there was no familiarity with Christians against which to measure the Gospel. But some professing Christians in today's world do not help the cause of Christ through the testimony of their life. The early Church had no history of evangelism to overcome. Today we have too many biased people who, because of what they have seen done under the banner of evangelism, have no interest in it. The first-century church had no organized practices and programs to maintain; evangelism could be pursued without trying to fit it into a niche in the program. There were no institutional by-products such as fund raising to detract from the real center of attention. The early church was also living in the afterglow of Christ's earthly ministry.

The church must stop and take some sightings and determine its real position. We may be like the man on the iceberg who walked ten miles in one direction while the iceberg floated fifteen miles in the opposite direction. When a congregation takes its evangelistic responsibility seriously, and when it places a major emphasis upon people, results follow.

In Acts 1:18 we read, "But you shall receive power when the Holy Spirit has come upon you; and you shall be My witnesses both in Jerusalem, and in all Judea and Samaria, and even to the remotest part of the earth" (NASB). This is the commission of the Christian. After Jesus had said this, He was taken up while they were watching, and a cloud swept under Him and carried Him out of their sight.

Jesus went up. The Holy Spirit came down. The disciples went out. These disciples were lowly men with no special talents. Their hopes had been dashed to pieces at the cross, but fifty days later they were at Pentecost. There they received access to a new power, became aware of their purpose, and were given a plan.

The Saviour seeks sinners through the saints. These saints, in order to be effective witnesses, should be prepared in mind and heart. It was shown by a survey that 99 percent of the church members questioned believe that witnessing is the primary responsibility of the church, but only 8.6 percent of their churches have an active program of witnessing.

Witnesses not only must love to work for the Lord but must love people. Their minds must be saturated with Scripture. Their hearts should be clear before God. "If I regard iniquity in my heart, the Lord will not hear me" (Ps 66:18). The witness must have a passion for the lost. The Lord Jesus was "swept as with a storm" with compassion when He saw the lost. Witnessing takes persistence. Five leading insurance companies discovered that they did 80 percent of their business after the fifteenth call.

There is certainly a need for power. Noise does not always indicate power; it takes 500 times as much power to turn on a light as it does to ring a bell. It is the Holy Spirit who regenerates (Jn 3:5), convicts (Jn 16:7-8) and seals (Eph 4:30). When on the Day of Pentecost the disciples were obedient, expectant, prayerful, and united, the power came.

It is necessary to have a gift for pleading. *Come* is God's favorite word, occurring some 640 times in Scripture. The winsomeness of the Spirit must be evident as individuals are called to satisfaction (Is 55), serenity (Mt 11:28), and salvation (Rev 22:17).

Donald McGavran and Winfield Arn, in *How to Grow a Church,* refer to three types of evangelism. "Evangelism 1" involves talking to one's intimates, friends, relatives, and business associates. "Evangelism 2" involves reaching those who live on the other side of a culture barrier. This is the type of evangelism reaching into new communities. Home Bible studies provide a good base for developing "Evangelism 2." "Evangelism 3" is carried on where there are different languages and races as well as different education and financial backgrounds.[4]

There are many different approaches to the work of evangelism in our day. Several "Fisherman's Clubs," or "Andrew Clubs," have been organized. These are made up of men who work in industry or trades. The gold fishhook emblem is often worn on their lapels.

The recreational approach to evangelism is illustrated by the Young Life movement. The leaders develop friendships with the young people within the context of sports and then talk with them about their relationship with Jesus Christ. Many churches organize athletic teams and use this as a vehicle for evangelism.

There is a Christian-center evangelism which uses a youth center as its main location for evangelism. This may be located in a section of the city where there is a special need due to a variety of nationality backgrounds. The center is often governed by an independent board of directors representing major Christian groups within the city.

Coffee house evangelism has become popular in recent days. In America there are now more than one thousand coffee houses being used for evangelism in the broad sense of the term. These coffee houses offer coffee, an unhurried manner, dialogue, a neutral reaction to hair and clothes, folk music, and a variety of presentations on a wide range of subjects.

Hubert Mitchell, founder and director of the Interchurch Ministries of Chicago, is the acknowledged originator and promotor of telephone evangelism. It is referred to as "televisitation." Televisitation has proved a significant factor in helping housewives, students, laboring people, and businessmen learn how to win a hearing for the Gospel in their neighborhoods and communities.

Other methods of evangelism include child evangelism, camping evangelism, radio evangelism, and house-party evangelism. Some churches have sponsored guest nights for evangelism; others have developed "carload" evangelism, which involves group-visitation techniques.

In evangelism, we should not overlook the harvest field within the organized church. It was Canon Green, the famous Anglican, who said, "I am convinced that the most fertile field for evangelism in America is among the unconverted church members."

In our approach to individuals, we should be simple and understandable in what we say. We should be sympathetic, remembering that everyone has problems. We should be optimistic. It might be a good idea to read Philippians just before making a contact. We should remember that the common people heard Christ gladly. People really want what Jesus can give them. The Master's greatest opposition came from the organized religious groups of His day and not from the common people. We can contact folk for Christ at school, at work, on the highways, in a restaurant, at the door of a home, and at church. George Whitefield rode 100,000 miles on horseback in order to tell people about Jesus. John Wesley was "out of breath pursuing souls." His last sermon, at the age of eighty-eight, was based on the text, "Seek ye the LORD while he may be found" (Is 55:6).

There are some additional summarizing suggestions which may be helpful in contacting for Christ. Remember that words are important. We can be perfectly sincere, devout, and earnest; but if we use the wrong word at the right time we can short-circuit the whole process. Avoid personal condemnations, and use Scripture instead. Be a good listener. Do not try to answer all questions; some questions may be inserted as a stall for time. Bear your own personal testimony for Christ. This will be one of the most effective portions of your whole contact. Lead the conversation by asking questions. Begin by asking questions about their relation to the church. You may then want to direct the conversation toward a discussion of Christ and the home. The climax of the conversation will be a discussion of their personal relationship to Jesus Christ as Saviour and Lord. Use only a few leading verses such as Romans 10:9-10; Romans 6:23; Isaiah 53:6; and John 1:12 in your conversation, lest your listeners become confused by too many verses of Scripture.

Becoming a Christian involves a change of mind; this is referred to as repentance. Instead of boasting of his sin, a person is sorry about it and is sorry enough to quit it. It involves a change of direction; this is conversion. The new Christian's life is headed toward fellowship with God. Becoming a Christian involves a change of conversation; this is confession. The individual confesses that what the Bible says about Jesus—namely, that He is the Son of God—is true; and that what the Bible says about the individual—that he has sinned—is true. When one becomes a Christian, there is a change of confidence. His confidence is no longer in self but in the Saviour to keep him (2 Ti 1:12).

The following four concepts can be identified in the book of Romans and can serve as a pattern to follow in pointing a seeker to the Saviour.

1. *You must realize that you are a sinner.* (Show him Romans 3:10 and 3:23.) If all are sinners, then am I a sinner? (Yes) If all are sinners, are you a sinner? (Yes)
2. *You must realize that you are condemned by your sin.* (Show

him Romans 5:12 and 6:23.) Adam sinned, and the curse of death came upon the human race. The same is true today. Complete death means the body goes back to the ground and the soul is cast into hell. (Revelation 20:14-15 may be used if needed.)

3. *You must realize that Jesus paid your debt on the cross.* (Show him Romans 5:8.) Jesus never committed a single sin. This means that He did not deserve to die, but *He did die.* If He did not die for His sin, for whose sin *was* He dying on the cross? (For ours)
4. *You must realize that if you will receive Jesus, you can become a Christian.* (Show him Romans 10:13.) According to this verse, if you were to ask God to forgive your sins and save you, what would He do? (He would save me.)

We must rethink the Great Commission (Mt 28: 19-20). Our monumental churches and professional workers are calling to the community and saying, "Come, we are ready to receive you!" The Great Commission tells us, "Therefore, go and make disciples of all nations, baptizing them in the name of the Father and of the Son and of the Holy Spirit, and teaching them to obey everything I have commanded you. And surely I will be with you always, to the very end of the age" (NIV). What is your response to the Great Commission?

Additional Reading

Brown, Stanley C. *Evangelism in the Early Church.* Grand Rapids: Eerdmans, 1963.

Downey, Murray W. *The Art of Soul-Winning.* Grand Rapids: Baker, 1957.

Ford, Leighton. *The Christian Persuader.* New York: Harper & Row, 1966.

Hale, Joe. *Design for Evangelism.* Nashville: Tidings, 1969.

Noyce, Gaylord B. *Survival and Mission for the City Church.* Philadelphia: Westminster, 1975.

Schaller, Lyle E. *Community Organization: Conflict and Reconciliation.* Nashville: Abingdon, 1966.

———. *Impact of the Future.* Nashville: Abingdon, 1969.

Stanfield, Vernon L. *Effective Evangelistic Preaching.* Grand Rapids: Baker, 1965.

Sweazey, George E. *Effective Evangelism.* New York: Harper & Row, 1953.

Whitesell, Faris D. *Basic New Testament Evangelism.* Grand Rapids: Zondervan, 1949.

———. *Evangelistic Preaching and the Old Testament.* Chicago: Moody, 1947.

Wood, A. Skevington. *Evangelism: Its Theology and Practice.* Grand Rapids: Zondervan, 1966.

CHAPTER 13

Updating Our Worship

The beginning and end of all worship is the awareness of God. Every form of worship, both in its content and conduct, should be a disclosure of God. These forms of worship should set forth His existence, power, character, and demands. God takes the initiative toward us in our worship because He loves us and He judges us.

There is, perhaps, no point where present Protestant church life exhibits a greater poverty than in worship. Why do many attend Sunday school who refuse to attend the church services? If the church worship services were cancelled, would they really be missed? We call them worship services, but are they? Many typical church services are devoid of a sense of the holy presence of God. A church may be filled with creative ideas and be overflowing with good works, but if there is no sense of the presence of God, the glitter has no glory. We may feel reverence, awe, and wonder, but the most important thing is that we relate ourselves creatively to Him. We are to respond to His presence in adoration and praise, confession of sin, and thanksgiving for mercies received. God, and not our own consciousness, is the object of worship.

Worship does not usually mean the imparting of new knowledge or the transmission of new information about God. It involves, rather, a rediscovery of that which we already know but constantly forget. We rediscover what we once knew, professed, and forgot—that everything in the world depends upon God.

Albert Palmer, in *The Art of Conducting Public Worship*, says that the success or failure of a worship service may be measured in three ways. The first measurement is whether or not there is a sincere outreach toward God and an act of real self-dedication on the part of the leader and worshipers. The next is whether or not the service held the attention and commanded the respect and participation of the congregation. Except for very unusual congregations, our basic approach to worship must be congregational; we must involve the members in worship. The third factor involves the presence or absence of inherent qualities of beauty, dignity, and artistry which will appeal to all in proportion to their ability to judge and appreciate.[1]

Our worship should be constructed around a healthy respect for the varieties of people. No longer can we afford to offer, as it were, a menu with only one dinner listed on it. Some churches have given the impression that those who attend may either "like it, or lump it." There is another alternative open to the people, and that is to leave it. We should give consideration to the people who worship as well as to the God whom we worship. Few present-day clergy realize how classical the presuppositions of their education have been or how rigid and inflexible their mentality is. Our knowing what is best for a congregation needs to be based on more than standards of good taste that we learned years ago in the seminary. We need to be willing to accept rather than to merely prescribe. The time has come when the question of liturgical forms should no longer be decided merely on the basis of traditional prejudices. We must be willing to make candid investigations and be willing to accept change. There should not be an unprofitable laxity or an oppressive uniformity.

Present-day Protestant worship is largely a consequence of the communications revolution of the fifteenth and sixteenth centuries. There had been written formularies from at least the third century. The printing press made the formularies available to all the people. Reading made changes in the people. A literate laity could participate in worship in a more meaningful way. In 1884, A. B. Dick's invention of the duplicating process also brought changes in the appreciation and conduct of worship. Protestant worship was shaped by the same forces that were shaping men at that period of time. It was characteristic of Protestantism that it allowed people to worship in the forms most natural to them.

There is a strong emphasis, in many quarters, on entertainment in worship. It is important that we realize the connection between the medium and the message. We must be clear about the message before we try to express it. Not all that entertains educates. Experimentation which involves theological shortcuts may be thrilling, but it may tear down more than it builds up in the community of faith. The period between 1920 and 1970 was the period of respectability for Protestant worship in this country. Much of our society is now far less inhibited in its response to life. It appears that the fastest growing churches here and abroad tend to lean toward more spontaneity in worship.

It is difficult for us in this day to recapture the resolute spirit that carried the early believers to their corporate worship. Just as force cannot compel belief, neither can penalties stamp it out. In spite of all handicaps, great masses of people came together in a humble, listening, and waiting attitude before their God. Through the years, much of the resolute spirit behind worship attendance dwindled away. In some cases, attending worship services became a conventional thing to do. In other cases it was regarded primarily as a mark of respectability. There is need in our day for the Holy Spirit to impress upon our conscience the Lord's appeal to and obedience to the first commandment of God's law: "Thou shalt worship the Lord thy God, and him only shalt thou serve" (Mt 4:10). This worship will involve drawing near to God, the plea for mercy and forgiveness, the adoration and praise of God, the listening to God's voice, and the dedication of self to God. An analysis of Genesis 22 and Isaiah 6 provides the essential components of true worship.

In order to increase the meaningfulness of worship, the minister should devote himself to a more careful and spiritual preparation. There should be the cultivation of the reverential spirit among the people. Emphasis needs to be placed upon the development of the social spirit in worship. Excessive individualism in worship hampers its effectiveness.

The Meaning of Worship

Worship is God's way of revealing Himself to His children and their way of responding to Him in faith. It is a two-way relationship between God and man. It includes God's initiative and man's response. Worship functions for the glorification of God and the sanctification of man.

Our English word *worship* is a combination of *worthy* and *ship* and denotes a recognition of value in a person or object. The dictionary says that to worship is to attribute worth to a deity. There are two Greek words for *worship*. One means "to fall down" and the other means "to serve." These imply that Christian worship is motivated by a sense of awe and of love. Christian worship is offering as well as appreciation. The New Testament words for *worship* stress the act. The Greek word is traced to the idea of a dog which crouches at its master's feet. Worship is an act in which the devout soul prostrates itself before God in humble homage and entire submission. The Old Testament words for *worship* also convey the idea of prostrating oneself before God. Worship is essentially looking from ourselves to God.

In an attempt to develop a definition of worship, reflect upon the following statements which have been gathered from numerous sources.

"Worship is the outward expression of religion. It is the formal communion between God and His people. In it God speaks to man and man to God."

"Worship is the occupation of the heart, not with its needs, or even with its blessings, but with God Himself."

"Worship is man's response to the nature and actions of God."

"Worship is an act of praise and thanksgiving to God offered at any time, in any place by those who have identified themselves with the mystical body of Christ."

Christian worship consists of four elements. The first of these is the observance of time. The chief function of time in Christian worship has been as a means of recovering key events in the history of revelation. This is evidenced by the Christian calendar. The element of initiation marks the beginning of our life with Christ. The ordinances remind us of the person and work of Christ. The divine office is the fourth element in the canon of Christian worship. In Protestantism this refers to the preaching service. These four elements in Christian worship have endured for twenty centuries.

The Word of God is an essential constituent of Christian worship. Without the Scriptures, the church would simply be a conglomeration of people of good will without any identity. Corporate worship is the response of the Christian fellowship to God's love as revealed in His Word.

Public worship must have design. It should, like a building, express the idea behind its erection and fulfill its function with singleness of purpose. Another characteristic of worship is unity. This is not the unity of a single idea, necessarily, but is more akin to the unity of a symphony in which there is a sequence of movements voicing different states of feeling. Leaders in worship must acquire the artistic powers to arrange and carry out a service so that a waiting God and seeking people may be joined in fellowship. The levels upon which men have fellowship with one another throw light upon God's communion with us. There is fellowship through a sense of physical presence. "Surely the LORD is this place" (Gen 28:16). There is fellowship through an exchange of current thoughts and, finally, through a oneness of purpose.

THE PURPOSE OF WORSHIP

It would be interesting and profitable to discover why people attend a worship service. When asked, some might respond that it makes them feel better, behave better, and live better. Some attend for worldly advantage. The politician may attend just before an election. The businessman may attend with a hope of making business contacts.

People sometimes respond positively or negatively to worship depending upon the personal satisfaction that it affords. This personal satisfaction may be supplied by the preacher, music, ritual, or the kind of people who attend. The primary purposes behind worship participation should not be that we might feel better or experience particular sensations but that we might respond to God for His great redemptive love in Christ. When entertainment substitutes for worship, we should take a hard look at the order of service. Displays of technical ability may make us happy, but they sometimes distract from spiritual reflection and meditation. The entertainment complex creates a few stars and many spectators.

There is a pedagogic usefulness in worship. We learn to be better Christians and to encounter God, the world, and our neighbor. There is a sociological usefulness, since worship brings people together and gives them a sense of fellowship. There is also a psychological usefulness in that worship provides the faithful with a sense of stability, peace, and joy.

Congregational participation will be most effective when individual members have prepared themselves for worship. Very little preparation is demanded of a spectator, but much is demanded of a participant. Participation in worship means appropriation, applying the various parts of the worship service to our own life and needs.

The motivation for sharing in worship might be stated in terms of need, duty, and love. There are four needs which the worship service should meet. The first is the need for friendship and companionship. People are also searching for stability in the midst of the perplexities of life. There is the need for reflection and recollection in a peaceful environment. The person who is carrying a heavy load desires the supporting prayers of the faithful.

A sense of duty often motivates us to worship. We have a sense of duty to acknowledge His lordship over life and express our gratitude for His gifts. Many who attend worship do so because of their love for worship itself.

The Elements in Liturgy

The New Testament has no specific liturgical terminology. The word *liturgy* itself has a secular origin, coming to us from two words meaning "people" and "work". When a citizen of ancient Athens paid for work or entertainment, or supplied equipment for the armed forces, he was said to have performed a liturgy. The early Christians restricted the word *liturgy* to the public functions of the church presided over by its official ministers. In its root meaning, the word means an act performed for the good of the community. In its restricted meaning, it refers to the public rites and ceremonies authorized by the church.

A liturgy consists of three elements: order, ritual, and ceremony. The *order* of a liturgy is its structural framework, its shape and design. Order is important, because the people cannot participate unless they know what is supposed to happen next. ***Ritual*** is the vocal organ of the liturgy, the words which are spoken or sung. The ritual words are uttered in prayers, songs, reading, and preaching. The *ceremony* includes the things that are done in worship. It includes the actions of both the leader and the congregation. The visual aids of worship are generally included as belonging to the ceremony. In liturgical formulation, it is imperative that the worshipers understand what is taking place, understand the language of worship, and be able to hear what is said in worship.

RITUAL

Ritual involves the logical and accoustical aspects of liturgical expressions. Wording is very important in worship. It is impossible to have a standard wording for every group. Each group develops its own words and phrases, which become familiar by repetition. The wording must be simple, and it must be clear.

The highest form of worship, and another element of ritual, is prayer. The language of prayer should be simple and direct, yet dignified and elevated. There are two basic conditions necessary for Christian prayer. The first is that the requests be for things which God desires to do, and the second is that the prayers be made in faith. There are five main forms of Christian prayer: thanksgiving, confession, petition, intercession, and dedication. All five of these should be included in the worship service if it is to be complete.

Special attention should be given to the preparation and presentation of public prayers. Even a great preacher such as Robert Hall of England poured his soul into his sermons but left his prayers to care for themselves. He gave them little thought and no preparation, and the world remembers. Public prayers should be marked by comprehensiveness, orderliness, concreteness, objectivity, freshness of thought and language, variety, and brevity. The real danger of an unprepared prayer is that it may lead nowhere; it may be just a disorderly dance of words. An unprepared prayer may also tend to run too long. Cotton Mather prayed at his own ordination for an hour. Spurgeon would often pray publicly for as long as fifteen minutes. Five-minute prayers are considered maximum for our day. It is better to have more and shorter prayers rather than fewer and longer prayers.

Some of the common faults of public prayers are lack of preparation; excessive length; poor delivery; monotonous references to Deity; pointed, personal references; preaching disguised as prayer; and finally, private prayer rather than public prayer. For prayer to be the intimate conversation between God and the worshiper, which it is intended to be, all disturbing difficulties should be removed.

Ritual includes not only the words that are spoken in prayers but also the words that are sung. Vocal music in public has a twofold function; it is a means of expression and a means of impression. Hymns should have good, lyric verse in simple form and language. The hymn must express a wholesome fellowship with God and a fellowship appropriate for every Christian. The doctrine contained in the hymn should be in accord with the teaching of Scripture. The hymn should provide a means whereby God may fellowship with the worshipers.

The anthem sung by a choir should not be discarded but is certainly secondary in liturgical importance to congregational singing. There are times when an anthem is needed. Too often, however, the anthem has been forced into the service with no clear idea of its liturgical function or purpose.

Albert Palmer in his book, *The Art of Conducting Public Worship*, provides a list of questions which may be used for evaluating church music in worship.

1. Does the music glorify God? Is it interpretative of the attributes of God?
2. Are the musicians intelligently sensitive with regard to their function in the service?
3. Do the hymns used in each service facilitate the progress or movement of the service?
4. Are all the hymns, in both text and tune, worthy of use in public worship?
5. Is due respect shown for each hymn and musical composition in its original form or as the author intended it to be used?
6. Is the universal character of Christian hymnody appreciated by both minister and people?
7. Do the hymns and responses win intelligent appreciation and hearty use by the members of the congregation?

8. Is the music consistent with the general setting of the worship service?
9. Under the leadership of the choir, the organ, and the minister, does the entire congregation worship through the use of the hymns?
10. Are the special musical numbers so constituted and rendered that the members of the congregation consider them to be integral and appropriate parts of the order of worship?
11. Is music used effectively to cover up the mechanics of the services?
12. Are the mechanics of the music successfully hidden?
13. Are the musicians careful not to constitute distractions from worship?
14. Are the musical instruments, including the organ, in good repair and worthy of use in the services?
15. Whenever vocal music is being accompanied by an organ or piano, does the accompanist confine his playing to merely adequate support for the singers?
16. Are members of the congregations having musical talent encouraged to qualify for leadership and honored service in this field?
17. Are the musical features of the service in keeping with the skill or ability of the musicians?
18. Is the music on such a cultural level that members of the congregation can recognize and appreciate it?
19. Do the processional and recessional, if used, reflect special study of these features of public worship?
20. Are the stories of the hymns and hymn writers used appropriately in helping worshippers to get a better understanding and appreciation of the hymns?
21. Is prayer offered at choir rehearsals?
22. Does the music committee really function?

ORDINANCES

Whenever the church performs the ordinances, it performs a liturgy. It engages in a corporate action that has a prescribed form, an essential ritual, and a necessary ceremony.

The Lord's Supper. The basic text for this ordinance of the Lord's Supper is 1 Corinthians 11:17-34, with its context of 1 Corinthians 10:14–11:16. This ordinance draws together the local church in an assembly. No other religion has as a regular feature the frequent assembling of its initiates for worship, instruction, and fellowship. This is a "supper" peculiarly "the Lord's" in contrast to the "cup of devils" (1 Co 10:21).

The absent Lord is the Host of the supper. The elements used are presented to Him before distribution. Our Lord is absent in the body but present in spirit and in His vicar, the Holy Spirit (Mt 28:20; Jn 14:16-18). Some churches set chairs for elders and deacons at the table, with an empty chair at the host's place to symbolize this reality.

The church is at worship as it shares in this ordinance specially instituted by the Lord. Though it was passed to the Corinthian church by Paul, it was instituted by Jesus Himself. To participate in the Lord's Supper is to share in something from the immediate, personal, visible presence of the Lord Jesus.

The ordinance is a mutual, symbolic participation in Christ. It is a mutual remembrance of Jesus Christ. It is a collective testimony of the Gospel. It is a mutual expression of hope.

The ordinance should be observed expectantly (1 Co 11:26), with self-examination (1 Co 11:27-28), in a worthy manner (1 Co 11:27), with mutual judgment (1 Co 11:31), and with mutual consideration (1 Co 11:33).

When the elements are ready for distribution, the presiding elder should make it clear that the participants are to wait until all have been served, and then partake together. While the elements are being distributed, portions of Scripture can be read to the congregation.

There are churches where many members have to work on Sunday morning and therefore cannot share in the communion service. It might be wise occasionally to have an evening communion service. Some churches have found it profitable to hold a service including the Lord's Supper on the Lord's Day afternoon.

Many churches read the church convenant either at the service of the Lord's Supper or at the prayer meeting held during the prior week.

If a communion offering or fellowship offering is received during the observance of the Lord's Supper, careful preparation should be made. The plates should be available and the ushers instructed.

Some churches merely place offering plates at the door at the close of the service. This offering is normally kept as an elder's fund and is used for the alleviation of need among the members. The names of the members helped through the offering are never made public.

Baptism. The observance of the ordinance of baptism involves the performance of a liturgy. There is a prescribed form, an essential ritual, and a necessary ceremony.

The Great Commission recorded in Matthew 28:19-20 says, "Go ye therefore, and teach all nations, baptizing them in the name of the Father, and of the Son, and of the Holy Ghost: teaching them to observe all things whatsoever I have commanded you: and, lo, I am with you alway, even unto the end of the world." Baptism is the outward symbol of that which has already transpired in one's life. Through faith in Christ, the individual has died to sin and has been raised to newness of life in Christ. The individual should be baptized only if he believes with all his heart in Jesus Christ as his Saviour and Lord.

The Bible teaches baptism by immersion by the very word used. The Greek word "baptizo" means "to dip, to plunge under, to submerge." Baptism by immersion fulfills the typology of the act including death, burial, and resurrection. This is emphasized in Romans 6:3-6.

The minister who baptizes is customarily but not necessarily ordained. If a minister is not ordained, he may ask an ordained minister to do the actual baptizing.

The baptistry in a Church should be located so that everyone in the audience is able to see the service and the participants. The minimum size of the baptistry would be eight feet by six feet. An exit should be provided at each end of the bapistry with handrails for the assistance of the candidates. Changing rooms should be located near the baptistry. If the baptism is held outdoors, cottages or tents can be used for changing of clothes. Have helpers who will guide the candidates in and out of the water. The minister should not walk back and forth with each one.

Clear instructions should be provided for the candidate regarding the meaning of baptism prior to administering the ordinance. A written communication can be sent prior to the service giving instructions regarding wearing apparel and other pertinent information.

SYMBOLS IN CEREMONY

In addition to the logical and accoustical elements of liturgy, there are the visual. Since 1970 we have seen an increased emphasis being placed upon symbols. The peace symbol and the flag are just two of the many symbols which have drawn special attention. Man lives by and for his symbols. He desires something to make the intangible tangible and the invisible visible.

The words *symbolism* and *symbolics* are derived from the Greek *symballein*, meaning "to make a comparison." In Greece, when two parties made a contract, it was customary to break an object. Each party kept a piece (a *symbolon*, or *symbol*) as proof of identity when one or the other presented his piece. In ecclesiastical usuage the word easily adapted itself to denote an identifying confession whereby a person's theological position could be ascertained. Thus the Apostles' Creed was called a symbol from the fourth century onward. The scientific study of the distinctive doctrinal characteristics of church bodies is called "symbolics."

In the early Christian Church, symbols were freely used as convenient fixatives of doctrinal points for the many Christians who could not read, and during periods of persecution as a secret language. In our day, symbols are used on church windows and furnishings for the purpose of indicating pictographically the cardinal elements of Christian faith, tradition, and teaching. Symbols present to the eye an interesting and valuable supplement to preaching and religious education.

In a certain sense, the great creeds are collections of symbols which do not and cannot compass the complete content of Christian faith. Nobody has ever compiled a creed that can remain unaffected by the passage of time, because the medium of expression is words which, in a living language, are subject to change in meaning and force and, even in a dead language, are not protected against misapprehension over long periods of time. Words have in them the inherent limitations of expression characteristic of all symbols. The statements of a creed are suggestive of meaning largely in the same way that pictured symbols are, and it is for this reason that the theological term *symbolics* is used for the study of creeds and confessions of faith.

A symbol is a tangible representation of an intangible moral or intellectual concept. The symbol is an object or image which has properties similar in nature to the moral or intellectual concept to be illustrated. For instance, the idea of endless love is conveyed by the ring, which has no end. Love cannot be pictured or photographed; but the ring is a picture which indicates, or represents, enduring love.

For the early Christians there was a very practical motive for the free use of symbols. The persecutions to which they were more or less constantly subjected made it necessary for those Christians to avoid the suspicion of their enemies. For this reason they made wide use of symbols, even adapting some pagan symbols to their use. The symbol was practically the only means that could safely be used to communicate with other Christians when an oral message was not possible. Symbols were also used to guard the holy mysteries from profanation. Thus, while symbolism is essential to every kind of external worship, it was especially necessary in the worship of the early Church.

Three great, fundamental truths that vitalize the soul of a Christian are represented by symbols which are common to Christian churches everywhere: the cross, the holy Trinity, and the resurrection.

The cross, the most important of all Christian symbols, symbolizes Christ and His death on the cross and the redemption of mankind. The cross, as a sign of a Christian and an emblem of his faith, speaks of the self-sacrificing life Christ's followers are expected to live. More than four hundred representations of the cross are in use.

The holy Trinity is typified by triple windows; three steps; triple arches; the trefoil, three lobes in one figure; three circles of identical size, intertwined; arcs of three circles joined; the equilateral triangle with its apex upward, indicating equality of the persons in the Godhead; and other triform figures.

The resurrection and life hereafter are symbolized by the vertical movement expressed in arches, elongated windows, pillars, lines, pinnacles, and spires leading the eye upward to heaven.

In interpreting symbols, consider the following:

1. The interpretation of symbols given by the Scriptures is the foundation for all further studies in symbolism. When the Scripture interprets a symbol, then we are on sure ground. These interpretations may be used as general guides for all further studies in symbols.
2. If the symbol given in Scripture is apparently not interpreted, we suggest the following:
   a. Investigate the context thoroughly. It may be that in what is said before or after, the idea behind the symbol is revealed.
   b. Using a concordance, find other passages which use the same symbol, and see if such cross-references give a clue.
   c. Sometimes the nature of the symbol is a clue to its meaning (although the temptation to read the meanings of our culture into these symbols must be resisted). The preservative character of salt is common knowledge, as is the ferocity of lions, the docility of doves, the meekness of lambs, and the filthiness of pigs.
   d. Sometimes comparative studies of Semitic culture reveal the meaning of the symbol. Perchance, too, in archaeological materials the clue will be discovered. If we are not able to turn up any clues to symbols uninterpreted in the text, it is wiser to be silent than to speculate.
3. Be aware of double imagery in symbols. There is nothing in the symbolism of the Bible which demands that each symbol have one and only one meaning. This appears to be the presupposition. The lion is at the same time the symbol of Christ ("the Lion of the tribe of Judah") and of Satan (the lion seeking to devour Christians [1 Pe 2:25]). Water means "the word" in Ephesians 5:26, the Spirit in 1 Corinthians 12:13, and regeneration in Titus 3:5. Oil may mean the Holy Spirit, repentance, or readiness.

The Environment of Worship

The environment of worship prescribes the form the worship will take. Where one worships and when one worships will have a great deal of influence upon his understanding of worship. Too often church buildings have failed to reflect the nature of the Church. Large monuments do not convey the thought of a servant church. Churchill is quoted as having said that we shape our buildings, and ever after they shape us.

Church buildings should be marked by utility, simplicity, flexibility, and intimacy. They should be built to be used, not to serve as scenery. They should be built, in other words, to be functional rather than to be admired. If new forms of worship are to develop, our churches must be liberated from rigidity. Very few major changes in worship can take place as long as furniture and furnishings are unmovable. In discussing architecture we should think primarily of worship.

A church is unlike any other building. One may worship in any kind of building, but not equally well in all. If any kind of building were good enough, why would we bother with a church at all?

In a church building there are some things that of themselves contribute to worship. A church building should be such that one would feel like sitting down in silence and worshiping whether there was a service or not. No style of architecture is better suited for such a purpose than Gothic. The arches and piers and vaulted ceiling lift the eye and attention, and even as they do so, they tune the soul to an attitude of prayer and meditation and peace. What if a dozen or so seats become obscured from the pulpit? Should high arches and the whole effect be destroyed for the sake of those few seats? After all, the most practical church building is not one in which a person can see the pastor and the choir but where he learns to see God. Perhaps you have been in a church building where the clash of colors and design have made you feel uneasy, disturbed, and tired. No matter what the preacher said, he could not overcome what the church building said. Low ceilings and stingy sanctuaries are common enough, for "practical" purposes. But why not help lift up the soul and widen its vision of God by making the building speak of room and height and depth? Beauty is more important in a church than whether one can see all the building in one glance. The church structure should be such that it grows on one's mind and helps the worshiper find gradually, in hidden places, some unknown truth or symbol of truth.

In an ideal church, the spire pointing upward should be a reminder of things above, "where Christ sitteth on the right hand of God" (Col 3:1). Its bell should proclaim the priority of worship over work and play. The open door of the church should say, "This is a house of prayer for all people" (cf. Is 56:7). Its cross on the spire should remind us of the words of the Saviour: "I, if I be lifted up, will draw all men unto me" (Jn 12:32).

In the past, many Protestant churches in America have been built with slight regard for the worship functions a church sanctuary should fulfill. One can see at a glance that the governing idea in their construction was to provide an all-purpose auditorium that would serve on almost any occasion. This object is understandable because, in many cases, the congregations could not afford to construct buildings adequate to meet their needs. But most of these all-purpose buildings make little or no contribution to worship. If the services of worship in them are uplifting, it is generally in spite of the uninspiring surroundings. Many of these buildings can be positively depressing to a sensitive person.

The Methodology of Worship

The updating of our methods of worship will involve first of all a careful evaluation of the present state of worship in our churches in order to become convinced of the need for improvement. To many, this need will be obvious. We must then become clear in our own thinking about the real, biblical purpose of worship. In worship, we come before God in reverence to acknowledge His worth, to praise Him, and to thank Him for His redemptive work in our lives.

A survey of the Scripture and a study of history provide information from the past which may prove helpful in the present. It will not be adequate, however, to make our worship merely an extension of tradition. One by-product of worship must be edification for the worshipers. It should help them to love one another in Christian love. Our aim is not that the worship be novel but that it be meaningful.

Participation helps make worship more meaningful. There are several areas of worship which provide excellent opportunity for participation. One of these is the area of music. Some churches tend to bring special musicians to the church rather than using the talent which is already there. But this practice ignores the principle that if we do not use our people, we will lose our people. A church choir can aid congregational participation in worship if its function is to train people in singing and not to perform for an audience. Lay people can participate in the prayers, Scripture lesson, stewardship, and the proclamation of the Word. (Several suggestions for encouraging participation in preaching can be found in my book, *Biblical Preaching for Today's World*, p. 93-103.)

One of the most refreshing approaches to worship is described in the book, *Full Circle*, by David Mains (Waco, Tex.: Word, 1971). His emphases upon having a unifying theme in the worship service, having the service divided into purposeful parts, and having a place for interaction are especially thought-provoking.

In regard to a unifying theme and purpose, I would suggest that the sermon be determined before the planning of the worship service. A good sermonic proposition is timeless. It presents truth which was valid in biblical times and is still valid and relevant today. As the core of the sermon, it provides the unifying theme for the worship. Relevance and purpose are important. We begin with purpose and then proceed to plan and performance.

When you have the thrust of the sermon in a declarative, timeless, truth sentence, the second step is to prayerfully select an attribute of God which is basic to this timeless truth. The center of worship is not man but God. The worshipers must realize that it is God's Word which is presented. They must realize that it is God who is worthy of their praise. They must recognize that their whole purpose in life should be to worship and to serve God. In this step, the worshipers prepare to express to God their appreciation for who He is. This can be done through prayer, music, use of Scripture, and giving. It is important to remember that these are all to be directed toward God.

The third step in developing a worship service is to consider ways and means in which the timeless truth of the sermon, which is the theme of the whole service, can be shown to be applicable to daily experience. The worship service theme should be meaningful for daily life. In many churches, this matter of application has not been emphasized in connection with worship and, sad to say, has been overlooked in much of the preaching.

These three parts of the worship service, from the standpoint of presentation, are adoration, edification, and application, in that order. From the standpoint of construction, we would change the order to edification, adoration, and application. We begin, therefore, with the theme, which is the center or proposition of the sermon. We prepare to praise God for having made that truth available. We conclude the worship by showing the practicality of that truth to our maturing in Christ.

These three steps are set forth rather clearly in Psalm 19. In Psalm 19:1-6, the emphasis is upon the glory of the Author of the Word. We are given a glimpse of the greatness and glory of God. The very heavens declare their Creator. In Psalm 19:7-10, the emphasis is upon the greatness of the contents of the Word. It is identified as law, testimony, precept, commandment, and described as being perfect, sure, right, pure, clean, and true. It will restore the soul, rejoice the heart, and enlighten the eyes. We have a great God who has given us a great Word. In Psalm 19:11-14, the emphasis is upon the gracious conviction which comes through the Word. In verse 12, we read of grace to purge; in verse 13, of grace to preserve; and in verse 14, of grace to perfect. The psalmist pleads for cleansing, preservation, and acceptance. The three parts of this psalm demonstrate the three steps in the worship experience. It begins with the adoration of God, proceeds to the speaking of God through His Word, and ends with the application of the Word of God to the life of the listener.

God has been pushed out of so many areas of our life that it becomes increasingly difficult to find Him. He is still there; He never left. We have wandered away and need to get back. A five-minute devotional each day is not enough to satisfy the spiritual hunger of the soul. Let us worship God together.

> Seek ye the LORD while he may be found,
> call ye upon him while he is near:
> Let the wicked forsake his way,
> and the unrighteous man his thoughts:
> and let him return unto the LORD,

and he will have mercy upon him;
and to our God, for he will abundantly pardon (Is 55:6-8).

Additional Reading

Baxter, J. Sidlow. *Rethinking Our Priorities.* Grand Rapids: Zondervan, 1974.

Blackwood, Andrew. *The Fine Art of Public Worship.* Nashville: Abingdon-Cokesbury, 1939.

———. *Leading in Public Prayer.* Nashville: Abingdon, 1957.

Gibbs, Alfred P. *Worship.* Fort Dodge, Iowa: Walterick, n.d.

Mains, David R. *Full Circle.* Waco, Tex.: Word, 1971.

Randolph, David J. *God's Party.* Nashville: Abingdon, 1975.

Segler, Franklin M. *Christian Worship: Its Theology and Practice.* Nashville: Broadman, 1964.

White, James F. *New Forms of Worship.* Nashville: Abingdon, 1971.

Williamson, Robert L. *Effective Public Prayer.* Nashville: Broadman 1960.

Wygal, Winnifred. *How to Plan Informal Worship.* New York: Association, 1955.

CHAPTER 14

Making Wise Use of Time

"Lost yesterday, somewhere between sunrise and sunset; two golden hours, each set with sixty diamond minutes. No reward is offered for they are gone forever" wrote Horace Mann. As short as life is, we make it even shorter by wasting time. Time is fleeting and irrevocable. It cannot be hoarded; it must be spent. A man without a plan for using his time is like a moving automobile without a driver.

Today's minister is expected to do too much. Some of his many responsibilities include worship, evangelism, missions, Christian education, study, devotions, visitation, counseling, pastoral services to individuals, administration, financial planning, caring for facilities, maintaining community relationships, mimeographing, running errands, and church decorating. And sometimes people would even like to add to this list! In trying to accomplish some of these tasks, the average minister is said to work on an average of over ten hours a day. Under this kind of work load, some ministers of large churches cannot be shepherds but only ranchers. The pastor must realize the importance of exegeting his datebook as well as exegeting the Greek text. Ecclesiastes affirms that there is a time for everything. This presents a special challenge to the pastor.

Most of us are not proficient at estimating time. It is imperative that we watch the clock and check the time in the course of our daily routine. But it is possible to become more proficient in estimating time. Remember that we tend to underestimate the time when we are engaged in something we like to do, and we tend to overestimate it when we are involved in less desirable activity.

Even when we think we have enough time for our duties, interruptions and unforseen developments upset our schedules. We should remember, however, that these are not interruptions in God's plan for our lives.

Auren Uris, in *The Executive Deskbook*, lists ten areas of executive concern, with time saving and time scheduling at the top of the list. Other items in the list include effective communication, decision making and problem solving, planning, delegation and assignment, building group effectiveness, leadership and motivation, dealing with problem people, dealing with interpersonal problems and improving one's own effectiveness.[1]

The pastor's tasks are essentially nonroutine. There is a need for flexibility. The pastor must be willing to set aside one task for a more important one. He must also be willing to drop everything in case of an emergency. If he manages his time on a demand basis, he must make sure that the demands which he honors have highest priority. There will be very little coasting time; there is no neutral gear. The quantity of time spent on the job is less important than how that time is spent.

It is important to talk with God in prayer about our desire to serve Him and the frustrations which face us in the use of our time. We need to ask Him for a calm, unhurried intelligence as we face the matter of time planning. Time is God-given, and we will be held accountable for its use (Ps 90:12; Eph 5:16; Col 4:5).

There are several suggestions which may prove helpful in guiding the pastor toward a more productive use of the time at his disposal.

Make a Time Inventory

To discover how you are actually using your time, record your activity for a week. Begin by selecting a normal work week. (That which begins normally may not end that way, but you can study the variations later.) Keep your record sheets close at hand, and note the starting and stopping time of each activity. It may be wise to divide the days into fifteen-minute segments. Be sure to include everything you do. A series of telephone calls and trips to the mailbox can add up at the end of the day.

At the close of the week, analyze the data which you have collected. Categorize and evaluate your activities. Draw a chart with a series of headings such as visitation, administration, sermon preparation, recreation, or any other general category. Under each heading, list your activities and the time you spent. By using such a chart, you are better able to evaluate your time expenditure.

The third step is to revise your time schedule to make it more efficient. You may be able to group similar tasks, change the timing of important items, and make room for items which were not included but should have been. This revising should take into account your own physical peaks of energy. We all have times when we feel more energetic than at other times. Put the difficult tasks in the high-energy periods. Save routine work for those periods when you know that your alertness will be at a low ebb.

Establish a Practical Time Schedule

In formulating a time schedule, there are actually four steps which must be taken. List your activities, decide whether or not they are assignable, evaluate their priority, and then proceed to schedule.

In step one, consider your obligations and the activities which they suggest. Four or five mornings each week must be set aside for study, meditation, and creative sermonic and administrative work. As a pastor, you may feel that you have an obligation to set aside four afternoons and four evenings in the week for pastoral calling, committee work, and office and administrative details. Sunday will be given entirely to church activities. This will mean that you will have one day and two evenings free for other obligations. This may not be enough time to meet all of those obligations.

At this point, you may want to take some time and consider your ideals in relation to this matter of the use of time. These ideals must be fitted into reality. Chart a day from seven in the morning until eleven at night, and divide it into one-hour segments. Jot down within these time segments the tasks which, ideally, you would like to accomplish. How does your actual meeting of obligations compare with the way you would like to use your time?

You may want to sketch out a week using this same approach. Formulate a chart of the week in which you divide each day into six sections, listing morning, prelunch, lunch, postlunch, late afternoon and evening. This will help you to visualize and analyze your use of time. You will then see the difference between the ideal use of time and the actual use of time.

A schedule should not be a straitjacket for the pastor, but it should provide helpful guidelines. He must be willing to change his schedule without being overcome with feelings of frustration and dismay.

Determine Your Priorities

Determining priorities involves a sorting process. At first, you may feel that everything you do has a high priority. After more sober reflection, though, you will realize that there are primary and secondary uses of time. All elements of your job have some importance. It is necessary, however, either on paper or in your mind, to rate these according to priority. This will help you determine the relative amount of time to reserve for each task and will also give you an idea as to the order in which matters should be undertaken. It may be wise to seek the counsel of others in determining priorities. Their experience may save you time and confusion.

To begin, consider those activities which are essential, such as the following:

1. Private devotional life
2. Preaching and the conduct of worship
3. Teaching
4. Study
5. Administration
6. Visitation
7. Office hours for counseling
8. Answering correspondence
9. Fellowship with the family
10. Physical exercise

Lyle Schaller, in *The Pastor and the People*, suggests that a set of cards be made, with a description of an activity or responsibility on each one. Sets of these cards could be distributed to church board members, committee members, or selected members of the congregation to arrange in the order which they feel represents the way the preacher is spending his time. The results may be used to indicate how they feel the minister *should* spend his time.[2]

The pastor should be aware that there is often a wide discrepancy between the way in which his people assume he is spending his time and the way in which he is actually spending it. There may also be a great difference between how they feel he should spend his time and the way in which he feels his time should be spent.

When your list of priorities has been established, write a second list of those activities which could be classified as secondary uses of time. This might include some of the following items:

1. Attending local ministerial meetings
2. Helping in odd jobs around the church
3. Traveling to broaden knowledge
4. Writing for publication
5. Attending religious community-events
6. Attending nonreligious community-events
7. Watching television
8. Playing games
9. Reading novels
10. Attending sports events

When the activities have been given their priority rating, the next step is to employ some principles for accomplishing them. There will always be some tasks which can be completed with less effort and time than the others. Do them first. This means that a few items can be cleared from the roster in short order. Not only is this encouraging, it also starts the work rolling. Be aware of deadlines for various activities. Priorities are established not only on the basis of value but also on the basis of time factors.

Your mental and physical fitness should be taken into consideration. Do the more difficult tasks when you are fresh and alert. Important tasks should be given prime time. Early hours of the day are generally uninterrupted hours, and your head may be clearer in those hours. Studies have shown that the peak of efficiency is at

8:00 A.M. It goes down gradually until about 8 P.M. when it is 2 percent better than it was at 4 P.M. After 10 P.M. efficiency goes down again. Save the more routine matters for times when you are weary. Interperse work on priority items with less pressing duties. Remember that a change is as good as a rest.

Learn to Delegate Responsibility

Dwight L. Moody has been remembered for many of his sayings, one of which is, "Put ten men to work rather than do the work of ten men." The pastor who fails to delegate responsibility forfeits a ministry of multiplication. Delegation not only recognizes the gifts and abilities of responsible laymen, it frees the minister for priority tasks. It is important, therefore, to spend time in training workers.

No matter how good an administrator one is, his responsibilities will always be greater than his personal capacity to carry them out. There is nothing wrong with this, for a person should undertake a job which holds a challenge rather than one which is easily accomplished and stifles creativity and motivation.

Use selective delegation. It is wise to delegate routine tasks and tasks which have low priority. It is often wise to delegate a task of even medium priority to someone who has expertise in that particular area. You may choose to delegate tasks to others not only for the accomplishment of the task but also for the personal development of the one to whom the task is assigned. A task may enlarge someone's understanding and increase his sense of satisfaction.

Be sure that the task is clearly explained before it is delegated. Be careful in selecting the person to whom the task is assigned. A leader builds his reputation as a leader partly through his wise choosing of helpers. Give moral and material support to the ones to whom you assign tasks. Show interest in them and their work by being willing to check and evaluate their progress.

Watch Out for Time Wasters

There is sometimes a temptation to give too much time to a pet project. That project may be intriguing and stimulating, but it may also have a low priority. We are so human that we will have a tendency to spend time where we are most interested rather than where necessity demands.

Some activities should be recognized as posing this problem. They should either be curtailed or be kept under control. Some of the items which may pose special problems for the pastor are membership in secret societies; excessive time spent before the radio or television; lingering with the morning paper before beginning to study; useless socializing in visitation; browsing in magazines; conversing at length with friends; and sleeping late.

Duplication of work is another time waster. In visitation work, this can be avoided somewhat by allocating calls to staff members. Making an appointment before making the visit will save time and travel. Good communication between visitation groups will avoid duplication of calls, and a wise geographical planning will avoid useless duplication of travel between calls.

One of the greatest time wasters in church work is an excessive number of committee meetings. Do not hold a committee meeting because it is scheduled but because there is something which needs to be decided. It is certainly unwise to use the time of five committee members to make routine decisions. If the meeting is not important enough to merit an agenda, then it is not important enough to be held. Committees can often make simple tasks appear very complex. This has caused someone to comment, "A camel is a horse put together by a committee."

Plan Ahead

Some churches have found it practical to give their minister a two-week sabbatical each year. During this period, the pastor may review his past goals, procedures, and results and establish some short- and long-term goals for the future. He may outline a loose schedule for the church year which will serve as a guide for church activities, emphasis, and preaching. He may also develop a helpful bibliography for the coming year. Some churches make provision for the minister to take some concentrated seminary-courses during his sabbatical. Some pastors work better in the routine of a class schedule than they do on their own.

At the close of each day, take a pencil and paper and make some plans for the next day. Give consideration to the tasks which must be done and those which you would like to accomplish. Take a look at the whole racecourse before you get to the starting line.

The United States Navy has developed a management tool called "PERT," the Program Evaluation and Review Technique. A study of this system provides some helpful hints for improving time management within a pastorate. Select a job which confronts you. List everything that has to be done in connection with carrying out this project. Arrange these tasks in sequence, and estimate the time which each one will take. Draw a wire diagram of the entire project indicating the sequence of activities and highlighting any possible bottlenecks in the operation. Estimate the total time for the job, and proceed to carry out the sequence of tasks toward the completion of the entire project.

Multiply Your Time

There are several suggestions which, when taken individually, may appear rather unimportant in time saving; but when combined, these items can help you multiply the work you can accomplish within the time at your disposal. It is important to accomplish the maximum in each moment and each activity.

Determine the purpose behind each activity. Ask yourself, Why am I doing this? Is this activity really helping me reach my goal?

When you are faced with decisions, make them. We sometimes have the tendency to merely sit and dread the moment when we will have to decide. Set a deadline for making the decision, and decide.

Learn to say no to others and to yourself when you are tempted to become involved in activities for which you have no time.

Maintain some type of filing system so that you can find needed items without going through unproductive activity just searching.

In many cases it is possible to do two things at once. While driving to an appointment, you might be able to listen to tapes or you might be able to do some dictating on a machine. This will often save time for your secretary as well. Try to design some dual-purpose activities.

Before spending time reading a book, glance through it rapidly to determine whether it will be profitable for you to spend your time reading it. If you do read it, take notes while reading so that you can review the notes at the end.

Always carry a book with you for reading during waiting or traveling times. Travel time can also be used for listening to tapes and preparing for meetings. When out-of-town meetings are necessary, try to arrange to have them at the terminal so that you will not have to waste more travel time. By the way, do not travel if a letter or telephone call can accomplish the task. You will save both time and money. If it is necessary to be there in person, schedule the trip at a time when you will not be too pressed.

Allow "think time" in your schedule. This will allow you to think a project through before becoming involved. It is important to schedule this time rather than merely waiting for a break in your schedule. This provision will help you in planning, problem solving, and creative development. This time for thinking may be scheduled for an hour before others arrive in the morning or for the evening, after others have retired and you are free from distractions.

When you make appointments, schedule a beginning and a closing time. Avoid having between-appointment breaks which are too short for getting down to work. Always have something to do in case an individual is late for his appointment.

Prepare well for your meetings. The secret of a good meeting is in the adequacy of its preparation. Five minutes of preparation could conceivably save an hour of meeting time.

You can multiply your time by having your secretary screen telephone calls. Routine return-calls can be made late in the day, thus saving interruption. Grouping your calls into one time span can save time. Only emergency calls should get through to you and be allowed to interrupt your labors.

You will improve the use of your time by taking breaks as you need them. As you return refreshed, you will accomplish more within the next period of time. Alternate between physical and mental work; the change will be as refreshing as a break.

Review and Evaluate

It is important, especially in leadership, that our attention be fastened not only upon today but also upon yesterday and tomorrow. Stop once or twice during the day to reflect and project. You may find that you will want to change the order of work in the middle of the day. Plans are made to be helpful and should not become straitjackets. At the close of a day, take some time to reflect upon the accomplishments and failures of yesterday. Take note of those matters which must be dealt with tomorrow. Lessons learned from yesterday can be of help to us tomorrow.

The procedure of review should be applied not only on a day-to-day basis but also over longer periods of time. After six months, survey the past and project into the future. Review your progress in terms of general purposes and also in terms of the more specific goals. By making wise use of time, everyone can help the church get on target.

Additional Reading

Drucker, Peter F. *The Effective Executive.* New York: Harper & Row, 1967.

Engstrom, Ted W., and Mackenzie, R. Alec. *Managing Your Time.* Grand Rapids: Zondervan, 1968.

Uris, Auren. *The Executive Deskbook.* New York: Van Nostrand Rheinhold, 1970.

CHAPTER 15

Assessing Problems and Progress

Assessment is the final step in the administrative process after recognizing need, planning, organizing, and stimulating. When we speak of assessment as the final step, we do not refer to chronology but only to the point of discussion. Assessment should take place throughout the administrative process as well as at the close of the project.

The process of assessment involves an examination, or appraisal, focusing upon potential future possibilities. Analysis, on the other hand, often produces a negative response. Assessment is designed to develop positive reactions.

There must be some standards of evaluation in order for the process of assessment to take place. Do not evaluate only in terms of statistics. The evaluation must also be from a spiritual perspective. We are not interested just in getting numbers but in comparing numbers. We are not interested just in checking the amount of benevolent giving but in checking that amount against the total giving of the church. We are not interested just in checking the number who left the church but in comparing that number with the total of those entering the church.

Church board meetings often seem to imply by their order of business that the major purposes of a church are to increase membership, achieve a balanced budget, operate a large Sunday school, and maintain the property. There appears to be a tendency to emphasize money and real estate. Someone has suggested that most of the questions with which we deal relate to nickels and noses. We do not seem to be concentrating upon ministering to people.

The church should appoint a program review committee. Just as it is wise to have an auditing committee to check financial records, so it is wise to have a committee to survey the church program and evaluate its effectiveness. This committee may recommend the launching of a new program or the termination of an obsolete or irrelevant program. It is not wise to try to pump life into a dead program. If God wants it to die, then let His will be done.

The process of evaluation will help us to get from where we are to where we want to go. It will help us bring to reality our hopes and expectations for the future. The process may reveal places of irritation over which we should place a "band-aid" to prevent scratching them and thus spreading the irritation. The process helps us get a clearer view of our purposes, goals, and objectives. It provides assistance in differentiating between means and ends.

Self-evaluation devices, such as surveys, have proved helpful in locating problems and evaluating progress. Five self-evaluating devices are included here as samples. These can be drawn up by the administrator and adjusted to fit the particular circumstance. The statements should be formulated so they will not evoke a yes or no answer. They should be formulated so that the individual can indicate his response on a continuum connecting two extremes of response. The individuals responding to these surveys should not be asked to include their names. The responses can be tallied and some conclusions drawn. The use of this type of device gives participants an opportunity to express their opinions apart from pressure. It is a means of giving the people a voice.

A. The Mission of the Church in This Community

1. One of the major responsibilities of the church is to minister to the physical as well as to the spiritual needs of people.
   Agree ____ ____ ____ ____ ____ ____ ____ Disagree
2. This church has clearly defined goals for its ministry to people in the community.
   Agree ____ ____ ____ ____ ____ ____ ____ Disagree
3. This church is now as active in ministering to the physical and

economic needs of people in the community as I would like it to be.

Agree ____ ____ ____ ____ ____ ____ ____ Disagree

4. The church has an obligation to help its members minister to others in everyday life.

Agree ____ ____ ____ ____ ____ ____ ____ Disagree

5. The church ought not to get involved in controversial political issues.

Agree ____ ____ ____ ____ ____ ____ ____ Disagree

6. The church ought not to get involved in controversial social issues.

Agree ____ ____ ____ ____ ____ ____ ____ Disagree

7. I feel free to express to others in this church my views on controversial social and political issues, even though I know many persons disagree with me.

Agree ____ ____ ____ ____ ____ ____ ____ Disagree

8. The minister ought to take stands on issues even when he knows many disagree with him.

Agree ____ ____ ____ ____ ____ ____ ____ Disagree

9. This church provides me ample opportunity for working with others in ministering to persons in the community.

Agree ____ ____ ____ ____ ____ ____ ____ Disagree

B. The Climate of the Church Organization (how it feels here)

We are interested in the overall climate, or atmosphere, of this church. While climate is not a tangible thing, there is usually general agreement as to what it is, what it feels like at any given time.

The main question is this: How does it feel when you work with other people inside this particular church?

Check each pair of words or phrases below. Don't worry about whether you are precisely accurate, but give your best estimate of the feel of this organization.

The Climate of This Church Organization

alert ____ ____ ____ ____ ____ ____ not alert
mistrustful ____ ____ ____ ____ ____ ____ trustful
cooperative ____ ____ ____ ____ ____ ____ uncooperative
personal and close ____ ____ ____ ____ ____ ____ impersonal and distant
creative ____ ____ ____ ____ ____ ____ uncreative
insensitive ____ ____ ____ ____ ____ ____ sensitive
facing problems ____ ____ ____ ____ ____ ____ avoiding problems
conservative ____ ____ ____ ____ ____ ____ innovative
unconcerned ____ ____ ____ ____ ____ ____ concerned
listening ____ ____ ____ ____ ____ ____ not listening
fearful ____ ____ ____ ____ ____ ____ not fearful
rigid ____ ____ ____ ____ ____ ____ flexible
feelings ignored ____ ____ ____ ____ ____ ____ feelings count
divided ____ ____ ____ ____ ____ ____ unified
relaxed ____ ____ ____ ____ ____ ____ tense

C. How Do I Feel About Our Worship Service?

1. The worship service reflects the desires of the total congregation.
   Agree ____ ____ ____ ____ ____ ____ ____ Disagree
2. The worship service is regularly evaluated and reviewed.
   Agree ____ ____ ____ ____ ____ ____ ____ Disagree
3. The worship service provides the kind of participation I want.
   Agree ____ ____ ____ ____ ____ ____ ____ Disagree
4. There is flexibility and adaptability in the worship service.
   Agree ____ ____ ____ ____ ____ ____ ____ Disagree
5. The hymns we sing reflect the preference of the congregation.
   Agree ____ ____ ____ ____ ____ ____ ____ Disagree
6. The congregation has a sense of expectancy and anticipation.
   Agree ____ ____ ____ ____ ____ ____ ____ Disagree

7. The sermon helps my worship of God.
   Agree ____ ____ ____ ____ ____ ____ ____ Disagree
8. There are elements in the worship service that need change.
   Agree ____ ____ ____ ____ ____ ____ ____ Disagree
9. The length of the worship service is satisfactory.
   Agree ____ ____ ____ ____ ____ ____ ____ Disagree
10. Change in the worship service upsets me.
   Agree ____ ____ ____ ____ ____ ____ ____ Disagree
11. Therc are some things in the worship service which should be omitted.
   Agree ____ ____ ____ ____ ____ ____ ____ Disagree

D. Questionnaire on Congregational Purposes

This is an instrument designed to help you describe your understanding of the purposes of this congregation as described in the church constitution. There are no right or wrong answers. Check the space which best expresses your perception.

1. The purposes of this congregation are clear to me.
   Agree ____ ____ ____ ____ ____ ____ ____ Disagree
2. The purposes of this congregation are merely implied.
   Agree ____ ____ ____ ____ ____ ____ ____ Disagree
3. Someone else has established the purposes of this congregation.
   Agree ____ ____ ____ ____ ____ ____ ____ Disagree
4. My personal purposes are consistent with the purposes of this congregation.
   Agree ____ ____ ____ ____ ____ ____ ____ Disagree
5. I have been involved in establishing the purposes of this congregation.
   Agree ____ ____ ____ ____ ____ ____ ____ Disagree
6. It is clear to me how we are moving to achieve our purposes.
   Agree ____ ____ ____ ____ ____ ____ ____ Disagree
7. The purposes of this congregation are unexamined by our present congregation.
   Agree ____ ____ ____ ____ ____ ____ ____ Disagree
8. Our church program is planned in accordance with our purposes.
   Agree ____ ____ ____ ____ ____ ____ ____ Disagree

9. Some parts of our program are not in accord with our purposes.
   Agree ____ ____ ____ ____ ____ ____ ____ Disagree
10. List what you feel are the purposes of this congregation.
    1.
    2.
    3.
    4.
    5.

E. Church Finances

1. Our church budget is too high for the number of contributors we have.
   Agree ____ ____ ____ ____ ____ ____ ____ Disagree
2. We should increase the percentage of our budget allocated for foreign missions.
   Agree ____ ____ ____ ____ ____ ____ ____ Disagree
3. Our church is doing a good job in stewardship education.
   Agree ____ ____ ____ ____ ____ ____ ____ Disagree
4. I am satisfied with the amount of financial information which the church provides to the membership.
   Agree ____ ____ ____ ____ ____ ____ ____ Disagree
5. There are some listed on our missionary budget whom I would hesitate to support financially.
   Agree ____ ____ ____ ____ ____ ____ ____ Disagree
6. Our church has a good financial reputation in the community.
   Agree ____ ____ ____ ____ ____ ____ ____ Disagree
7. I have a good knowledge of the amount and extent of coverage of our youth budget.
   Agree ____ ____ ____ ____ ____ ____ ____ Disagree
8. Our financial problems would be solved if we had more teaching and preaching on tithing.
   Agree ____ ____ ____ ____ ____ ____ ____ Disagree
9. More individuals and groups should be given a voice in establishing the budget.
   Agree ____ ____ ____ ____ ____ ____ ____ Disagree

10. Our present budget allows for:

	Too much	Too little	Enough	?
Music	______	______	______	______
Foreign Missions	______	______	______	______
Home Missions	______	______	______	______
Youth Activities	______	______	______	______
Heat & Light	______	______	______	______
Staff Salaries	______	______	______	______

Epilogue

True revitalization of the church begins with a valid conception of God, a recovery of the full revelation of the person and work of Jesus Christ, and a consciousness of the presence and power of the Holy Spirit. Many churches appear to be spiritually bankrupt. The last concern of the Lord Jesus before His ascension was that His followers might have power (Ac 1:8). There is no real substitute for spiritual reality.

That "old first church" of the second chapter of the book of Acts was a powerful church. It had an attractive ministry. Those who witnessed it were impressed by its enthusiasm, influence, and missionary vision. It presented an attractive message. It was Bible-centered, prayer supported, victorious in theme, and convicting. It had an attractive membership. Their qualifications, activities, and attitudes gave evidence of the working of the Holy Spirit in their midst. The Holy Spirit must be central in our planning for revitalization.

Give careful consideration to the first-century message to the twentieth century church as recorded in Revelation 2-3. These messages to the seven churches provide guidance for getting the church on target:

Beware of losing the first love for Christ (2:1-7).
Be willing to suffer with assurance (2:8-11).
Recognize when discipline is demanded (2:12-17).
Remember that sometimes there is tragedy in tolerance (2:18-29).
Make certain that there is reality in your reputation (3:1-6).
Take advantage of open doors of opportunity (3:7-13).
Watch out! It is possible to go from riches to rags (3:14-22).

A successful revitalization program demands that the workers have God's point of view rather than man's. Man says that success is measured by gaining, promoting self, and declaring profits now. God measures success by giving, presenting the Saviour, and declaring eternal profits (Mk 8:27–9:1).

Time is short. The church needs to get on target.

Notes

CHAPTER 1

1. *Journal of the Academy of Parish Clergy*, April 1971, pp. 63-64. Quoted in James D. Glasse, *Putting It Together in the Parish*, pp. 134-35.

CHAPTER 2

1. Dean M. Kelley, *Why Conservative Churches Are Growing*, p. 51.
2. Alvin J. Lindgren, *Foundations for Purposeful Church Administration*, pp. 53-87.
3. Amitai Etzioni, *A Comparative Analysis of Complex Organizations*, pp. 71-73.

CHAPTER 3

1. Arthur Merrihew Adams, *Pastoral Administration*, p. 13.
2. Alvin J. Lindgren, *Foundations for Purposeful Church Administration*, p. 60.
3. See Lloyd Perry, *Biblical Preaching for Today's World*, pp. 116-17.
4. Olan Hendrix, *Management and the Christian Worker*, pp. 61-63.
5. Ordway Tead, *The Art of Administration*, p. 105.
6. Herbert Simon, *Administrative Behavior*, pp. 2-21.
7. Gene Getz, *Sharpening the Focus of the Church*, p. 189.

CHAPTER 4

1. Adolph Deissmann, *Light from the Ancient East*, p. 112.
2. Augustus Hopkins Strong, *Systematic Theology*, p. 890.
3. Arthur Merrihew Adams, *Pastoral Administration*, pp. 57-60.
4. Edgar Schein, *Organizational Psychology*, p. 118.
5. Kenneth Kilinski and Jerry Wofford, *Organization and Leadership in the Local Church*, p. 143.
6. Ordway, Tead, *The Art of Administration*, p. 79.
7. Lyle E. Schaller, *The Change Agent*, pp. 58-70.

CHAPTER 5

1. Harold L. Fickett, Jr. *Hope for Your Church: Ten Principles of Church Growth*, p. 83.
2. S. P. Carey, *William Carey*, p. 256.
3. J. Oswald Sanders, *Spiritual Leadership*, p. 44.
4. Alvin J. Lindgren, *Foundations for Purposeful Church Administration*, p. 204.
5. Basil Mathews, *John R. Mott, World Citizen*, pp. 344-45.
6. P. James, *George W. Truett*, pp. 270-71.
7. A. E. Norrish, *Christian Leadership*, p. 28. Quoted in J. Oswald Sanders, *Spiritual Leadership*, p. 60.
8. Kenneth Gangel, *So You Want to Be a Leader*, p. 25.
9. Ibid, p. 27.
10. Warren Schmidt, *A Leader Looks at Styles of Leadership*, pp. 3-4.
11. Gordon Lippett, *Organizational Renewal*, p. 84.
12. Paul E. Sangster, *Doctor Sangster*, p. 109.
13. Ibid.
14. Sanders, pp. 66-67.
15. Ibid., pp. 142-50.
16. R. E. Thompson, "Missionary Dropouts—Is Leadership to Blame?" *World Vision*, February 1966, p. 4.

17. John Alexander, *Managing Our Work*, pp. 39-40.
18. Renis Likert, *New Patterns of Management*, pp. 7-11.
19. Kenneth Gangel, *So You Want to Be a Leader?*, pp. 94-99.
20. Chester Barnard, *The Functions of an Executive*, p. 194.
21. Sanders, p. 45.

CHAPTER 6

1. Cyril O. Houle, *The Effective Board*, p. 62.
2. Ibid., pp. 93-97.
3. Ibid., pp. 120-22.

CHAPTER 7

1. Lyle Schaller, *Hey That's Our Church*, p. 35.

CHAPTER 8

1. Lawrence O. Richards, *A New Face for the Church*, p. 146.
2. Lyle Schaller, *The Change Agent*, pp. 169-71.
3. Paul A. Mickey and Robert L. Wilson, *Conflict Resolution*, p. 12.

CHAPTER 9

1. Kenneth Kilinski and Jerry Wofford, *Organization and Leadership in the Local Church*, pp. 197-200.
2. Auren Uris, *The Executive Deskbook*, p. 153.
4. Ibid., p. 155.

CHAPTER 10

1. Lyle Schaller, *Parish Planning*, p. 52.
2. Lyle Schaller, *The Pastor and the People*, pp. 127-31.
3. For further information see Robert N. Gray, *Church Business Administration.*

CHAPTER 11

1. Findley B. Edge, *The Greening of the Church*, pp. 116-17.
2. Alvin J. Lindgren, *Foundations for Purposeful Church Administration*, pp. 147-52.
3. Edgar H. Schein, *Organizational Psychology*, p. 82.
4. Charles H. Cooley, *Social Organization: A Study of the Larger Mind*, pp. 23-57.
5. Gordon Lippett, *Organizational Renewal*, pp. 114-15.
6. Harvey Seifer and Howard Clinebell, *Personal Growth and Social Change*, p. 150.
7. George Beal et al., *Leadership and Dynamic Group Action*, pp. 23-30.
8. Lippett, p. 114.
9. Ernest and Nancy Bormann, *Effective Committees and Groups in the Church*, pp. 57-59.
10. Beal, pp. 103-9.
11. Bormann, pp. 32-34.
12. Robert Powell, *Managing Church Business Through Group Procedures*, p. 82.
13. For useful suggestions for Bible study groups, see Tom Rees, *Break-through.*

CHAPTER 12

1. Ralph Stoody, *A Handbook of Church Public Relations*, pp. 31-33.
2. Ibid., p. 34.
3. Ibid., p. 52.
4. Donald McGavran and Winfield Arn, *How to Grow a Church*, pp. 51-53.

CHAPTER 13

1. Albert Palmer, *The Art of Conducting Public Worship*, p. 4.
2. Ibid., pp. 195-202.

CHAPTER 14

1. Auren Uris, *The Executive Deskbook*, pp. 2-180.
2. Lyle Schaller, *The Pastor and the People*, pp. 45-55.

Bibliography

Adams, Arthur Merrihew. *Pastoral Administration.* Philadelphia: Westminster, 1964.

Alexander, John. *Managing Our Work.* Downers Grove, Ill.: Inter-Varsity. 1972.

Ayres, Francis O. *The Ministry of the Laity.* Philadelphia: Westminster, 1962.

Barnard, Chester. *The Functions of an Executive.* Cambridge, Mass.: Harvard, 1971.

Baxter, J. Sidlow. *Rethinking Our Priorities.* Grand Rapids: Zondervan, 1974.

Beal, George, et al. *Leadership and Dynamic Group Action.* Ames, Iowa: Iowa State U. 1962.

Beck, Hubert F. *Why Can't the Church Be Like This?* St. Louis, Missouri: Concordia, 1973.

Bennis, Warren G. *Changing Organizations.* New York: McGraw, 1966.

———. *Organization Development: Its Nature, Origins and Prospects.* Reading, Massachusetts: Addison-Wesley, 1969.

Bennis, Warren G.; Benne, Kenneth D.; and Chin, Robert. *The Planning of Change.* New York: Holt, Rinehart & Winston, 1969.

Bennis, Warren, and Slater, Philip. *The Temporary Society.* New York: Harper & Row, 1968.

Berne, Eric. *The Structure and Dynamics of Organizations and Groups.* New York: Grove, 1963.

Berton, Pierre. *The Comfortable Pew.* Philadelphia: Lippincott, 1965.

Beveridge, W. E. *Managing the Church.* Cambridge: Allenson, 1971.

Blackie, Bruce L. *Gods of Goodness: The Sophisticated Idolatry of the Main Line Churches.* Philadelphia: Westminster, 1975.

Bloesch, Donald. *Reform of the Church.* New ed. Grand Rapids: Eerdmans, 1970.

Bormann, Ernest, and Bormann, Nancy. *Effective Committees and Groups in the Church.* Minneapolis: Augsburg, 1973.

Brister, C. W. *Pastoral Care in the Church.* Evanston, Ill.: Harper & Row, 1964.

Brow, Robert. *The Church: An Organic Picture of its Life and Mission.* Grand Rapids: Eerdmans, 1968.

Brown, Robert M. *Frontiers for the Church Today.* New York: Oxford U., 1973.

Buckley, Walter. *Sociology and Modern Systems Theory.* Englewood Cliffs, N. J.: Prentice Hall, 1970.

Organizational Development. Fairfax, Va.: NTL Learning Resources,
Organizational Development. Fairfax, Va.: NTL Learning Resources, 1972.

Caplow, Theodore. *Principles of Organization.* New York: Harcourt, Brace & World, 1964.

Carey, S. P. *William Carey.* London: Hodder & Stoughton, n.d.

Casteel, John L. *The Creative Role of Interpersonal Groups in the Church Today.* New York: Association, 1968.

———. *Spiritual Renewal Through Personal Groups.* New York: Association, 1965.

Churchman, West C. *The Systems Approach.* New York: Dell, 1969.

Clark, Edward M.; Malconson, William L.; and Moulton, Warren, eds. *The Church Creative.* Nashville: Abingdon, 1967.

Come, Arnold B. *Agents of Reconciliation.* Philadelphia: Westminster, 1964.

Cooley, Charles H. *Social Organization: A Study of the Larger Mind.* New York: Schocken, 1962.

Daniel, James, and Dickson, Elaine, eds. *The Seventies: Opportunities for Your Church.* Nashville: Convention, 1969.

Deissmann, Adolph. *Light from the Ancient East,* 3d ed. Trans. Lionel Strachan. New York: Harper, 1927.

Desportes, Elisa. *Congregations in Change.* Project Text Pattern Series. New York: Seabury, 1973.

Drucker, Peter F. *The Effective Executive.* New York: Harper & Row, 1967.

Dunnam, Maxie D., et al. *Manipulator and the Church.* Nashville: Abingdon, 1968.

Edge, Findley B. *Greening of the Church.* Waco, Texas: Word, 1971.

Engstrom, Ted W., and Mackenzie, R. Alec. *Managing Your Time.* Grand Rapids: Zondervan, 1968.

Ernsberger, David J. *Education for Renewal.* Philadelphia: Westminster, 1965.

———. *Reviving the Local Church.* Philadelphia: Fortress, 1969.

Etzioni, Amitai. *A Comparative Analysis of Complex Organization.* New York: Free Press, 1971.

———. *Modern Organization.* Englewood Cliffs, N. J.: Prentice-Hall, 1964.

Evely, Louis. *If the Church Is to Survive.* Trans. J. F. Bernard. New York: Doubleday, 1972.

Fickett, Harold L. *Hope for Your Church: Ten Principles of Church Growth.* Glendale, Calif.: Regal, 1972.

Fisher, Wallace E. *Preface to Parish Renewal.* Nashville: Abingdon, 1968.

Fray, Harold. *Conflict and Change in the Church.* Philadelphia: Pilgrim, 1969.

Gamson, William A. *Power and Discontent.* Homewood, Ill.: Dorsey, 1968.

Gangel, Kenneth O. *Competent to Lead.* Chicago: Moody, 1974.

———. *Leadership for Church Education.* Chicago: Moody, 1970.

———. *So You Want to Be a Leader?* Harrisburg, Pa.: Christian Pub., 1973.

Geisinger, R. W. *To Revitalize the Church.* New York: Vantage, 1969.

Getz, Gene A. *Sharpening the Focus of the Church.* Chicago: Moody, 1974.

Gibbs, Alfred. *Worship: The Christian's Highest Occupation.* Fort Dodge, Iowa: Walterick, n.d.

Gilkey, Langdon. *How the Church Can Minister to the World Without Losing Itself.* New York: Harper & Row, 1964.

Gillaspie, Gerald W. *The Restless Pastor.* Chicago: Moody, 1974.

Girard, Robert C. *Brethren, Hang Loose.* Grand Rapids: Zondervan, 1972.

Glasse, James D. *Putting It Together in the Parish.* Nashville: Abingdon, 1972.

Gray, Robert N. *Church Business Administration.* Enid, Okla.: Phillips U., 1968.

Green, Hollis L. *Why Churches Die.* Minneapolis: Bethany Fellowship, 1972.

Group Development. National Training Laboratories Selected Readings Series No. 1. Washington, D.C.: NTL Learning Resources Corp., 1961.

Halverson, Richard C. *How I Changed My Thinking About the Church.* Grand Rapids: Zondervan, 1972.

Haney, David. *The Idea of the Laity.* Grand Rapids: Zondervan, 1973.

———. *Renew My Church.* Grand Rapids: Zondervan, 1972.

Hendrix, Olan. *Management and the Christian Worker.* Manila, Philippines: Living Books for All, 1972.

Hornstein, Harvey; Bunker, Barbara; Burke, W. W.; et al. *Social Intervention: A Behavioral Science Approach.* New York: Free Press, 1971.
Houle, Cyril. *The Effective Board.* New York: Association, 1960.
Howard, Walden. *Groups That Work.* Grand Rapids: Zondervan, 1967.
———. *Nine Roads to Renewal.* Waco, Texas: World, 1967.
Hubbard, David A. *The Church—Who Needs It?* Glendale, Calif.: Regal, 1974.
James, Powhatan W. *George W. Truett.* New York: Macmillan, 1939.
Johnson, B. C., ed. *Rebels in the Church.* Waco, Texas: Word, 1971.
Jones, Stanley E. *The Reconstruction of the Church–On What Pattern?* Nashville: Abingdon Press, 1970.
Judson, Arnold S. *A Manager's Guide to Making Changes.* New York: Wiley, 1966.
Kelley, Dean M. *Why Conservative Churches Are Growing.* New York: Harper & Row, 1972.
Kilinski, Kenneth, and Wofford, Jerry. *Organization and Leadership in the Local Church.* Grand Rapids: Zondervan, 1973.
Kraemer, Hendrik. *A Theology of the Laity.* Philadelphia: Westminster, 1959.
Krutza, William. *Decision . . . Ouch!* Grand Rapids: Baker, 1974.
Kung, Hans. *Truthfulness: The Future of the Church.* New York: Sheed & Ward, 1968.
Kung, Hans, and Kasper, Walter, eds. *Polarization in the Church.* New York: Seabury, 1973.
Larson, Bruce. *Living on the Growing Edge.* Grand Rapids: Zondervan, 1968.
Larson, Bruce, and Osborne, Ralph. *The Emerging Church.* Waco, Texas: Word, 1970.
Lawless, David J. *Effective Management: Social Psychological Approach.* Englewood Cliffs, N. J.: Prentice-Hall, 1972.
Lawrence, Paul, and Lorsch, Jay. *Developing Organizations: Diagnosis and Action.* Reading, Mass.: Addison-Wesley, 1969.
———. *Organization and Environment: Managing Differentiation and Integration.* Boston: Harvard, 1967.
Leas, Speed, and Kittlaus, Paul. *Church Fights: Managing Conflict in the Local Church.* Philadelphia: Westminster, 1937.
Leslie, Robert. *Sharing Groups in the Church.* Nashville: Abingdon, 1971.
Levinson, Harry. *Organizational Diagnosis.* Cambridge, Mass.: Harvard, 1972.
Likert, Renis. *New Patterns of Management.* New York: McGraw-Hill, 1961.

Lindgren, Alvin J. *Foundations for Purposeful Church Administration.* Nashville: Abingdon, 1965.

Lippitt, Ronald; Watson, Jeanne; and Westley, Bruce. *The Dynamics of Planned Change: A Comparative Study of Principles and Techniques.* New York: Harcourt, Brace & World, 1958.

Lippitt, Gordon L. *Organizational Renewal.* New York: Appleton-Century-Crofts, 1969.

Litwin, George, and Stringer, Robert, Jr. *Motivation and Organizational Climate.* Boston: Harvard, 1968.

Luft, Joseph. *Group Processes: An Introduction to Group Dynamics.* Palo Alto, Calif.: National, 1970.

MacArthur, John, Jr. *The Church: The Body of Christ.* Grand Rapids: Zondervan, 1973.

McGavran, Donald A. *Church Growth & Group Conversion.* William Carey Lib., 1973.

———. *Understanding Church Growth.* Grand Rapids: Eerdmans, 1970.

McGavran, Donald A.; and Arn, Winifield C. *How to Grow a Church.* Glendale, Calif.: Regal, 1973.

McNeil, Jesse Jai. *Mission in Metropolis.* Grand Rapids: Eerdmans, 1965.

Mains, David R. *Full Circle.* Waco, Texas: Word, 1971.

Mathews, Basil. *John R. Mott, World Citizen.* New York: Harper, 1934.

Mead, Loren B. *New Hope for Congregations.* New York: Seabury, 1972.

Metz, Donald L. *New Congregations.* Philadelphia: Westminster, 1967.

Mickey, Paul A., and Wilson, Robert L. *Conflict Resolution.* Nashville: Abingdon, 1973.

Miles, Matthew B. *Learning to Work in Groups.* New York: Teachers College Press, 1967.

Neighbor, Ralph. *The Seven Last Words of the Church.* Grand Rapids: Zondervan, 1973.

Neill, S. C., and Weber, H. R., eds. *The Layman in Christian History.* Philadelphia: Westminster, 1963.

Nelson, William R., and Lincoln, William F. *Journey Toward Renewal.* Valley Forge, Pa.; Judson, 1971.

Noyce, Gaylord B. *Church is not Expendable.* Philadelphia: Westminster, 1969.

———. *Survival and Mission for the City Church.* Philadelphia: Westminster, 1975.

Palmer, Albert. *The Art of Conducting Public Worship.* New York: Macmillan, 1939.

Paquier, Richard. *Dynamics of Worship.* Philadelphia: Fortress, 1967.

Paul, R.S. *The Church in Search of Its Self.* Grand Rapids: Eerdmans, 1972.
Perrow, Charles. *Organizational Analysis: A Sociological View.* Belmont, Calif.: Wadsworth, 1970.
Perry, Lloyd. *Biblical Preaching for Today's World.* Chicago: Moody, 1973.
Powell, Robert. *Managing Church Business Through Group Procedures.* Englewood Cliffs, N.J.: Prentice-Hall, 1964.
Raines, Robert A. *New Life in the Church.* New York: Harper, 1961.
———. *Reshaping the Christian Life.* New York: Harper & Row, 1964.
Randolph, David J. *God's Party.* Nashville: Abingdon, 1975.
Reddin, W. J. *Effective Management by Objectives: The 3-D Method of MBO.* New York: McGraw-Hill, 1971.
Reid, Clyde. *Groups Alive—Church Alive.* New York: Harper & Row, 1969.
Rees, Tom. *Break-Through.* Waco, Tex.: Word, 1970.
Richards, Lawrence O. *A New Face for the Church.* Grand Rapids: Zondervan, 1970.
Sanders, J. Oswald. *Spiritual Leadership.* London: Marshall, Morgan & Scott, 1967.
Sangster, Paul E. *Doctor Sangster.* London: Epworth, 1962.
Schaeffer, Francis A. *The Church at the End of the Twentieth Century.* Downers Grove, Ill.: Inter-Varsity, 1970.
Schaller, Lyle. *The Decision Makers.* Nashville: Abingdon, 1974.
———. *Hey, That's Our Church.* Nashville: Abingdon, 1975.
———. *The Change Agent.* Nashville: Abingdon, 1972.
———. *Community Organization: Conflict and Reconciliation.* Nashville: Abingdon, 1966.
———. *Impact of the Future.* Nashville: Abington, 1969.
———. *The Local Church Looks to the Future.* Nashville: Abingdon, 1968.
———. *Parish Planning.* Nashville: Abingdon, 1971.
———. *The Pastor and the People: Building a New Partnership for Effective Ministry.* Nashville: Abingdon, 1973.
Schein, Edgar. *Organizational Psychology.* Englewood Cliffs, N. J.: Prentice-Hall, 1965.
———. *Organizational Psychology.* 2d ed. Englewood Cliffs, N.J.: Prentice-Hall, 1972.
———. *Process Consultation: Its Role in Organization Development.* Reading, Mass.: Addison-Wesley, 1969.

Schein, Edgar H., and Bennis, Warren G. *Personal and Organizational Change Through Group Methods.* New York: Wiley, 1967.

Schindler-Rainman, Eva, and Lippitt, Ronald. *The Volunteer Community.* Washingron, D. C.: Center for a Voluntary Society, 1971.

Schuller, David S. *Emerging Shapes of the Church.* St. Louis, Mo.: Concordia, 1967.

Segler, Franklin M. *Christian Worship: Its Theology and Practice.* Nashville: Broadman, 1967.

Seifer, Harvey, and Clinebell, Howard. *Personal Growth and Social Change.* Philadelphia: Westminster, 1969.

Simon, Herbert. *Administrative Behavior.* New York: Macmillan, 1957.

Seiler, John. *Systems Analysis in Organizational Behavior.* 3rd ed. Homewood, Ill.: Irwin, 1967.

Smith, Clagett, ed. *Conflict Resolution: Contributions of Behavioral Sciences.* Notre Dame, Ind.: U. of Notre Dame, 1971.

Stedman, Ray C. *Body Life.* Glendale, Calif.: Gospel Light, 1972.

Stoody, Ralph. *A Handbook of Church Public Relations.* Nashville: Abingdon, 1969.

Stott, John R. W. *One People.* Downers Grove Ill.: Inter-Varsity, 1971.

Strong, Augustus Hopkins. *Systematic Theology.* 3 vols. Philadelphia: Judson, 1907-9.

Taguiri, Renato, and Litwin, George, eds. *Organizational Climate: Explorations of a Concept.* Boston: Harvard, 1968.

Tead, Ordway. *Administration: Its Purpose & Performance.* Tamden, Conn.: Shoestring, 1968.

———. *The Art of Administration.* New York: McGraw-Hill, 1951.

Thielicke, Helmut. *The Trouble with the Church.* New York: Harper & Row, 1965.

Thomas, Donald F. *The Deacon in a Changing Church.* Valley Forge, Pa.: Judson, 1969.

Thompson, James. *Organizations in Action.* New York: McGraw-Hill, 1967.

Thompson, R.E. "Missionary Dropouts—Is Leadership to Blame?" *World Vision,* February 1966, p. 4.

Trexler, Edgar R., ed. *Creative Congregations.* Nashville: Abingdon, 1972.

———. *Ways to Wake Up Your Church.* Philadelphia: Fortress, 1969.

Tucker, Michael R. *The Church That Dared to Change.* Wheaton, Ill.: Tyndale, 1975.

Urls, Auren. *The Executive Deskbook.* New York: Van Nostrand Rheinhold, 1970.

Vallquist, Gunnel. *Churches on the Move*. Philadelphia: Fortress, 1970.
Vaughan, Benjamin N. *Structures for Renewal*. London: Mowbray, 1967.
Visser 't Hooft, W. A. *The Renewal of the Church*. Philadelphia: Westminster, 1956.
Von Bertalanffy, Ludwig. *General System Theory*. New York: Braziller, 1968.
Walden, Howard, ed. *Groups that Work*. Grand Rapids: Zondervan, 1967.
White, James F. *New Forms of Worship*. Nashville; Abingdon, 1971.
Winter, Gibson. *The Suburban Captivity of the Churches*. New York: Macmillan, 1962.
Worley, Robert. *Change in the Church: A Source of Hope*. Philadelphia: Westminster, 1971.
Wygal, Winnifred. *How to Plan Informal Worship*. New York: Association, 1955.

Index